EVIL
INTENTIONS

EVIL INTENTIONS

The Story of How an Act of Kindness
Led to Senseless Murder

Ronald J. Watkins

WILLIAM MORROW AND COMPANY, INC.
NEW YORK

Library of Congress Cataloging-in-Publication Data

Watkins, Ronald J.
    Evil intentions / by Ron Watkins.
       p.   cm.
    ISBN 0-688-10270-0
    1. Murder—Arizona—Case studies. 2. Rossetti, Suzanne Maria,
1954–1981. 3. Murder victims—Massachusetts—Saugus—Biography.
I. Title.
HV6533.A6W38   1992
364.1'523'0979177—dc20   91-17897
                                                                                        CIP

Printed in the United States of America

First Edition

1 2 3 4 5 6 7 8 9 10

BOOK DESIGN BY M & M DESIGNS

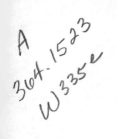

For Suzanne

AUTHOR'S NOTE

THIS IS A TRUE account of murder. It is based on official records and extensive interviews with all key participants, including the killers. Real names have been used except to spare the innocent and those innocently involved with the guilty. Even when names and descriptions have been changed, the roles of the individuals have been correctly portrayed. No character has been invented; no scenes have been manufactured. Thoughts and conversations are those reported.

There were discrepancies when more than one person reported the same incident. The account chosen is that determined to be most correct, given the history and personal character of the sources.

No photographs have been used at the request of the Rossetti family.

I know indeed what evil I intend to do,
but stronger than all my afterthoughts is my fury,
fury that brings upon mortals the greatest evils.
                              —Euripides, Medea

PROLOGUE

I will lift up my eyes unto the hills, from whence cometh my help.

—Psalm 121

Tears mixed with melting snowflakes on the policeman's face as he stood in the falling snow directing the solemn procession of cars. The continuous train of vehicles extended nearly two miles from the church to the cemetery. The snow fell silently, muffling all sound. The aged tombstones were crested with white. Slowly the mourners gathered about the gaping hole shielded by the black canopy. Poised above the earth stood a coffin.

It was a large gathering by community standards. Those who stood on the perimeter of the cemetery could scarcely hear what was said, but it was of little consequence. They were here to pay respects, to remember as much as their hearts could bear. The priest blessed them and this place, then, just before speaking, made the sign of the cross upon the coffin.

For well over three hundred years the townspeople have been laid to rest in even rows overlooking the gentle river. Those dead of aging, of disease, of mischance, and of war, all are here, but in the memory of anyone, there is only one murder victim.

The town has existed in the lowlands of Massachusetts for nearly four centuries, a place not distinctively different from hundreds of others in the region. Located a convenient but significant distance from Boston, the town's economic situation may have altered with the years, but not the character of the place or its people. Residents are polite, inward-looking, and embrace their own with candor and warmth. The children of one family are the children of all; forces threaten only from outside. Children take up their adult lives nearby, and a move of twenty minutes away is considered far. Making one across the United States is like journeying to some primitive corner of the Earth.

Parents accept that their children must go away; they accept because they have no choice. And if in their hearts they dread the nightmare of every parent, they hold that thought to themselves, for when tragedy befalls one of their own its dark presence touches each of them. They have made a pact with fate that as long as the dread is never uttered, it will never strike.

In 1981, that unspeakable tragedy occurred and on this early February day, the townspeople stood in the intermittent snowfall as the murdered daughter was laid to rest. As the coffin was lowered into the frozen earth, each member of the family tossed a crimson rose into the grave. The mourners wept in grief and sympathy and could only ask themselves, How could this happen? What kind of men could do such a thing?

Parents stared at their adult children with fresh uneasiness. Anything could happen. Anything. Even the nearby towns, where their offspring lived, were now more distant and foreign. Nothing was the same.

PART ONE
SUZANNE

"It's nice to be important, but it's more important to be nice."

—Suzanne Maria Rossetti

It is an all-American city. Saugus, Massachusetts, is the kind of place most towns claim to be, but rarely are. With a population of 27,000 people and less than ten miles outside of Boston on the North Shore, it is a quiet city. Although the townspeople commute to the metropolis for work, there is a deep sense of community and of history. The children grow up honest and industrious; couples more often than not grow old together.

There are two centers to the town, located approximately one mile apart. At Cliftondale Square are a street rotary and the business district with a grocery store, small restaurant, post office, and St. Margaret's, the Catholic church. Across the street is the Saugus Federal Credit Union and Peter A. Rossetti's Insurance Agency.

Saugus is seven miles from Lexington and only four miles farther from Concord. History has not marked its name with theirs, but the Revolutionary War had scarcely begun before the farmers and merchants of Saugus mustered five companies of 247 men.

A mile away is the government center for Saugus and the town library. There is a rotary here also, but this one is larger and bears a war memorial. The Yankees of Saugus served in the Civil War and 160 of the dead are neatly listed on it. The town hall across the street is relatively new, having been built in 1875. Another memorial announces that 792 of Saugus's young men fell in what was then called the Great War. And so it is for the Second World War and Korea and Vietnam. There are memorials for all the wars and the name of each of the dead is meticulously inscribed, the stark lists muting the tragedy each name bares.

Saugonians are proud their town is older than Boston. In 1629, just nine years after the landing at Plymouth Rock, settlers sailed down the coast from Salem into the mouth of the Saugus River. It flows just a few miles inland, but it was a safe harbor for fishing vessels and offered ready access to the bountiful Atlantic ocean.

Today the Saugus River has filled with silt and is more marsh than river. It is difficult to understand its significance to the first settlers, but in those days, one could sail several miles inland. The first iron foundry in America was constructed at Saugus for that reason. The ore and products moved up and down the river with regularity for more than a century.

The river flows quietly beside the government center of town and is overlooked by the Riverside Cemetery, the final resting place of Saugonians.

There is a large Italian community in Saugus, although they are in the minority and Catholicism is not the dominant religion. There are Christian churches of most sects; well maintained and well attended, and away from the highway, there are more churches than liquor establishments.

Townspeople gather on the sidewalks and chat near the rotaries, joggers run along the winding streets with impunity, the neat clapboard houses rest on modest parcels of land thick with vegetation. There are oaks and birches, beeches and maples. Spring is ripe with mayflowers, hellebores, violets, azaleas, and rhodoras. The narrow streets meander through the hills and the bordering trees often meet in a graceful arch. The land is no longer wild and nearly all of it that can be occupied, is. This is hilly country, luxuriantly green, but rarely can one see for more than one hundred yards. The four seasons last their allotted three months and mark the steady passage of the years with comforting regularity.

Saugus is not without its faults. Citizens speak forcefully of unwholesome influences from Boston and not an African American can be seen on its streets. There is an openly expressed relief that foreign elements, mainly East Indians and Pakistanis, have made no inroads into their town. Town politics can be as self-serving and exclusive as anywhere. But basically these are decent, law-abiding citizens who believe in and live the American Dream.

Peter Rossetti, Sr., was born in Saugus, one of nine children raised by an Italian immigrant father who supported his family as a laborer. They raised chickens and rabbits to have meat. The Rossettis worked hard, attended and supported their church, and lived life by society's rules. Peter's father often said that if you follow the rules in America it will be good to you. There are Rossettis throughout the North Shore. One relative stopped counting Peter's first cousins with the Rossetti name after reaching fifty.

When the Second World War broke out, Peter secured a naval commission, then was disqualified because of an impairment in one eye. He took a position as a manager in the shipyards of Boston. In 1945, Peter attended a cousin's wedding and met Louise May Bernazani, the date of the best man. Soon after the war he and Louise were married.

Peter is shorter than average but solidly built, with powerful hands. He is full of energy and optimism, and is by nature a gregarious man, the product of a happy childhood. Peter is a man who believes in the basic decency of others and treats people accordingly.

When he was free to leave the shipyard, Peter obtained his insurance license and opened his own business. He and his bride took an attic apartment in Saugus two miles from Cliftondale Square and worked as a team. Here were no false salesmen's smiles or feigned interest. Peter and Louise were a genial, outgoing couple who instinctively cared for others. Clients sensed the concern and became genuine friends.

Louise had been raised in nearby Everett and also was one of nine children. She was not quite five feet tall, perhaps one hundred and five pounds. She had always been athletically disposed and was amazingly fit in a time when almost no one thought of such matters. For all her optimism and unselfishness, Louise was nevertheless a woman of strong opinions and reserved the right within the marriage to voice them; but this was a traditional family and if he wished, Peter always had the final say.

Life for the couple was a single continuous circle. Professional and personal activities were intermixed with no attempt at separation. Peter worked out of his attic apartment initially because he could not afford an office; later there was no need to change. In 1950, having eyed the house across the street for a time, Peter and Louise bought it. It was a clapboard Colonial-style home, three stories, white with cranberry trim, typical of the houses in that vicinity. That same year Louise gave birth to their first child, Peter Jr.

Peter had each part of the interior of the new house rebuilt during the first years. His tiny office was on the second story, down the short hallway from the bathroom. In 1952, they had a daughter, Donna Louise. And two years later, Louise bore their third and final child, another daughter, whom they named Suzanne Maria.

Now the children were part of the Rossetti team. They learned to answer the business phone with a polite, "Hello, this is [Peter or Donna or Suzanne] Rossetti speaking. May I help you?" They took notes with meticulous accuracy.

Each year, the same clients came to the Rossetti home to have their taxes prepared or to discuss insurance. The children would take their nightly baths down the short hall, and it seemed the door was always open. The children, especially the Rossetti girls, would squeal as they played in the water, then run to their rooms with little towels wrapped partially around them.

After they were ready for bed, they would be presented to whomever was visiting. The clients would smile and ask the sisters questions, tell them how much they had grown. Clients took to bringing gifts for the children, especially for the two girls. The sisters would ask sweetly who was coming that night, then try to remember what they had received the year before. At first it was hard, but by the time they were six they came to know who could be relied upon for fresh-baked cookies, or hard candy, or cupcakes. At an early age, the Rossetti sisters could walk on their hands and entertain clients by walking this way upstairs. The girls sat on the visitors' knees, talked of school, and told stories as the clients smiled broadly, telling the father what fine children he had.

Peter Jr. was a quiet boy, given to his studies and to books, which he often read with a flashlight under the sheets at night. He planned to become a doctor. Later, when the porch was converted into an office, the attic was made into his room. He had posters, love beads, strobe lights, and a television set. It was a wondrous room, and the two younger sisters were always envious of it.

The girls each had a room at the end of the second-floor hall, separated by the bathroom. Though they were two years apart, they were more like twins than sisters in temperament. From the beginning, they were the best of friends. Suzanne was always very small, while Donna was of average size. Often Donna would visit in Suzanne's room at bedtime and they would giggle. It was not unusual for Donna to crawl into one of the twin beds in Suzanne's room and stay the night, just to be close to her younger sister.

Like twins, the sisters could anticipate each other's thoughts and feelings. Often they communicated with hardly a word, or with no more than a glance. Even when they were apart, it was uncanny the way they could sense what the other had been feeling or experiencing.

They visited their extended family who lived nearby, and from the time the girls were very young, for birthdays and holidays or simply on the occasion of a visit, aunts and uncles, great-aunts and great-uncles presented them each with a silver dollar to save. Suzanne's collection of these special gifts grew steadily.

When the girls were of age, the activities began: dancing and swimming lessons, religious instruction, Brownies and Scouts. The parents' car took the children everywhere. When Peter or Louise went to pick up one of them, they automatically gave a ride to all of the other children.

The Rossettis loved the "kiddos." When Peter rebuilt the interior of the house, he converted the basement into a giant recreation room. Louise kept the pantry stocked with goodies, and after school the neighborhood kids automatically flocked to the Rossetti residence. With children and relatives dropping by, there always seemed to be a crowd in the house. If a mother could not find her child, she called the Rossettis. On Fridays, it was virtually a party, with games and music and, most of all, laughter. Peter would arrive after work, weighted down with soft drinks and snacks. The children, sometimes as many as thirty, would stay until bedtime, when they would scatter home, except for the privileged few selected by Peter to be the clean-up crew. These slept over after their chores and in the morning were treated to hot chocolate and a gargantuan breakfast. Parties at the Rossettis' were a Saugus institution.

Despite the busy schedule, the children did homework each night without interruption and the family invariably ate together. Peter would quiz them on their schoolwork, and many nights promise a treat after they had cleaned up the kitchen and washed the dishes. Then he would pile the kids into the car and take them for ice cream, or to visit their grandmother. About once a week, the family went out to dinner, and the Rossetti parents were proud that the children knew table manners and how to order from a menu at an early age. Suzanne had little trouble ordering since she always wanted a tuna fish sandwich.

Suzanne was the one who always remembered the jokes and loved to make people laugh. Often called "Suz" in the family, she had a winning way with her father. When the older children wanted something, they would say, "Suz, you go ask," knowing their father was not likely to tell the baby of the family no.

By 1958, Peter was elected to the school board, and that same year he helped organize a vocational school district. He was voted on that board and served continuously thereafter. He was a Saugus town meeting member and served on the parish council at St. Margaret's where his family was in regular attendance. His business prospered, and increasingly Peter was respected as a leader and opinion maker in the community. He refused several job offers because he did not want to be on the road and away from his family, once declining a substantial job in Rome, Italy.

When Suzanne was still a very little girl the family took a vacation to California and Arizona. On board their flight, a drunken passenger attempted to hijack the airplane by holding a knife to the throat of a stewardess. Suzanne stood in her seat and watched, frightened. When the plane landed, the hijacker was taken into custody.

Louise commented to Peter that the man was obviously unhappy over the breakup of his marriage, and that the arrest would now make him miss his connecting flight to Hawaii. "It would have been better," she said, "if he had gone to Hawaii." Peter laughed. He could not believe that their lives had just been threatened and here Louise was concerned about the happiness of the hijacker.

Suzanne liked her dance recitals the best of anything she did. She loved to perform. There was a local talent show on television, broadcast on Sunday mornings, called "Community Auditions." Her family and friends laughed at her spunk when eleven-year-old Suzanne informed them that she would be appearing on the show. Suzanne mailed cards to everyone she knew so that they would watch. She rehearsed her dance routine religiously, then performed it with agility and enthusiastic energy. She tap-danced, did ballet, and threw in a series of impressive gymnastic maneuvers. She was very satisfied with her job, even though she did not win. For years, those who saw her performance recalled it with a grin. That was Suz.

Louise took her girls with her to the YWCA on Saturdays during family swimming hours. Suzanne was always the daredevil. One day she attempted a dive from the board, and managed to land on the deck and split her lip. She required eight stitches, but bravely ate dinner with the family at a restaurant that night, wearing her bandage like a badge.

Louise had an aunt who owned a modest cottage in the seaside town of Duxbury, just north of Plymouth. For a month each summer, and during many weekends, the Rossetti children and Louise would go to the beach. Donna met Joy Crisafulli, who was one year older, and through her Suzanne met Joy's younger sister, Debbie, who was her own age. A saying in Duxbury is that "summer friends are the best friends," and so it was for the four girls.

The cottages at Duxbury were scarcely luxurious and the Rossettis' had no bath. Adults and children alike used a garden hose for bathing. There were also no modern entertainments as such. Children in swimming suits had the run of the town; they would play cards, and rent bicycles, boats, and water skis. They bought penny candy and five-cent ice cream cones. Suzanne and Donna tasted their first, and only, disgusting cigarette one summer at Duxbury.

Children stayed out after dark and parents experienced little concern. At night the kids played on the beach, where they would build huge bonfires and roast wienies. Or they would hang out, lying on the seawall, staying up very late, talking and dreaming under the stars as the waves lapped below them.

In her early teens, Suzanne was four feet eleven inches tall and weighed ninety-five pounds. She looked beautiful in a swimming suit. Her dark hair was thick and she grew it very long and very straight in the style of the sixties.

At the beach was the Green Harbor, a dance hall made available to various children's age groups on different nights. Suzanne had to prepare first on these nights because her hair took the longest to dry. Then she stayed on the dance floor all evening.

The fathers came on weekends. On the way, Peter would buy five dozen doughnuts for the kiddos. The hour before he arrived, the girls would position themselves so they could spot the car before anyone else, then would run to meet it, so they could have first pick.

At times there were so many staying at the cottage, upwards of thirty on weekends, that many of the children had the fun of sleeping in the cars. The Rossetti family cottage was the one with the crowd, the one with the mob of laughing children, just as it was in Saugus.

Peter Jr., being the oldest and the only boy, had a special place in the family. Suzanne, because of her temperament and being the youngest, had a special place as well. Donna languished in the center. Not that she dwelt on it, or that it caused her unhappiness, but she often felt uncertain of her abilities. However, Donna was so popular, and such a gifted artist, many never noticed her insecurity.

When summer ended, friends lined up as the Rossetti sisters left. Everybody cried and promised they would see each other the next year.

In 1965, Peter finally took an office outside his home, just down the street. Peter Jr. worked after school and served as a runner; the sisters were responsible for cleaning up. Donna, however, would leave early and shop at nearby Fred's Grocery for dinner. Following Louise's instructions, relayed over the telephone, she would cook. When she ruined the occasional meal, it was a humorous event, and the family ate cereal or went out. Donna was, after all, thirteen years old.

As she reached adolescence, Suzanne began taking photographs of everything. She would carefully place them in albums, then write witty sayings beside them. Her friends pored over them for hours.

At this time, a troubled teenager burned down several of the local schools before being finally apprehended, requiring double sessions in those schools that survived. Peter Jr. was sent to board at Brown and Nichols, a prestigious Cambridge high school considered a training ground for those headed to Harvard.

In her school Donna seemed active in everything. She started playing the oboe in the fourth grade, but gave it up to be a cheerleader at Saugus High School, just like her cousin. Donna was on the student Board of Directors, performed floor exercises with the gymnastic team, served on the yearbook staff, and belonged to many clubs.

In middle school and later at Saugus High, Suzanne too lived at a feverish pace. It seemed as if her life was so full of wonderful things that she could hardly find the time for them all. She had met Freddie Quinlan even before middle school. At first he was just part of her group and went along to the movies or ice skating. He played hockey and starred at football. He was very large, and when he and little Suz began dating in high school, they were a memorable couple. Despite his size and athletic prowess, the girls considered the soft-spoken, scrupulously polite Freddie to be a teddy bear.

Carolyn Peters was one of Suzanne's friends at school. When Carolyn became a drum majorette and her father, who was in the local police department, presented her with a charm in the shape of a baton, she went to the Rossettis' to display her gift proudly. There the girls had pajama parties, ironed their long hair straight, played records, talked about boys, and nibbled on pretzel rods until they were sick. Peter bought them by the gross lot, and on weekends brought ten pounds of cold cuts, two sheet cakes, and at least a case of soda pop for the gathering. The teenagers did not leave behind a trace of it.

Suzanne was class vice president at Saugus High, served on the student Board of Directors and the student council, was a member of the National Honor Society and the French Club, and performed with the gymnastics team.

With her sister Donna, she often double-dated. Going out in groups was the practice. Donna obtained her driver's license ahead of the boy she was dating and she drove the family car for everyone.

The Saugus High cheerleading squad, known as the Sachems, a name of reputed Indian origin, was composed of four juniors and four seniors. Donna was selected captain her senior year. The cheerleaders dressed as Indians, and each fall, during the school's largest rally on Color Day, the day before Thanksgiving, wore full costumes and war paint during their performance. This was the weekend of the biggest football game against the school's arch-rival, a contest that went back nearly one hundred years. Each class made a float for the parade, and though the seniors usually won, the teachers reminded the students there had been one year when they had not.

Suzanne became a high school cheerleader her junior year, and because Donna had been captain of the squad, she set her heart on doing the same. The selection was made by an adult panel after each girl performed before them. At her tryout, Suzanne delivered her best; an athletic, gutsy, enthusiastic routine. When another girl was picked ahead of her, Suzanne was devastated. It was the most crushing disappointment of her young life, and she cried all that night. When she arrived at school the next day, all spunk and grit with bright red-circled eyes and smiles for the winner, everyone knew she had cried her heart out. She never expressed a word of disappointment and supported the new captain.

Soon this loss was dwarfed by a more significant event as one of the cheerleaders began dying slowly of leukemia. The girl had to drop from the squad after just two games. Like Suzanne, she had everything, and students slowly came to terms with their own mortality. The girls in the rec room at the Rossettis' now talked of death, and their church activities became more important to them. Suzanne and Carolyn Peters attended a retreat that year, sponsored through the Catholic Youth Organization, and emerged from it with positive feelings. But when their friend died that winter, there was anger at a God who would allow such a terrible thing to happen to someone like her. The girls spoke to Father Creed at St. Margaret's in an attempt to understand. He was the priest who worked the closest with the Catholic teenagers of Saugus.

When the dead girl's mother attended the last game of the season wearing her daughter's letter jacket, the cheerleaders performed through hot tears.

2

Freddie remained Suzanne's boyfriend throughout her high school years. It was a relationship that met with the approval of both sets of parents. Freddie was good at hockey, but in football he began attracting the attention of scouts. Not without reason did he entertain thoughts of a professional career.

Freddie and Suzanne were not merely another cute high school couple; they were in love. First love is conceived and maintained in innocence, and never really ends. During their senior year, they began to talk of marriage. When everything felt so right it was very hard to wait. But they were also the practical children of practical parents, and both of them were directed toward college. It was simply out of the question that they not attend, so they planned to go to the same college and marry following graduation.

Freddie was tied to those colleges that offered an athletic scholarship, while Suzanne, who was an honor student, could be more selective. She had her eye set on Boston University, and was eventually accepted there, as she was by Northeastern. But the first college to notify her of acceptance was small North Adams State in far western Massachusetts. During that last year at Saugus High, Suzanne drove with her parents and Freddie to inspect the campus. She was at once enamored, and returned from her visit enthusiastic about attending the school.

When Freddie received a scholarship to another college too distant for them to see each other as often as they wished, the couple reasoned that their love was strong enough to survive the separation.

In April of her senior year in high school, Suzanne traveled to France with the French Club for one week, escorted by one of the school's language teachers. The intent was to expose the students to French culture and to the language as it was spoken in its native land. Theoretically, the students were not to speak English, even among themselves. Instead, the trip turned into a hectic rush in a crowded bus to see all of France in a few frenzied days. The sleepy-eyed teenagers, exhausted from the grueling schedule, took in France through the streaked windows of their bus. The Rossettis also traveled to Europe at the same time, where they met up with Suzanne.

Graduation from Saugus High was a poignant moment as lifelong friends first realized that nothing would be the same thereafter. In the yearbook, called the *Tontoguonian,* Suzanne smiles directly at the camera, her long straight hair parted in the middle. Under the picture is the entry "Popular Suz . . . bundle of happiness . . . our peppiest cheerleader . . . stale pretzel rods . . . Friday night over Suz's . . ."

North Adams State College was founded in 1894 and is one of hundreds of similar liberal arts colleges in the Northeast. It sits comfortably in the aged Berkshire Hills, a lovely campus in a picturesque locale. At that time the surrounding town had a population of 19,000; the college itself had just 1,900 students.

The seasons are spectacular in the mountains of northwestern Massachusetts. Winter sparkles with icicles and crusted snow everywhere. The students tramp to classes in ski parkas and heavy mittens. The air is crisp; the environment, wholesome. There is nearby skiing, sledding, and ice skating. In the fall and spring, hiking and weekend backpacking are popular.

North Adams State was more like a high school than a college, and the teachers knew their students by first names. In the spring, the student body celebrated Fling at Fish Pond. The pond had little water, but was located a convenient hike from the campus. There were Frisbees, and beer, and good-natured games throughout the day. It was typical of the tone of life at the college.

It was the pull of the outdoor life and congeniality of the campus and community that attracted Suzanne to North Adams State, and she remained enthusiastic over her selection throughout her last year at Saugus High.

Suzanne had matured into an attractive young woman, though it was hard for her to see it. Now five feet tall, she was always the shortest in her group and like her mother she was busty. She was not muscle-bound but was so physically fit that her friends remarked with friendly envy that Suzanne had not an ounce of fat on her. Dressed for a date with Freddie, she was soft and feminine, with a trace of warm perfume.

The Rossettis were pragmatic parents, and Suzanne had learned to be conscientious with her money. She saved, and she understood that college would not be a free ride, even though her parents could afford it; she would have to do her part financially. During her four years in college she often worked as a waitress in town. When she drove off to North Adams State, she took the family station wagon that would be her car for the next several years.

The departure of their last child brought changes to the Rossetti household, with both Donna and Peter Jr. in college as well. Louise increased her involvement in physical activities and took to bicycling and running with enthusiasm. She became a regular fixture at the many local ten-kilometer races and began to acquire what would become an attic full of T-shirts and trophies from each event.

Peter continued with his work. His breathing suffered a bit from the asbestos to which he had been exposed at the shipyard during the war, but otherwise his health appeared robust.

In her freshman year at North Adams State, Suzanne was assigned to Hoosac Hall, an all-girls dormitory, where four girls had their own bedrooms and shared a common living space and kitchen. The first day, Suzanne met Joanie Saltzberg, also a freshman, from Waltham, Massachusetts, a half-hour drive from Saugus. They were not roommates that year, but Joanie's boyfriend and Freddie car-pooled so they could visit the girls on many weekends from their colleges.

Not long into the year, Suzanne and her roommates put their hair in curlers, smeared on brightly colored facial masques, stuffed pillows under oversized shirts, and walked around the dorm presenting themselves as typically pregnant housewives. Around Christmas, they acted out *The Grinch Who Stole Christmas* and dressed as Who people. They were always a hit, and Suzanne was the instigator.

That first year, Carolyn Peters and friends joined Suzanne and Freddie for a day's outing at Island Pond in New Hampshire. Carolyn's father told everyone to be careful. Despite the warning, Carolyn managed to fall off a toboggan and break her leg. Suzanne nursed her and saw to it that the girl was taken to a doctor, the whole time frightened that Mr. Peters would never let her see Carolyn again.

In nearly every regard Suzanne repeated her high school years at North Adams State. She was a cheerleader, was on the gymnastics team, and she performed acrobatics. At 5:30 most mornings, during a time before the sport was popular, she was up and ran five to eight miles.

Suzanne continued to take photographs of almost everything she did, and everyone she knew. She processed her film in triplicate and distributed the extras to her friends. She was punctual, so punctual other students joked about it, and though she was open when first meeting someone, she did not give rides to strangers, or extend her trust without exercising judgment.

To those who knew her, Suzanne remained the same happy and concerned person she had always been; the first to think of someone's feelings, or defend another, the one who remembered the special occasion, the one who enjoyed cooking a surprise meal for her room-mates. When the dorm was having one of its frequent parties, it was Suzanne who went around to be certain that everyone was included.

But in many ways Suzanne lacked confidence in her accomplishments. She preferred to brag about Donna, and Donna's artistic achievements, which impressed her so. Suzanne was also especially uncomfortable whenever her looks were complimented, for she did not consider herself attractive.

At the beginning of her second year in college, Suzanne's relationship with Freddie came to an end. The strain of distance had been too great, and the weekend visits had come less and less often. Over the Christmas holidays, they spoke of it. Suzanne had taken the words of the Beatles song "In My Life," written them down beautifully, and had the verses framed. She presented this gift to Freddie. They had believed in their love, and when it had not endured, they ended their special relationship with a sense of loss. They agreed to see each other, but they would now date others.

Suzanne had many male friends who talked to her about other girls, about dating and broken hearts, both at Saugus High and at college. Young men were drawn to Suzanne, as a friend. When she had had Freddie, that had seemed normal and correct to her. But when she was available to date, her relationship with the male students did not change. She was still Suz—or occasionally Rose for Rossetti

—the friend to talk with when you were having girl troubles, Suz to take hiking, or to liven up the party. Rarely was she the date.

Though she concealed her unhappiness from most who knew her, she occasionally told Joanie how frustrating it was. Suzanne had come from a happy family. She wanted a husband and children of her own one day. But that would never happen as long as she remained just plain Suz.

Despite the envy of the other girls over her figure and fitness, Suzanne remained uncertain of her ability to attract men. One night the girls were listening to music in the dorm when "Pretty Woman" began to play. Suzanne turned to Joanie and said, "I guess they're not talking about me." Joanie's assurances made no difference. Suzanne was more inclined to consider herself an ugly duckling than as the vivacious and attractive woman she had become.

Her senior year, Suzanne went on a diet that concerned her friends. In an attempt to give her body an unnaturally slim line, she crash-dieted to an unhealthy, even gaunt, ninety pounds. Joanie often expressed her concern and was relieved when Suzanne finally stopped, and returned to normal meals and her now-usual one hundred pounds.

During Suzanne's years at North Adams State, the Rossettis regularly drove the three hours to the campus to visit their daughter. Her closest friends would pile into the family car and be treated to dinner. Suzanne was proud of her parents and regularly showed them off around campus. Peter Jr. often made the long drive as well as to visit his little sister.

It was quite natural to those who knew Suzanne that she should major in sociology, and it appeared for a time that she might actually go into social work. During her senior year in college, however, she was assigned to work as a court intern as part of her curriculum. At first she was enthusiastic to be of help, and worked with one woman in whom she took a special interest. But she soon found her inability to effect change in people's lives frustrating, and when her favorite client stole money from her purse, Suzanne told her parents that this was not something at which she could make a career. She completed her major, but not with the intent of working in the field.

Suzanne's basic personality was now firmly established; it had remained fundamentally unchanged from the time she was a young girl. She was invariably of a sweet disposition, always vivacious and fun loving. If she had a dark side, it was fleeting and passed in private.

No one recalls ever seeing it; no one who knew her believes it ever existed. Suzanne had been reared in a world of love, of mutual respect and of kindness. She did not see the bad in anyone, and was quick to embrace a new acquaintance as a trustworthy friend, something against which friends occasionally cautioned her. Rather than being a hostile place, she believed that the world was populated with basically good people, and one could live with the expectation that strangers would act with decency and consideration.

She was, however, not a Pollyanna. She had been raised to exercise caution, to lock her car doors, to avoid the worst parts of Boston, to see to her own safety. The Rossettis had reared their daughter to be self-sufficient; able to take care of herself.

Suzanne and Freddie maintained contact after breaking up and still saw one another over the summer and during holidays. But whatever expectations Suzanne may have had concerning their future were shattered when she learned in May of her senior year that Freddie had married a girl he had been dating at his college. Suzanne did not speak directly of it to anyone, but clearly the unexpected marriage troubled her. A wall descended between the two of them now that had not existed, even after they had stopped dating.

In May 1976, when Suzanne graduated from North Adams State, Peter and Louise took her to stay with them at their new condominium in Scottsdale, Arizona, to watch the Celtics and Suns' playoff game. Louise's sister, Frances Chubinski, had lived in Phoenix since 1952. Through a niece, the Rossettis had bought the condominium in September 1975 as an investment and to use as a winter vacation home. It was a modest, two-bedroom, two-story place off Granite Reef Road.

Following the ball game, the family took a day trip to the South Rim of the Grand Canyon, where Suzanne was interviewed for work in the summer as a Harvey Girl. The Harvey Company had a long history, going back over a hundred years, of bringing young, attractive eastern women to the West. Joanie Saltzberg had worked the previous summer at Glacier National Park and had enthusiastically related the experience to Suzanne.

Suzanne had come to love the out-of-doors at North Adams State College, and decided to spend a few months working out West following graduation. She was hired, and soon left Saugus in her station wagon, driving across country from one friend's home to another as she made her way to Arizona, never once staying in a hotel.

During work hours at the Grand Canyon, she was a waitress or cashier. After work, the young people would hike and backpack, then throw a party at night. They were college students or, like Suzanne, just graduated from college. It was a great deal like life in a dorm, only the Grand Canyon was right out the window. Suzanne would sometimes load friends into her car to spend free time in the Rossetti condominium in Phoenix. The utilities were shut off, so the young people slept in sleeping bags and cooked on camp stoves. One time Peter and Louise flew out for a surprise visit and literally stumbled over a sea of bodies scattered across the living room floor, sound asleep.

After leaving the Grand Canyon, Suzanne joined a girlfriend in New Orleans and worked as a waitress. She remained through Mardi Gras, then took a job in California at Sequoia National Park.

During May 1977, Suzanne visited her parents and attended the wedding of a friend. There Suzanne saw Freddie for the first time since his sudden marriage the previous year. They danced and talked awkwardly. Suzanne told him that she was going to move out West, that she simply did not want to remain in Saugus. Freddie tried to dissuade her. He had understood her need to travel this past year, but he did not want her living so far away. He was afraid that he would never see her again. Suzanne told him there were too many bad memories for her to remain at home.

For some time, Peter had been experiencing heart difficulties, for which he was taking medication. That year he had a triple-bypass heart operation, and though he recovered his strength, the family paid particular attention to the condition of his health. Peter Jr. had graduated from Northeastern, then attended medical school, but when his father became ill he stepped in to run the family business, found out that he enjoyed it, and remained.

Suzanne established her residence in the Scottsdale condominium. She loved the West, and spoke rapturously of it in her telephone calls home. Although flat with little vegetation, Phoenix was flanked by mountains, and to the east the famed Superstition Mountains were visible. She loved the mountains, the barren rock formations, and the delicate, pastel-colored flowers. If the Rossettis were bothered by their youngest living there, they kept their concern to themselves. They vacationed in Arizona two or three times a year, and both Peter Jr. and Donna paid Suzanne visits. On frequent telephone calls her parents cautioned her to be careful to reassure themselves.

Suzanne waitressed for a time and then found a job with Youth

Services supervising teenagers who worked cleaning up city parks. She did not care for the job much, but it was a beginning. She traded in the large family station wagon and replaced it with a blue 1977 Pinto station wagon with only a few thousand miles on it. Although small and economical, it had the room she needed and a distinctive luggage rack. In her private life, Suzanne set out to establish a network of friends and began living a life very similar to the one she had led in Saugus and at North Adams State College.

Suzanne was now a fully grown young woman of twenty-three. She had suffered the loss of love, graduated from college, driven cross-country alone, and supported herself. She was loved and admired by those who knew her. She had been taught to play by the rules, and did. She had been raised to be a perfect child, and succeeded. She was altruistic, industrious, honest, and sincere.

If Suzanne Rossetti had a fault, it lay in her inability to perceive evil, and the evil intentions of others.

PART TWO

LOGAN

"Everybody wants to be a cowboy."

—Michael David Logan

3

The Crazy Mother Fuckers, the CMFs as they liked to be known, were a teenage biker club of wannabes. Not old enough for the adult outlaw biker gangs such as the Renegades, they emulated them in look and, they believed, in action, hoping to make a name for themselves. Members joined as early as age fifteen, while others were as old as twenty one. They all rode Harley-Davidsons with extended forks, "ape" handles, and sissy bars, all except for one who rode a Triumph. He was different in other ways as well, with his headband and moccasins. They called him "Indian."

Indian was born Michael David Logan in 1953 in Detroit. His parents were of French and Indian descent, a common ethnic background in Detroit at that time. The Logans had five sons, of whom Michael was the fourth. The youngest child was a daughter. Michael's father had returned to Detroit after serving in the Second World War. He was a hard drinker who worked loading Chrysler cars for shipment.

The Logans lived in the Jeffries Project in downtown Detroit, rough country even then, though not as rough as it would later become. The Logans were in the minority, being white, and Michael was forbidden by his mother to play outside the crowded apartment, except in the company of his older brothers.

As a group, the Logan boys were proud of their ability to take care of themselves and tolerated no interference with any member of the family. The boys fought routinely, and the line was clearly drawn:

us against—everyone. Michael was safe with his brothers, safe from the hostile world just outside the front door.

The Detroit of the 1950s and early 1960s was experiencing an economic boom that masked the fundamental decay just beneath the surface. She was like an aging courtesan who still attracted patrons with candles, ingenious makeup, and knowing gestures. The old game had worked so well for so long that when the fall came, it was an elemental shock. The Detroit of Michael's youth was poised for that shock.

At night Michael's father staggered home and the eldest son put him to bed. It was a dreary, unhappy life that abruptly changed when Michael was six years old and his father stopped drinking. The housing project was deteriorating rapidly and he was going to move his family away from the "niggers," as they were called by the Logans, and away from the violence. Michael's father bought a house in Warren, an all-white suburb ten miles to the north. Michael always referred to it as "heaven." At this time his father also quit his job loading cars and opened a "party store," a beer and wine establishment.

Warren may have been heaven, but the basic orientation of the Logan boys toward outsiders remained unchanged. They were the local toughs, and fights remained a daily occurrence, with Michael beginning to join in.

In Warren, Michael's mother allowed him to play outside, and he soon had friends other than his brothers. When Michael was ten years old, his mother spotted him in a park with his new friends smoking cigarettes. She dragged him home, spanked him, and washed his mouth out with soap.

Though Michael Logan was unaware of it, he was of better-than-average intelligence and maintained his C average with no effort. It was sports that interested him. In parish football he was a halfback and defensive back, in Little League a right fielder and power hitter. The team was called the Apaches, and appealed to the maverick in him. His father had strong Indian features and Logan had inherited his dark hair. Otherwise there was little resemblance. Logan's eyes were set far apart, and his face tapered to a weak chin. He liked the image of the Indian and was proud to be an Apache. He continued playing ball in junior high and Babe Ruth.

Rules, of course, were not meant for Logan. He had learned early on that the Logan brothers made their own. He routinely ran afoul of team discipline, such as it was, for his age group. He was kicked off his baseball team for a season when he was caught smoking cigarettes with two other players in the locker room.

Logan had trouble with school discipline as well and routinely talked back to his teachers. Rebellion was part of his nature. He resented any authority except for the force his brothers exercised. Once, when he was fourteen years old, he was taken from the classroom into the hallway with others to be paddled for misconduct. The teacher kept a well-worn paddle in his desk for these occasions, and applied it indiscriminately to his students as required. Though Logan knew he was not being singled out for punishment, he was angered by it. As they were being sent back into the classroom, Logan suddenly seized the paddle and flung it against the wall, causing it to split apart. The teacher grabbed Logan's ear and pulled him along to the principal's office, where Logan was no stranger.

The principal inexplicably sent for his older brother, and as he prepared to paddle Logan, the older brother unexpectedly stepped forward and quietly removed the paddle from the principal's hand. He was a large, thoroughly intimidating youngster. Logan was suspended for a week, but never received that second paddling.

The summer he was fifteen years old, Logan ran away from home. One of his brothers had worked at a Detroit racetrack and Logan had helped him out with the horses. He stayed with an older acquaintance that summer in a rural town and worked at the track "hot walking" horses just in from their workout, rubbing them down, mucking out the stalls, and running errands.

Mostly though, he partied. He began drinking beer every day, all day, and smoked "weed." He and his friends would get drunk and stay drunk, or stoned, or both. There were girls now, but Logan preferred the beer and the marijuana.

Logan came to love the horses as much as he distrusted and disliked people in general. Only infrequently did he extend his loyalty beyond the circle of his brothers. He enjoyed walking the horses with their pungent smell as they cooled from their workout in the crisp morning air. Afterward he rubbed their gleaming coats.

Logan was fascinated by the veterinarians and watched them intently, having his own dreams of being a vet, and coming into the stalls as these learned men did, knowing all of the answers, being looked up to and respected.

There was more to learn than how to tend horses at a racetrack. Track people are an itinerant lot, not unlike carnies, traveling from track to track in a seasonal circuit. They form their own subculture with its own rules. Logan found them and their lifestyle immediately appealing.

Drugs were a constant theme. Jockeys often depended on illegal pills to keep their weight down or, they believed, to heighten their performance. Substances of every description were used on the horses when the opportunity was afforded, but drugs were consumed primarily by the employees for recreation. The trade in narcotics was routine among racing people and carefully concealed from the track stewards and fans.

Violence was part of the racing life as well; welshing on private bets led to beatings. Violations of any of the unwritten rules of the track subculture meant more beatings and potential expulsion. There was an undercurrent of danger in this world that Logan found exciting and inviting.

Logan returned home and enrolled in school at summer's end. He experienced his first serious love affair that year with a girl named Patty,* an all-American beauty, with auburn hair and light eyes. He was on his best behavior with her and was crushed when she abruptly dropped him. In spite of this, his affection lingered.

After the adult freedom of the past summer, school was a restraint he could no longer tolerate; even success in sports failed to raise his spirits. During the long, bitterly cold winter, he became depressed and chafed at the limits imposed on his life.

When spring came he turned sixteen and was no longer legally required to attend school. He dropped out, moved from his parents' home, and joined the Crazy Mother Fuckers. In 1969, there were perhaps thirty motorcycle clubs in Detroit, most of them outlaws. The best known had a national reputation and informal ties with other regional outlaw bikers such as the Hell's Angels or the Banditos. The CMFs had a charter crafted from a real outlaw club.

Outlaw bikers are as regimented as any military organization. Every aspect of their life is controlled by a rule. Yet even within the CMFs, Logan carved a place for himself apart from the rest. He alone wore a headband and moccasins, and only he rode a Triumph.

But he did enough to fit in. When the boys took turns having sex with one of the teenage girls who hung out with the group, Logan

* Pseudonym

stood dutifully in line. He usually disdained having an "old lady," as their girlfriends were called, but when the occasion required, a girl would be with him. He was sufficiently accepted to be elected treasurer, even though in one unusual area he was insistent. His mother had taught him that the body is sacred in the eyes of God and was not to be intentionally marked. Enough of her teaching had rubbed off on Logan for him to refuse the usual club tattoos, and the members teased him over it by calling Logan "Mr. Clean" whenever the subject came up. Otherwise, he was known as Indian.

Despite their look of toughness with colors, chains, and conspicuous weapons, the CMFs were basically partyers. The only violence they found appealing was whatever they could visit on an easy victim. They wanted to look tough, not be treated accordingly.

They also had no criminal enterprise with which to support themselves. If they had attempted to branch into one, that would have brought them into immediate conflict with an older and genuinely tough outlaw club. The CMFs were content to look and play the part for the unknowledgeable, and their own egos.

Having no place of his own, Logan crashed with others or slept overnight in someone's van. For money he would work a few days as a roofer, help out in his father's store, or steal, if the theft was relatively risk-free. Logan spent most of his time in pool halls and considered himself to be something of a hustler. He played cards as well and was always on the lookout for easy pickings. Because he considered himself to be cleverer than he was, he was not nearly as successful at either endeavor as he imagined.

This was the time of free love, even in Detroit. The city's streets were filled with runaways, and the CMFs on their bikes were obviously rebels and exotics. Indian was routinely flagged down for a ride and would end up smoking weed in someone's van and having sex.

For Logan, however, the best part was the beer with the occasional whiskey chaser. He loved beer, and started each day with a single long pull from a can. Even before he was out of bed, he would pop the can he had left beside him with which to jump-start the day. Cold or warm, it made no difference. Throughout the day he always kept a beer at hand. He consumed it at a steady pace and maintained a level of intoxication that allowed him to function, and kept up the numb, low-key buzz he craved and increasingly needed. Logan constantly smelled of alcohol, the stale odor that oozed from him and from the fresh beer that he continually drank. Late at night, he would gradually sink into an alcoholic stupor, and the pleasant taste of hops sucked from a can of beer was his last memory before sleep.

There was also the weed that he smoked and there were pills, lots of them. Primarily uppers, but downers as well. And LSD, when he could find it. He drifted through two years of life like this, working no more than required, drunk and stoned every waking moment, sleeping wherever he found himself that night.

This pack of teenagers was shocked in 1970 when two CMFs were killed, one after the other. These were the gang's first fatalities. One of the older outlaw motorcycle clubs would have gone to war, or at least have made a show of force and kicked butt, as they put it.

The first to die was a member of the CMFs known to Logan as a serious drug addict. No one was especially troubled by his death. It was understood that he had been killed when a petty drug transaction went awry. But a few weeks later another CMF was beaten to death. He was not known as a drug addict, and his death frightened members. The CMFs did not see these events as coincidence. Fraught with fear, the club fell apart.

By this time, Logan was nearly eighteen years of age and believed he had outgrown the CMFs. Some CMFs recruited others and formed a club of older bikers called the Zigzags. To them the name appeared a clever double-entendre. It evoked in their minds outlaw bikers zigzagging along the city streets, envied or feared by everyone who saw them. It was also the name of the paper in which they wrapped the weed they smoked.

Compared to an authentic outlaw biker club, the Zigzags were the semi-pros. Proof that they were closer to the real thing came when, after a few months, the Renegades and the Outlaws recruited a few of their members. Still, they had no criminal enterprise with which to support themselves, and though this was a step up, they were not an organization to be taken very seriously. In both the CMFs and the Zigzags, Logan found the same kind of familiar us-against-the-world orientation in which he had been reared with his brothers.

In Detroit there were good and decent people going about work and diversions, but Logan saw none of this. He lived in an outlaw subculture that was his whole existence. Straights existed to be conned or to rob; the world in which he moved was a threatening place from which he required protection. It was natural then, when the CMFs dissolved, that he would help organize another club to replace them.

One day Logan was working at his father's store when Emily Lewis* came in to make a purchase. At one time, she had dated a friend of his and Logan thought she was good-looking. Emily was tall and slender and had "great tits," as Logan put it. She wore her black hair long with bangs and used glossy red lipstick. Even though she disapproved of the Zigzags and of Logan's lifestyle, they began to date.

Logan had become so used to willing girls, he was at first put off by the fact that Emily would not sleep with him. She demanded respect. And the more she saw of him and continued to refuse him, the more Logan did respect her. He kept Emily away from his other life as much as he could. After a year she began sleeping with him.

In the fall of 1971, Logan had been drinking coffee in an all-night coffee shop with two Zigzag brothers in downtown Detroit. At 2:00 in the morning, they were riding in a pickup truck when four cars of black youths suddenly blocked their route. The white men piled out of the truck wielding chains, ready to fight. The other two Zigzag members were in front of Logan, and no one was covering his back. Just as the fight began, Logan felt a terrible blow to the side of his gut. He turned and flailed away at his assailant with a motorcycle chain, but the pain only intensified. Suddenly he collapsed. He reached down and his hands were bathed in warmth. When he looked, he saw steam rising from his side and bloody hands. With a sinking heart, he realized he was clutching his intestines.

He made it the few feet to the truck and leaned on the horn until the youths scattered and his two buddies came to help him. He could hardly speak, and Logan knew beyond doubt that he was dying. He gasped to the others that he had been stabbed. The men ran the truck wide open to the nearest emergency room.

For two weeks, Logan lay in the hospital with tubes protruding from him. Emily visited almost daily. He was released, weak and unsteady on his feet, on the first day of December.

Shortly after New Year's, they were entering a pinball parlor when Emily abruptly told him she was pregnant. With hardly a missed beat, Logan said, "We'll have to get married." She nodded her head, looked relieved, then followed him in to play pinball.

Even after Emily had begun sleeping with him, Logan respected her no less. It never occurred to him not to do what he thought was right when she told him she was pregnant. He never doubted for a

*Pseudonym

moment that he was the father. Not only did he respect Emily, he loved her.

Because she was not a Catholic they were married the following month by a judge. Logan rented a place to live and landed a steady job as a roofer. Emily quit working at a dress shop.

Three months after his marriage, Logan went off to settle his unfinished business. He spoke to a cop with whom he was friendly, a man who despised "niggers" as much as Logan, and learned the name of the man who had stabbed him and where he could be found. The cop told Logan there had been no reason for the attack other than Logan and his buddies being white.

The Tip Top Café was in a transition area between black and white Detroit. Logan was very drunk when he barged into the black café. He had no idea what the assailant looked like and tried calling him out to fight. He held his fists up and shouted that the two of them would settle this face to face, no tricks. When no one stepped forward, Logan called them "niggers" and challenged the café full of men to a free-for-all. They ignored him except for one who called the police. Informed of that, Logan took off unsteadily on foot.

Not far away a cop called out to Logan, "Are you the one?"

" 'One' what?" Logan shot back with slurred speech. Logan was accustomed to dealings with the police, and if a veteran had challenged him he might have responded differently. But this cop did not look any older than he did and Logan mouthed off. Since he was worked up, easy enough, given the adrenaline from the Tip Top Café and his drunken state, he told the cop to take off his badge and gun and they would "go at it" right in the street. Several police cars soon arrived and Logan was arrested for disorderly conduct.

Instead of calling Emily, Logan asked his boss to come down and pay the nominal fine. However, he was not released until morning, so Logan simply went straight to work. That evening Emily demanded to know where he had spent the previous night. Rather than lie to her, he refused to answer. Finally, she told him she already knew. His boss had called to let her know Logan was all right. Unexpectedly she let it go, which was fine by Logan at the time. Emily, he was to learn, was the kind of wife who preferred to bank her grievances.

Logan decided to go straight, to his way of thinking. Emily was big by now and she always seemed to be holding one grudge or another against him. She never tired of telling him that his so-called friends were bums, and no good for him. He dropped out of the Zigzags and shed the persona of Indian for good, but he still hung out with a few of the brothers and members of other biker clubs. His drinking remained unchanged and he would have been angry had anyone, even Emily, said anything to him about it. That was his business.

If he thought giving up formal involvement with the Zigzags would fix things at home, Logan was mistaken. The men with whom he associated, the manner in which he lived, his constant drinking, all caused Emily to be angry with him. Logan would listen to none of her complaints.

Eight weeks after Emily gave birth to a son, she moved in with her mother. Logan was thunderstruck. They were married, for God's sake! Wives didn't leave husbands.

Logan dropped by from time to time to see Emily and the child. Emily, however, began behaving strangely toward him. Logan called her best friend, Stacy,* and pressured her about his wife's behavior. Stacy finally admitted that Emily was dating someone else. Logan felt betrayed, and though they patched things together and reconciled a few weeks later, his feelings for Emily were changed. He did not trust her any longer and he was tortured by thoughts that another man had kissed the breasts he loved, and that she had spread her legs for someone else. He spied on her and challenged anything she did or said that struck him as out of place.

Emily took a job because their financial situation was so desperate, but she soon found herself pregnant again. Logan's behavior went unchanged, despite the reconciliation. Though he did not pop a brew from beside the bed the moment his eyes opened, he did take one from the refrigerator to suck on as he stood over the toilet urinating. He still drank all day, every day, and in the morning there were empty cans of beer beside the bed.

Despite Emily's protests, Logan maintained the same friends. Nothing had changed, except that once again she was pregnant and Logan was more distrustful and surly. And so in the last month of this pregnancy, Emily came home one night, accompanied by Stacy. Logan was in an alcoholic stupor, seated at the kitchen table with one of his friends she disliked. The pair were cutting a kilo of marijuana for resale.

* Pseudonym

"I'm getting a divorce," Emily announced at the door.

It took a moment to sink in. Still seated, Logan finally managed, "Why?"

"I'm going to stay at my mother's. We can talk about it in a few days."

Still without rising, Logan shouted drunkenly, "Why can't we talk about it now?" Instead of responding, the two women left.

Logan's friend had stopped parceling the weed when the confrontation began. Now he said, "Wow!" Then, "Do you want me to leave?"

"There's no reason," Logan said, and they returned to cutting the kilo.

Logan and Emily had little to do with each other after that. Less than a month later, Logan telephoned Emily at her mother's. Stacy answered by saying, "Donnie?" As a consequence Logan no longer cared whether Emily filed for divorce. Within months, Emily married Donnie. Soon after that Logan stopped seeing the babies and ceased paying child support.

Logan was now twenty years old. His one attempt at a normal life had been a failure. He had demonstrated an inability to make and carry out meaningful plans. He had demonstrated that, like his father, he knew how to be a drunk.

Logan still ached for Emily, however, and the thought of her with another man raised murderous thoughts in him.

His animosity toward people in general continued to grow. Almost no one meant anything to him, and more and more he sought privacy and distance between himself and others. Now he moved in a new direction, still clutching the ever-present can of beer. Though it was too late to save his marriage, he severed all contacts with bikers, believing they had cost him Emily. He took a job at a racetrack where once again he groomed horses, "hot walked" them after their morning run, mucked out the stalls, and watched the vets with keen interest and distant dreams.

This time, when the racing season ended, he hooked up with the track gypsies and moved on to the next state. He had come to despise Detroit with its huge population. As a boy, his mother had friends who were Australian, and he had loved listening to their accent. Since that time, he had read magazine articles on Australia, and was especially drawn to the Outback because almost no one lived there.

For the next two years, Logan traveled across the United States, though all he saw was an endless stream of liquor stores and bars, and look-alike racetracks. The cast altered at each track, but there were always familiar kinds of people with different faces. He worked in Ohio, Nebraska, California, and nearly every state in between. His last stop was near Clearwater, Florida.

Until now he was enjoying this life. The more alienated he became from the world in general, the more he came to love horses, the open spaces between cities, and his dreams of Australia. Logan experienced an affinity with horses he could not with people. That suited him.

Logan's life in the subculture of the racing world was not so different from the one he had led when he was sixteen years old. He was not well paid and was always in search of an easy score. There were many such opportunities, from selling drugs, to administering beatings, to committing arson. He had developed a reputation, which served him well, of being a stand-up guy. He did not snitch, and if he took money, Logan did what he was paid to do. At night there were parties with plenty of beer, weed, pills, and women. Nothing, however, meant as much to him as the beer, and no woman was worth the effort if he had to work too hard. If it was convenient, Logan was not a man to say no.

One day at the track near Clearwater, Logan was holding a "$1,200 horse," as they are called, with a leather strap called a shank, while the vet was cleaning its teeth. He struck a sensitive spot and the horse abruptly reared in the air and flipped on its back. Logan dove head first out of the stall, escaping just in time. The vet was laughing like hell and through his tears reminded Logan that the first thing you do is position yourself so something like that cannot happen. Logan was not amused, and his fine opinion of vets took a fall.

Toward the end of the season, one of the women working around the track discovered the tires to her car were flat. Having neither the time nor the money for repairs, she asked one of the older, year-round employees to keep an eye on her car until she could return for it. Logan knew she kept a record collection in the trunk; perhaps she had told him he could use it, but probably not. In any event, he helped himself to the records and two days later was arrested for breaking and entering, and possession of stolen property. He served eighty days in jail waiting to receive probation. By now, the track was closed for the season, and rather than follow the circuit, Logan went home to Detroit.

He returned to the biker clubs. Though he never formally joined one, his reputation in that world was solid, and he was treated to honorary membership privileges. He roofed a little, stole a little, went on an occasional road trip.

By December 7, 1977, Logan was looking for a big score. For two years he had paid no child support, and his brothers cautioned him that Emily had taken legal action. There was a warrant outstanding for his arrest. Logan figured he needed $14,000 to square with her and to take care of other needs. That was a great deal of money for him, a sum he wanted to make in a single score, not with nickel-and-dime deals.

That day, Logan learned of such an opportunity. He knew an elderly man named Vic* who ran a porno shop on the west side of Detroit where a buddy of Logan's made bets. That was Vic's actual line of work: bookmaking. In an area heavily populated by Iranians, Logan met with others that night in a bar, men who had already agreed to help him roll Vic. One was Fat Al** another biker and, like Logan, a heavy drinker. Another was Hog†, a Yugoslavian drug addict. Hog knew Vic the best, and he had stopped by to see the bookie at his store earlier to be certain Vic was coming to the bar as he did every night after work. According to Hog, Vic would be carrying $40,000 in a wad thick enough to stop up a toilet.

Logan, Fat Al, and Hog hung out at the bar getting wasted and planning how they would rob Vic. Hog was to take Vic nearby for pizza. When they left, he would lead Vic down a quiet street. By then, it would be very late. At a certain signal, Logan would toss Vic's coat over his head and Hog would flee, since according to the scenario, he too was a potential victim. Then Fat Al would grab the stash, while Logan held the struggling old man.

By the time Vic entered the bar and greeted Hog, the three men were pretty well tanked. True to form, Vic flashed bills and bought the house a couple of rounds. Soon he and Hog left to eat. After the beer and talk, the plan looked workable to everyone. Nobody would get hurt and everybody would do well financially except Vic, who had plenty anyway and should learn not to flash money around like he

* Pseudonym
** Pseudonym
† Pseudonym

did. Before the bar closed, Logan and Fat Al had one more and then moved out into the frigid night to take up their planned positions.

By the time the bar closed at 2:00 A.M., Logan was standing in an alley, shivering in the wind. Not long after that, Vic and Hog left the pizzeria. When Hog gave his signal, Logan jumped Vic as arranged, but before Fat Al could locate the money wad, plainclothes cops were everywhere shouting, "Freeze!," pointing handguns. Hog, Fat Al, and Logan fled in different directions.

While the men had been swilling beer and talking big plans, plainclothes policemen had been sitting in the bar eavesdropping. Later, Logan recalled that the cops had bought them a couple of rounds.

Logan fled down an alley, so drunk that in the dark he sprawled flat on his face while running. Just then shots were fired. There was an organized effort to stop street crime in Detroit and the police were playing rough. Logan looked up and believed he could make out holes in a nearby wall. He fled again, thought he had evaded the cops, and finally crawled under a car. A few minutes later Hog, who had started off in another direction, slipped in beside him. Logan was furious at sharing his hiding place, but there was nothing he could do.

The police had cordoned off the area and were conducting a systematic search. All the commotion and shooting had roused the neighborhood. One woman looking out her window, spotted Hog and Logan freezing under the car. "There they are!" she screamed, and pointed her arm at them.

4

Logan was a convicted felon on probation in Florida and had little choice other than to accept Michigan's best offer on this new charge. He received the going sentence of three to fifteen years. After his plea and sentencing, Logan was transferred to Jackson State Prison north of Detroit, at one time the largest walled criminal institution in the world.

Logan found incarceration not unlike the world in which he lived; the unwritten rules there were the same rules by which he had grown up. Because he knew more than a few of the inmates, Logan attached himself to a group of incarcerated bikers for protection, then set about serving his time without trouble.

Except for the close proximity of so many lowlifes and blacks he despised, it was not a bad life. To earn good time and an early release, he was required to attend Alcoholics Anonymous, and pass a high school equivalency test. After a while, he stopped thinking about beer every minute.

Logan was released to outside trustee status where he was held in prison by cyclone fences and guards. After serving a total of twenty-seven months, he was released to a halfway house while in transition to street parole. He still had a fifteen-year prison sentence hanging over him should he violate the conditions of his release. He was twenty-five years of age.

Logan returned to the Detroit track where he had worked previously, because his reputation was still untarnished and he was known there. The people who handled such matters told him they would check out his Florida problem to be certain it was not something that tainted him with them. In the meantime, he could have his old job back. Because of his time in prison, Logan had made even more underworld connections. He returned to drug dealing, committed arson occasionally, and now dealt in guns.

Logan had a vague idea of getting Emily and his two children back. He had not thought things through enough to consider whether or not she wanted him, or what she would do with her current husband; he just knew he still wanted her. Though he had plenty of cash from his illicit activities, the staff at the halfway house wanted proof of his means of income, and that was going to be a problem. Before he could work it out, events intervened.

One of the services Logan had rendered across the country was to place official bets for those whom the track prohibits from doing so. He was pulled from the betting floor by security heavies and told he was not allowed to make wagers. He was also told that that was something he should have known. Before he could explain himself, he was off the track and blackballed.

In the ten days he had been in the halfway house, Logan had worked at not drinking. Since he was not required to attend AA, he did not. Without his track job and with the halfway house pressing him for pay stubs, he went on a drunk. Once he did not return, he became a fugitive. Logan spent the next two nights with different friends and settled into his old routine of steady drinking. Loitering the third day in a store parking lot, considering his next move, he spotted Laurie.* Laurie had been an old lady in the Renegades to a biker named Snake. Logan offered to help carry her groceries.

Laurie was thirty years old. She had lived a hard life in biker clubs and had the usual tattoos. When he was a boy, Logan had seen the movie *Snow White*. He had always been fascinated by the raunchy Laurie when he watched her with Snake because she looked, in his eye, exactly like Snow White. Snake had left Laurie with two children; she was on welfare and unhappy. They talked standing by her car and Logan turned on the charm until she suggested he spend a few nights with her while he looked for a permanent place.

Logan lived with Laurie for six months under an assumed name

* Pseudonym

and continued supporting himself with various criminal enterprises.
He sold drugs, ran guns, performed contract beatings. He drank thirty
to forty cans of beer a day. He had a theory that if he stayed drunk,
never really allowing himself to become sober, he would never experience a hangover.

To his surprise, Logan actually enjoyed his life with Laurie. One
of her two children was a girl with her mother's looks. She was sharp
and entertained Logan with her stories and drawings. As for Laurie,
she was just glad to have a man around, to help with the groceries,
to spend money, and take her out once in a while.

One very cold night when it had been snowing heavily, Logan
and one of his buddies had been drinking as usual. On their way home,
the drunks drove the car into a snowbank and could not break free.
After a time, a police car stopped to help the men, and because of
their condition, the officer asked to see identification. Logan had a
false ID, but not on him. Pressed for a name, he told the cop he was
one of his brothers. The officer had heard of the Logan boys and ran
a record check on the name. Logan's brother, he learned, was wanted,
of all things, for not paying child support. Logan was arrested, and
five days later one of the guards passed by his cell and called out his
false name derisively as he flashed Logan's fingerprint card. They now
knew who he was and shipped him back to Jackson.

After a few weeks, Logan's brief time on the streets seemed as if
it had happened to another person. Once again he was required to
attend AA. He was effective in winning over one of the prison coun-
selors, who was impressed by Logan's apparent earnestness and verbal
candor in his meetings. The counselor was filled with high expectations and expedited Logan's release. Logan served a flat year behind
the walls and received direct parole without outside trustee status or
a halfway house.

Within a few days, Logan ran into his high school love, Patty.
It had been nearly ten years since he had last seen her and his old
emotions were renewed. She had a little girl, and Logan took an
immediate liking to the tomboy. He needed a place to stay and Patty
was agreeable. Logan was determined never to return to prison.

Unfortunately, there was a perpetual recession on in Detroit and
Logan could not find work. He did not want to return to his usual
criminal activities, and he was no longer welcome at the track. He
was becoming desperate and began thinking about making a big score

again when he saw a "Help Wanted" sign at a fiberglass company and inquired. He was hired on the spot. Exhilarated, he decided to test his luck further. He walked into a service station just down the street and was hired as a night attendant.

For most of the next year, Logan's life settled into a routine. During the day, he worked making fiberglass products. When that job ended, he walked down the street and pumped gas until midnight. Slowly, he returned to drinking.

One night friends dropped by a for a visit. A condition of Logan's parole prohibited him from entering a bar, so they had brought a load of beer. While the men drank, Patty and the women went out together and a few hours later called, very agitated. There was a fight going on in the background and she told Logan to come and get her, now! The men piled into a car to help, although Logan remained outside once they arrived. The bar brawl continued until the police arrived. Logan was questioned, then arrested for outstanding traffic warrants. Patty bailed him out that night, but when he went to see his parole officer, he was told to hold his hands out while a pair of handcuffs was slapped on them. The police report of the bar incident said Logan had been fighting inside the bar. Logan begged his PO not to revoke his parole without first checking the report. The parole officer agreed, but for eight days Logan languished in jail. When his story was confirmed, Logan was released to the streets, only to learn that the eight days had cost him both of his jobs.

Logan resumed his habit of continuous heavy drinking. Patty had made it clear that she would not tolerate it, and within days she threw him out. Logan crashed with friends and no longer saw his parole officer. Within a month, in a drunken stupor, he passed out in a car. When a policeman asked him his name, Logan was so intoxicated he could not remember the one he was using. He had purchased a false ID, which he handed to the officer. Then he told the man a different name.

His parole was revoked and he was returned to prison. His counselor was very disappointed and visibly angry with Logan. "I really thought you'd make it this time," he said. Then he reminded Logan that he still faced most of his fifteen-year sentence. No matter how many times Logan violated parole, he would always come back to Jackson and begin over again. At that moment, Logan made up his mind to escape at the first opportunity. He maintained his easy surface charm with the counselor, and after only two weeks in isolation for classification, persuaded the man to transfer him to outside trustee status.

By now, Logan was six feet tall and weighed 185 pounds. He stooped slightly when he stood, and it presented a false illusion of even greater height. He had long arms and oversized hands. Already his long, unkempt hair was receding; and as a consequence, his large forehead appeared to grow with each year, which only accentuated the space between his eyes and the distance to his weak chin. His face presented a distinctly triangular aspect.

Most disturbing was his inability to meet people's eyes. What appeared to be a direct gaze on close examination was, in fact, an almost imperceptible twitching of his eyes, as if he were staring at each corner of one's pupil, unable simply to look at whom he was speaking. In his manner he appeared detached and uninterested, but in reality he was observing closely, seeking to blend in while not depriving himself of a fortuitous opportunity.

Most ominous was his fish-eye stare once he was determined to accomplish something and was set on his obsessive course.

Outside trustee status was still prison, but life there was easier. Men were free of many restraints behind the walls and were allowed to wear civilian clothing. Usually OT was used as a transition point for men on their way to a halfway house or parole. That was why Logan had been assigned there his first fall at the prison. Now he was thinking primarily of the fences, of the lack of security, of what he would do once he reached the nearby highway.

When he was on the streets, Logan existed in the perpetual haze of the alcoholic. His thoughts were muddled and he found it impossible to organize his life for more than a few consecutive hours. Each day was a crisis and he was always searching for the quick fix, the big score that would make everything right for him.

In prison, he was a different man. With plenty of rest, free of the alcohol that permeated his body, in a world where he was more intelligent than nearly everyone, including the staff, he could establish a goal and work to attain it. During his first two periods of incarceration, he had focused on manipulating the system by being dutiful in his AA meetings, penitent with his counselor, respectful to his superiors. Both times he had secured releases as quickly as they ever came. Now all Logan could see ahead of him was an endless succession of releases and increasingly lengthy reimprisonment. What he needed was a new start, and the more he considered it, the more he reasoned Australia, with its sparse population and vast Outback, was the solution. But first he had to escape.

Each morning before dawn, the cell doors in OT were opened for breakfast. The inmates mingled with relative freedom after that, going about their assigned work until lockdown that night. Money is forbidden in prison, so there is always lucrative trafficking in it. In OT the inmates were issued silver-colored plastic tokens against their accounts, which they could use as currency at the commissary. Logan made contact with other inmates he knew to be stand-up guys and explained that he had business on the outside. He used his tokens to buy what he reasoned he would need to make good his escape and traded the rest at the rate of two for one to acquire cash.

Since most of the inmates in OT were on their way to early freedom, few escaped, but they knew how it was done, as did Logan.

There was a soft place in the ground under the cyclone fence. Shortly after lockdown on an early morning in August 1980, Logan scooped up the loose soil from under the fence, squeezed through, and took off. OT had some security in that it was located within a larger, contained area. The mistake most men made, Logan reasoned, had been to attempt getting out of that area immediately. He would be missed nearly at once and the veteran guards could place bets on his location one hour after the morning doors had sprung open. Logan had spotted an abandoned bus once used by the prison for transporting inmates, gutted and resting flat on the ground. It was of no use and lay ignored a distance from the OT fence, but within the larger security area.

Before the sun was fully up, Logan had squirmed under it and found a black hole in which to hide. With candy bars and a can of soda pop, he passed the time and lay there through the day while the search for him ranged unsuccessfully farther out. He heard no one approach the bus. When it was dark, he shucked his soiled prison garb and slipped into a new jogging suit he had bought at the commissary. He made his way to the outside perimeter and crawled over the tall cyclone fence.

Logan took off on the bordering highway at a steady gait, as if he were a jogger out for a run. He was in terrible physical condition, but was strongly motivated to maintain the charade, though by the time he reached the interstate he was ready to collapse. He ran for a while on the freeway before it occurred to him it was illegal and he was asking for trouble. He stuck out his thumb and very shortly a refurbished police car pulled to a stop. Logan smiled and slipped in beside a uniformed prison guard on his way to work at Jackson. Of all the luck, Logan thought.

Logan explained that he was on the Ann Arbor cross-country team and was on a long-distance training run. Instead, he had become very tired and decided to hitch a ride to his parents, who would drive him back to the campus. The coach would never know.

The guard got an obvious kick out of the story. Logan quizzed him on what it was like inside a prison until he reached his turnoff, then thanked him with a long sigh of relief.

Logan hitched a second ride which took him straight into Detroit, and then crashed with a friend who expressed surprise that Logan had been released so soon. The next day, Logan confided in him and after the friend rounded up clothes for him, Logan collected old debts. Through one of his brothers, he bought a quick identification card just in case he was stopped. Then he blew nearly all of the money after that on a weeklong drunken party.

The longer he remained in Detroit, Logan thought, the greater was his risk. The plan was to begin moving in the direction of Australia. Along the way he would look for the big score that would pay his way. One of his brothers had lived a time in Tempe, Arizona, just outside of Phoenix. Arizona was open country, which appealed to Logan, and if things became too hot he could jump over the border to Mexico. Most importantly, Arizona was in the right direction, toward Australia and a new life.

He bought a bus ticket for Phoenix with what money remained, then smuggled beer and Southern Comfort on board and sat in the rear, where he gathered others for a card game and party.

For many years, Logan had enjoyed what he viewed as the mystique of being the Indian. He had cultivated the look, carried the moniker. As he headed to Arizona, he formed a new identity. "Everybody wants to be a cowboy," he said. Now Indian was going to become a cowboy. He was excited as he considered the prospect, and played cards continuously until the bus pulled into the terminal in downtown Phoenix on Labor Day night, 1980.

The Logan who escaped from Jackson State Prison was a desperate man who had just spent over three of his last four years in prison. When he stepped off that bus, he was a wanted fugitive and was determined that nothing, and no one, was going to get in his way. He was prepared, absolutely committed, to doing whatever was necessary to remain at large and reach the haven of Australia.

PART THREE

·

GILLIES

"Everybody dies."
—Jesse James Gillies

5

———•———

When Yolanda Gillies* first set eyes on her fourth child in 1960, the one she would name Jesse James, she knew that she could never love him. His had been an unwanted pregnancy, and she saw ahead only heartache because of his birth. Uneducated, unmarried, with three children already, she considered this child an undesired burden in a life already weighted down with them.

She could pity her newborn; what Yolanda could not feel was a mother's love for him.

It was a godsend when her stepmother said that she and her husband would take Jesse. They would raise him as their own and adopt him. It would be the best for all concerned. Yolanda readily agreed, and shortly thereafter, Jesse went to live with his grandparents.

San Francisco in 1960 was much the same as it had been in the years since the Second World War. The Haight-Ashbury days of hippies and LSD were still a few years in the future. The city possessed a rough-and-tumble reputation and tolerated unorthodox lifestyles.

Yolanda lived in the decidedly unglamorous Mission and Sunset districts. Altogether, she would have five children who were to be raised in a life of chronic poverty. Jesse did not know, and would never meet, his father.

Sometime after a year, Yolanda came to regret having given Jesse

* Pseudonym

61

to her parents. She felt that the arrangement would be unfair to him in the coming years, as well as to his brother and sisters. She reneged on the agreement and retrieved him, determined to raise the boy herself, but her feelings toward Jesse remained unchanged.

That very first morning in her apartment, Jesse caused total dev-astation. He had risen before anyone else and proceeded to destroy whatever he could find. Magazines were ripped to pieces; knickknacks and pictures had been knocked off the walls and destroyed. In the kitchen, he had ripped apart everything he could reach in the refrig-erator; half gallons of milk flooded the floors, and pots and pans were scattered like islands. By the end of the first week, Jesse had ruined everything of value she possessed.

Yolanda responded by whipping Jesse vigorously after each in-cident. But he never cried, never showed the slightest hint of emo-tion. He bore punishments with lifeless eyes that stared unflinchingly at her.

When he entered school his behavior was unchanged. At least two of his grammar schools recommended treatment for young Jesse, but Yolanda could not afford it. One of them went so far as to arrange an appointment with a psychiatrist, but he never went. The child had become so unmanageable Yolanda shipped him off to her parents in Auburn, in the foothills of the Sierra Nevada Mountains.

This shuttling between houses would remain the pattern of young Jesse's life, and his chronic problems were never dealt with. He was reared moving back and forth between the two households. In both Auburn and San Francisco he routinely cut school and ran around all day.

Jesse became an accomplished liar and manipulator. He set fires, chased the smaller kids at school with a knife, and hitched rides hanging on the back of streetcars with a friend. He stayed out until midnight or later, and nothing his mother said or did could modify his behavior. He was beyond Yolanda's control.

Jesse's IQ would later test at 116, just above average. He had an active imagination and was inventive. He was usually a loner, though his propensity for having a companion to share in his mischief was well developed. He was also an habitual bed wetter, and a thrill seeker, driven by whichever impulse most compelled him at the moment. The world around him was a place from which he sought gratification. He could do, and often did, anything that came to mind.

Yolanda had moved to Daly City, but the change in locale made no difference; the troubles continued. She and her son fought constantly. His relations with the other students, especially minority children, were aggressively hostile. Yolanda was in steady, and unsuccessful, contact with school authorities.

Jesse added a new dimension to his misconduct by habitually running away from home. At first, the police simply brought him back, but soon they locked him up in Juvenile Hall as a deterrent. The juvenile court ordered psychiatric treatment, and he actually attended two sessions before he and a friend stole a car and were arrested in Roseville. His bed-wetting suddenly stopped. He was twelve years old.

Gillies was released to his grandparents, but when nothing improved, he was committed to a foster home. The first home did not work out, so he was sent to a second one, and then to a third. He ran away from all of them. His juvenile probation officer determined that Gillies was unsuited for family life and had him committed to a boys' camp near Los Angeles, where he remained for eight months. His stay ended when he and another boy ran away.

Yolanda had decided to move to Lincoln, California, in largely rural Placer County. Gillies pleaded with her not to send him back to the boys' camp. She relented and took him with her. He was promptly expelled from high school in Lincoln. His malicious behavior continued and he was arrested for robbery. When he was caught, he invariably denied his guilt and cast the blame on someone else. If there was a lesson to be learned from his experiences, it evaded him, and he kept getting into trouble time and again.

Following arrest for robbery, Jesse remained in detention and had counseling, but it did no good. In 1976, when Gillies was sixteen years of age, he was arrested again, this time for burglary and possession of marijuana. He served six months in another boy's camp.

For the two years Yolanda resided in Placer County, Gillies became well acquainted with the police, as he did wherever he lived. At home he frequently threw temper tantrums and knocked windows out with his fists, seriously cutting himself. He obtained a high-powered pellet gun and destroyed Yolanda's garage with it. Gillies was bigger now and routinely threatened his mother with bodily harm. She lived in terror of her son.

On one occasion, when he disappeared for two days, Yolanda was informed that the police had arrested him in a drunken psychotic state. They placed him on a seventy-two–hour hold at the Placer

County Mental Hospital for observation, where Jesse ranted over and over that he was Jesus Christ. Upon his release he was sent home to her.

Not long thereafter, Yolanda received an unexpected call from a doctor who told her he was treating Gillies for a severe reaction to alcohol. The doctor was not certain her son would survive. She rushed to Roseville Memorial Hospital. It had taken four grown men to restrain him, and he injured one of them in the process. His condition was improved and he was transported to Juvenile Hall to sleep it off. The next morning, when Yolanda went to pick him up, Gillies had no recollection of what had taken place.

In 1977, when Gillies was seventeen, Yolanda returned to San Francisco. Over the years her fear of him had increased. He no longer attended school and worked for a temporary employment agency, doing construction or rough electrical jobs. He was making $100 a week. Though he was well under age and looked it, he spent Friday nights in a bar, squandering his week's earnings. Monday he borrowed money from his mother to make it through the week.

Jesse's behavior deteriorated. By now, in addition to alcohol, he was using marijuana, PCP, LSD, cocaine, heroin, uppers, downers, anything he could find. His temper was a club he used against everyone around him. Gillies once commented, "When I get angry I really don't give a fuck anymore," and he was often angry.

He acquired a car and recklessly drove the streets with other hoodlums. Yolanda could do nothing to stop it. One day he spotted his younger brother with friends and drove as if he were going to run them over, and nearly did, terrorizing the children.

Gillies approached an older woman who worked as the bartender where he hung out and talked her into letting him move in with her. His drinking was constant. The woman had a daughter who was also seventeen, and one night when they were home alone, Gillies raped her. He was arrested and served six months in detention.

One of Jesse's girlfriends showed up with a baby she claimed was his. They stayed together a short while, but the girl became so frightened of Gillies, she took the baby and left the state.

Whenever Gillies had nowhere to go, or had no money, he returned to his mother, who had taken to hiding anything of value. Once he took his sister's expensive ring and sold it for five dollars' worth of marijuana. When he could find nothing to steal from his family, he wandered the neighborhood siphoning gas from cars to sell. Finally, he stole the bicycle of one of the younger children on the block, and Yolanda insisted he move back with her parents.

Now that Gillies was an adult, his criminal conduct intensified. In August 1979, he was arrested in Auburn for burglary. Three months later, he was arrested for passing bad checks and for petty theft. He was sentenced to three years probation and ordered to serve ninety days in jail.

At nineteen years of age, Gillies stood just over six feet tall and weighed 185 pounds. He was well muscled and a menacing presence to those with whom he came in contact, especially those who were weaker and more fragile than he. Because he had ignored his teeth, they were in very poor condition, with ugly staining and exposed cavities that caused him constant pain. His green eyes were set too close together, and he had a broad, straight nose. He wore his long, naturally wavy chestnut hair much in the style of a woman.

In manner he was hyperactive, and his attention was never focused on the person at hand; rather his restless eyes took in everything about him. Gillies spoke as if only a tiny portion of himself were actually involved in the conversation; the rest of him was directed elsewhere.

He was in constant search of the con, looking to have his way by manipulating others. Though he could be engaging, these moments were short-lived; he turned more readily to the threats and intimidation he enjoyed. He was utterly self-absorbed and nearly totally narcissistic in his behavior. His energy was consumed in getting what he wanted; the problem was that he hardly ever knew what that was.

Gillies loathed himself, and directed that loathing to the world around him. He regarded other people as flesh-and-blood mannequins for his use and pleasure. When he did not have his way, he flew into a rage; when he did, it was never enough. Most of all, he despised women, though he sought them out constantly. He was impulsive and, even for a nineteen-year-old, incredibly immature.

By the time he was released from jail, early in the spring of 1980, his grandparents had moved to the Wigwam Resort in Litchfield Park, Arizona. Gillies's uncle had run the resort stables for years, and his grandparents were going to work there. Gillies met with his probation officer and begged to be given a new start, in Arizona. Permission granted, Gillies joined his grandparents in Litchfield Park, a pleasant resort community several miles west of Phoenix, near the White Tank Mountains. His uncle took him on as a wrangler for incidental money and his keep at the stables.

Gillies knew something about horses from frequent stays with his grandparents and loved to be around them. He enjoyed nothing so much as riding horseback.

The new environment in Litchfield Park did not change Gillies. He did not like to work, even though he enjoyed the horses, and he continued to drink and rebel against the discipline imposed by his family. Gillies prowled the little community in his ten-year-old Buick, and by May his uncle had fired him.

Without money or prospects, Gillies stayed on, living unwanted at the stables. There was a little man with a serious speech impediment and mild retardation named Billy* who stabled his horse there and worked at the golf club as a busboy. On June 19, 1980, Billy went to ride his horse and was assaulted by Gillies at the Litchfield Road bypass. He threw Billy down, wrapped his hands around the man's throat and threatened to kill him. As Gillies choked him and severely bruised and scratched Billy's neck, he demanded money. He took Billy's radio and $23 in cash, then told him to come up with $1,000 the following day or Gillies would kill him and his parents.

A warrant was issued for Gillies's arrest that same day, and he was taken into custody. Told by the arresting officer that he was being charged, Gillies said, "Are you gonna believe me or a mental retard?" When it became apparent that his version of events would be discounted and these charges were going to stick, Gillies told the officer, "I'm gonna kick Billy's ass for this!"

Unable to meet the $2,240 bail set, and with no friend or family member willing to post it, he remained in jail until his preliminary hearing on July 9. That same day, he signed a plea agreement in which he admitted to the crime of theft, a felony, be placed on probation and, as a condition, serve one year in county jail. The judge ordered a probation officer to prepare a presentencing report before accepting the plea.

Gillies was assigned to adult probation officer Mike Hodge, who went to interview Gillies at the Maricopa County jail. Gillies refused to leave his cell, calling the detention officer a "motherfucker."

During his initial processing, Gillies denied having been arrested

* Pseudonym

previously. He also denied being on probation in California, and being a convicted felon there. He claimed he had lived in Arizona one year, attended real estate school, and still worked at the stables. All lies.

Though Gillies would not talk to Hodge, there was an abundance of official paperwork available for the probation officer. One of the intake officers had noted Gillies's probation status on his form. Hodge failed to see and report it.

Hodge wrote a report to the judge in which he recommended that the plea agreement be negated and Gillies sent to prison. This was at a time of intense prison overcrowding in Arizona. It was unlikely Gillies would serve more than one year in prison; it was far more likely he would serve considerably less time. The judge followed the recommendation.

On August 13, 1980, Gillies entered into another agreement, this one calling for him to go to prison. He received one and a half years, the presumptive sentence, with credit for fifty-five days in custody. He would be eligible for parole in six months. Had the original agreement been followed, Gillies would have served a full year in custody.

That Labor Day, 1980, as Michael David Logan left the bus terminal in downtown Phoenix, Jesse James Gillies was housed at an Arizona Department of Corrections facility for youthful offenders in Tucson. Each day passed slowly before him as Gillies marked his time in custody yet again, and waited for freedom, one last time.

PART FOUR
·
PHOENIX

"There's more takers than givers in this world, and they were one of the takers."

—Jack Hackworth

6

In the fall of 1980, after three years in Phoenix, Suzanne Rossetti was at last feeling good about her professional prospects. Following the disappointment of supervising teenagers with Youth Services, she had worked as a waitress. Finally, ten months earlier in 1979, she had landed a job with Armour Pharmaceutical at their Phoenix-based Burn Treatment Skin Bank. She had accepted an entry-level position supervising a half dozen employees, a position for which she was overqualified. But now she was informed that she was being promoted into management.

Her personal life was also more satisfying. She took jazz and improvisational dance lessons two nights a week, and she still performed acrobatics. Occasionally, she and a friend went to nearby Arizona State University to roller-skate for the evening. She attended church fairly regularly, and especially enjoyed the Sunday evening Mass celebrated by the Franciscan Fathers at their retreat on Lincoln Drive, La Casa de Paz y Bien. Service was held in a modest rotunda as the setting sun splayed against the stained-glass wall.

Suzanne participated in frequent ten-kilometer runs, ran up Squaw Peak in central Phoenix at least once a week, and jogged on other days. Her mother's sister, Frances Chubinski, joined Suzanne on more than one of her Squaw Peak runs. Suzanne would sprint to the top, while her aunt walked steadily up the trail. Then Suzanne would run down to Frances and walk the rest of the way to the peak while they chatted and laughed.

Suzanne maintained frequent correspondence with her friends, and a steady stream of them dropped in from out of state to visit. One of Suzanne's closest new friends was Brayton Willis, known to everyone as "Pug." He was a strappingly fit, soft-spoken man a few years older than she. In Boston he had become a good friend of one of the innumerable Rossetti cousins. When his marriage disintegrated in 1977, he relocated to Phoenix, and was given Suzanne's telephone number in Scottsdale. He called her in the fall of 1977.

During lunch, Pug was immediately taken with Suzanne's infectious grin, her spontaneous personality, and her can-do demeanor. She was, as he often told his friends, just a "pint of peanuts."

Once again she became the friend instead of the date. Pug had no interest in seeing anyone romantically at this time, and very quickly Suzanne was the sister he never had. She was Suz to talk with about his divorce, Suz to discuss other women with when he did start dating, Suz to take backpacking.

Pug was learning to rock-climb and he belonged to the Arizona Mountaineering Club. When he learned of Suzanne's activities and her experiences in the Berkshire Hills, he suggested she join the group.

The club was made up mostly of professional men, but there were a number of very fit and fearless women as well. Every other weekend, members of the club went climbing. Suzanne threw herself into the new discipline with enthusiasm, and she quickly progressed from simple to advanced climbs. It was her goal to become a team leader.

There was an esprit de corps among the club members that arose from a common love for the out-of-doors, and a commitment to mountain climbing. Occupations were rarely discussed. Late Friday or very early Saturday, a group of eight to twenty would pile into cars and four-wheel drives, and set out for one of the many excellent sites close to Phoenix. Often, it was a weekend undertaking, and a close bonding developed among the climbers, most of whom drew their social life from the club membership.

Suzanne wore heavy rock-climbing boots and a helmet. In the summer she wore Levi's shorts and a tank top; a men's heavy flannel shirt and full-length Levi's in the winter.

On the climb, members were roped together and slowly worked their way up sheer cliffs, sometimes more than a thousand feet in height. With the toes of their boots or with their bare hands, they gripped crevices and outcroppings as they inched up treacherous stone faces.

Suzanne rapidly became a skilled second. It was her job to move below Pug as they slowly made their way up a cliff, with the others looped in below her. The role of the second was vital to the safety of the team. The seasoned leader picked the course up the rock, and was the most vulnerable. Should that person fall, and it happened often enough to be a concern, he or she shouted, "Falling!" When Suzanne heard the cry, she would lock the brake on the line and brace herself against the cliff. It was essential that she hold her position. If the leader pulled her down with him, the weight and momentum of the falling pair would likely take the entire team with them. Suzanne was too small to be a traditional second, especially for someone of Pug's size, but she was so skilled, so incredibly fit and reliable, she was soon given the role.

One day the two of them were working their way up Granite Mountain in northern Arizona, an especially demanding climb. Pug was working above her and around a corner, out of sight. Without warning, he suddenly broke free of the wall. So unexpected was the fall that he did not have an opportunity to shout, and Suzanne was caught unprepared when his 190 pounds struck her line at full force, giving her small frame a hell of a shock. She clamped the brake down and clung to the surface furiously.

Pug recklessly climbed without a helmet, though he insisted that Suzanne and the others on his teams wear theirs. His long fall was very bad. When he reached the end of his safety line, he was thrown against the mountain violently and struck his unprotected head. He was dazed and disoriented. When his head cleared a little, he looked up 125 feet to Suzanne and made her out, grimacing with strain, holding the brake with a death grip. He was swinging free, completely dependent on her to stay alive.

As Pug shook the cobwebs out of his head, he called up, "Suz, are you okay?"

She said she was. "For a few seconds," she told him, "I didn't know if you were all right." He could hear the fear and concern in her voice. Then she asked if he was able to assume a position on the face of the mountain. "I'm really hurting," she said, near tears from the pain. The rope was cutting into her, and the strain of gripping the brake and the stone face was apparent. Pug located a spot to perch and remove the strain from her. A few moments later they resumed the climb.

In the nearly three years they had known one another, they had climbed every interesting peak in the state: Baboquivari Peak beside Kitt Peak outside of Tucson, Mount Lemmon to the north of that city, Pinnacle Peak near Phoenix, and, frequently, the Grand Canyon. The vast and inhospitable Superstition Mountains east of Phoenix were also favorites of club members and the two of them had climbed extensively there as well.

The previous Easter, a party of twenty-five had scaled Weaver's Needle in the Superstitions and spent the night at its summit. The next morning, they celebrated sunrise services as dawn broke over the magnificent landscape stretching below them. That fall of 1980, they were planning two hikes at the Grand Canyon. They would go South Rim to North Rim, then back, one hike before Thanksgiving, the other immediately after the holidays.

Suzanne carried her 35mm camera on the outings and was the unofficial photographer. As usual, she made copies of the photographs she took and handed them out to members of the club. Her pictures were not of professional quality, but they were excellent amateur shots. She had several of them enlarged and hung in her living room, and, later, in her office, along with photographs taken of her by others. There was a picture of Suzanne in full accoutrement, dangling precariously from a lofty peak with a majestic sweep of southwestern desert in the distance; another of her on the beach with Donna, the two of them grinning into the camera; others of vistas in Yosemite and the Grand Canyon, several of the delicate Arizona flowers, and one of a spectacular Arizona sunset.

She kept the camera in a brown canvas bag in her car when the weather was not too hot. Because she often exercised immediately after work, she also maintained an athletic bag in the car with her own towels and athletic clothing.

Between her many activities, Suzanne was a bit of a homebody. Alone in her condominium she would quilt or sew Raggedy Ann dolls to use as gifts for her many cousins and their children. The backyard to the condo was minute in size. As do many easterners who relocate to the Southwest, she planted a cactus garden. There wasn't room for much else. She strung a Mexican hammock across the tiny patio, and during the frequent warm desert months, she napped there.

The condominium was carefully arranged with cherished childhood items, like the collection of silver dollars which she kept in a special box. Mementos of her childhood and family were everywhere.

Her job at the Burn Treatment Skin Bank was considerably less glamorous than her mountain climbing. There were four offices to the front of the building and a larger processing area in the rear where about forty employees worked. The building was located at Twenty-fourth Street and Washington close by a commercial district. Near central Phoenix, it was just one block from the seedy, locally notorious East Van Buren Street.

Each day the bank received pig skin, packed in ice, from Nebraska. It was stripped of fat and hair, and placed in cleansing solution where it was processed and reprocessed until it became tissue thin. Used by physicians in treating severe burns, the skin became a life-saving, translucent medical bandage.

Teams worked around baths of fluids as the skin went from one step of the process to the next. There was a vaguely unpleasant chemical odor to the place, but everyone became accustomed to it. The employees talked through the day as they worked, and Suzanne quickly became everyone's friend. During breaks or in her office, employees were often seen chatting with her.

Jo Ann Heckel had worked at the bank for six years as a microbiologist. Once a week or so, Suzanne, Jo Ann, and others would walk one block to Twenty-fourth Street and Van Buren for the buffet lunch at the Kon Tiki Hotel restaurant; the best place that was close.

It was Suzanne's nature to get along with people, but at the burn center there was a manager who constantly spoke to the women in a condescending manner. Once Suzanne turned to Jo Ann with a look of anger. "He always thinks he's so much better than women," she said.

One employee mooched money from everyone, and ended up owing several hundred dollars to Suzanne. Suzanne had a personal savings account of $4,000, but she was becoming increasingly concerned about being repaid. When the employee quit her job and announced to everyone that she was moving to California, Suzanne told Jo Ann that she hoped the girl was going to pay her back. She did not.

Suzanne had talked to her aunt Frances about her money. Frances did not think it a wise idea for Suzanne, who lived alone, to keep cash around the house. Suzanne had an account with Valley National

Bank and acquired one of the new Automatic Teller Machine cards. Valley National called their machines "Ugly Tellers," and the cards issued to their customers bore a picture of the customer posed next to a potted plant.

Jo Ann was engaged, but her fiancé lived some distance away. Suzanne soon had her new friend jogging and participating in the frequent weekend ten-kilometer events in the valley. She also took Jo Ann with her up Squaw Peak, out to movies, and to Happy Hours with her other friends.

Jo Ann was not the only one at work Suzanne persuaded to start running. So many were involved that Suzanne posted a large chart on a wall logging distances. One of her friends drew a funny picture of a running pig and they had silk-screened T-shirts made. When Suzanne, Jo Ann, or any of the others ran in an event, they made a point to wear the shirt. They also wore them around town for fun.

That fall of 1980, the company created a marketing position for Suzanne and transferred her from the processing room to an office up front. She was retrained and soon represented the company at conferences. It was now her job to coordinate the sales force and develop new markets for the product. It was a sizable promotion, and the employees working in processing were very proud of her.

Suzanne also had been dating a bright, outgoing young man named Rick* who lived in Flagstaff, some distance from Phoenix. He was a handsome, popular man in the mountaineering club and was known for his machismo.

That summer Jo Ann and Suzanne, along with their boyfriends, had driven to Payson in the mountains of northeastern Arizona for a bluegrass festival. That night, they visited a country-and-western bar. During the evening they participated in a dance contest, which Suzanne and her boyfriend won handily. Afterward, the four slept in sleeping bags in the yard of one of Suzanne's friends.

Rick had earned a reputation as a hard-core climber and had more than once pushed Suzanne in directions in which she was not comfortable. Pug liked the young man well enough, but felt he did not appreciate Suz properly. It was also apparent that beyond climbing and hiking, Rick had little in common with her. Suzanne often attended the ballet and opera, activities which Rick did not enjoy with

* Pseudonym

her. On these occasions Pug was struck by the difference between Suz, the mountaineer, all sweat-stained, cut, and bruised from the rock, dressed in men's heavy clothing, and Suzanne, patron of ballet, in heels, gentle silk, and fragrant perfume.

Peter and Louise Rossetti came to Arizona more frequently and stayed with Suzanne, usually three times a year for a total of two months. They made a fall trip, a midwinter trip, and one in the spring, just after tax season. On one of these visits, Suzanne told Louise that she thought it was time to end her relationship with Rick. That summer the two of them had gone canoeing in Canada, and it had been necessary to portage the boat and equipment from lake to lake. She felt that he had given her little help, and often required her to carry far more than her share. When they returned to Phoenix, Suzanne thought she observed him eyeing other women as they were dancing.

Louise agreed with her daughter's decision. "Never mind, Suzanne," she said. "There's plenty of fish in the sea. You don't have to worry about him." There was plenty of time.

Despite the rational process behind her decision, Suzanne was crushed at the end of the relationship. More than once she had told Pug how the distance from her family caused her to be lonely. This time, she shared her feelings with Pug, crying as she related why she had broken up with Rick. Pug expressed his sympathy and told Suz that she should plan to marry and have children. Some women were born to be mothers, and Suz was one of them. She wondered aloud if that would ever happen.

Not long after that, however, Suzanne met a backpacker, a good-looking young carpenter named Eric Gregan.* Eric was gentler than her previous boyfriend, less arrogant and more reserved. He was interested in doing what she wanted, and he was more attentive to her needs. It was apparent to others that his sudden interest in mountain climbing was a measure of his affection for Suzanne, but she was very taken with his keen interest in her and her concerns.

Louise met Eric and thought he was nice, but not right for Suzanne. She believed he would help make Suzanne happy following the end of her relationship with Rick, however, and was pleased at that.

In October Suzanne and nine others hiked across the Grand

* Pseudonym

Canyon. Some in the party were members of the mountaineering club, others were not. Gary Reid, an FBI agent assigned to the Phoenix office, met Suzanne on this trip. He and his wife were an active couple. Reid had been reared in Arkansas and still retained a soft southern accent. As a CPA, he was assigned by the Bureau primarily to accounting cases, but worked in all types of FBI investigations. He was, in fact, on the Phoenix office SWAT team.

Reid was taken with Suzanne and her vivacious personality. Everyone in the party was upbeat and very fit. Usually on a hike of this type someone was out of shape and after the first few hours, when the blisters and aching muscles kicked in, there was a great deal of complaining. But none of this happened on this occasion; the group talked and laughed continually. Reid's wife was going to rendezvous with the group at the lodge on the North Rim and hike back with them. Reid spent most of that first day with Suzanne.

Whenever the group finished a break, it was Suzanne who shot to her feet and sang Willie Nelson's hit song, "On the Road Again." While she sang, she moved around the group, pulling people to their feet.

For a joke, Reid started slipping rocks into her day pack. Others joined in. Packs grow lighter during hikes as the water and food are used, but after two or three breaks Suzanne noticed her pack was heavier. She concluded it was fatigue and just gutted it out. Every time she said something about it, the other hikers smiled; when she could not see them they would meet one another's eyes.

As the hikers approached the north side of the canyon, Suzanne's pack was conspicuously heavy. She dropped it with a thud and dug around, finding the layer of rocks at the bottom. Everyone laughed. From then on at intervals, she would pick up a rock and pretend to throw it at Reid or one of the others. But after each break, she still shot to her feet and sang "On the Road Again" with gusto.

Reid and his wife stayed in touch with Suzanne after the trip. He ran with her in ten-kilometer races in Phoenix throughout the winter season, one of them at Papago Park near the zoo. And more than once Reid's wife climbed Squaw Peak with Suzanne and other friends.

The only serious problem in Suzanne's life had occurred several months before. In early summer her father had unexpectedly entered the hospital for prostate surgery and, in the family's opinion, had been released prematurely. He soon suffered a relapse and was rehospitalized. When he was released again, he was weak and in fragile health.

By the fall, however, Suzanne was able to commit herself to her new job, and the company told her she would be traveling frequently for them. After waiting on tables, supervising the cleanup of parks, and scrubbing hair from pig skin, it was all very rewarding and exciting.

7

On Labor Day night, 1980, Logan stepped from the downtown Phoenix bus terminal into a furnace. Though it was already late, the temperature was still in the high nineties. He had never known such miserable heat.

Phoenix was a city in the midst of an unprecedented boom. In the 1930s, it had been the same size as sleepy Santa Fe, New Mexico. By 1980 the population of Phoenix was over 800,000. Most of the growth occurred in the suburbs and, as a consequence, Phoenix had a stunted central core surrounded by a vast expanse of suburbia.

Visitors loved the place, especially if their stay had occurred during the long, temperate winter. The pace of life was measurably slower than nearly anywhere else, and everything was new, clean, and flat. Almost no one was a native, so it was easy to fit in. Newcomers often commented there were few blacks; the city's black population was, in fact, a steady 3 percent despite an overall growth rate approaching 50,000 a year.

People who moved to Phoenix were not hampered by the family and social ties of their birthplaces. It was easier to get divorced in Phoenix, easier to disregard obligations. People were not interested in becoming involved in the community, nor did they care to know their neighbors. Nearly everyone lived in single-family houses surrounded by high walls that shut them in and kept out their neighbors. Because people did not really know one another, there was a freedom in Phoenix that newcomers found nearly intoxicating. People could do whatever they wanted. There was no one to condemn or judge, no one to point out a duty, no one to tell. Many became disillusioned after a short time and moved on, others acclimated well. For every four new residents who arrived, three moved out. As a consequence, the population was in a constant state of flux.

On the outskirts of Phoenix, the desert proper began abruptly. With dirt bikes and four-wheel drive vehicles, it was often covered with trails and litter, but soon gave way to a pristine state such as observed by the early Spanish explorers.

Logan had little money, and only a modest bundle of belongings, as he struck out looking for somewhere to eat after getting off the bus. Because of the Labor Day holiday most of the restaurants were closed. After several attempts, he found a family-operated café still taking customers. He had always liked Mexican food, but had never tasted anything like this and left feeling very satisfied with his situation.

By walking and thumbing rides, he made his way across the empty Salt River bed, then up the slow rise toward South Mountain. He became disoriented and went to the wrong side of south Phoenix, but finally arrived at an address his brother had given him. The man's name was Ricardo, and he lived in a dilapidated wood frame house with his Anglo girlfriend.

Logan hung around for several days while considering his next move. Each day Ricardo and his girlfriend left for work, and Logan decided they must be doing something honest since they owned scarcely a thing—there was nothing for him to take. Logan walked several miles to the base of South Mountain, just off Central Avenue, because he had heard of a riding stable there called the Ponderosa. He spoke to the operator, a man Logan's age named Frank.* He and his young wife lived at the stables and were in need of another hand. The pay was one hundred dollars a month plus tips, and room and board.

Logan produced a false identification in the name of George Richardson, then he told the couple to just call him Mike. Logan bunked in their house in his own room, the same arrangement made for another employee, Rhonda.** Logan was a little taken aback at

* Pseudonym
** Pseudonym

the thought of a woman wrangler, but had worked with women around racetracks before.

Frank was adamant about employees not drinking on the premises, so Logan decided to try giving up beer. Things had been going his way ever since he broke out of Jackson State Prison and he did not want trouble.

The Ponderosa Riding Stables was a successful operation that catered to teenagers who wanted to ride horses in South Mountain Park, and to tourists desiring a taste of the real West. The wranglers groomed and tended the horses as well as escorted and cooked for parties on both breakfast and dinner trail rides.

Logan loved being a cowboy. He quickly acquired boots, a hat, and even a medium-cut racing saddle he used when he cut stock. Logan carefully mimicked the other wranglers' manner and speech. He dressed like them, and his quiet speech and reticent manner fit the image perfectly. After his first weeks, no one suspected he was an outlaw biker from Detroit.

Once he was settled, Logan went to the Arizona Motor Vehicle Division and told them a story about losing his wallet on a ride at work. He showed them his remaining ID in the name of George Richardson and was issued a state identification card.

When Logan had worked at the Ponderosa for two months, his boss, Frank, invited him to go drinking, but urged Logan do the driving. Because Logan had no license, he did not want to go and was adamant about not driving. Frank, however, insisted, and in the end Logan took the wheel of the pickup truck.

Logan hoped that Frank would just buy a bottle of liquor and drink it in the truck. To prod Frank in that direction, Logan told him he did not want to go into any bars. But Frank preferred barhopping and enthusiastically invited Logan to join him. Logan liked Frank, so after resisting initially, was soon sipping a long-missed cold beer.

Logan still wanted to stay at the Ponderosa stables and keep out of sight, but once he resumed drinking it was inevitable that he would continue going out. A group of stable employees and their friends hit a few of the nearby bars one night. Rhonda's sister, Karen,* and her boyfriend came along. Karen was a pretty girl, only nineteen years old, and Logan considered her an innocent. After having a few drinks, he found himself confiding in her that he was an escaped convict. A

* Pseudonym

jukebox played a country tune, and couples shuffled on the tiny dance floor. Karen was wide-eyed as she comprehended what he was saying. "I never would have guessed," she said. She cautioned him not to tell anyone else and promised that she would not reveal his secret to anyone.

At work, Logan hid liquor bottles and beer to keep customers from spotting them, or from seeing him drink. He was back to his established daily consumption, and he was drinking so much, people around him could not help but notice. Logan figured as long as there was no trouble he could do as he pleased, though he suspected Frank knew and chose not to say anything.

The owner of the Weldon Riding Stable, a lanky, moustached Coloradan named Jerry Schneider,* dropped by the Ponderosa on occasion to talk business with Frank. Schneider was a smooth talker always in search of a deal. He admired Logan's saddle and more than once offered to buy it. Logan declined, but it put the pair into conversation. Schneider routinely talked about what a big place he ran, how much better an operation Weldon was than the Ponderosa, and urged Logan to work for him. When he learned that Logan was interested in leaving the city altogether, Schneider spoke about going north to round up horses. Logan could make big money with him there, breaking horses. Schneider's persuasive talk fired Logan's imagination.

Logan did not always like the customers at the Ponderosa. While tourists enjoyed the expanse of desert, the excitement of the ride, and the feel and smell of the well-oiled leather saddles, they occasionally complained about the behavior of the horses he selected, or of their appearance. High schoolers enjoyed riding the hell out of the stock and did not appreciate it when Logan told them to knock it off. The horses and western gear sometimes caused men to show off for their girlfriends, and more than once Logan found himself in a confrontation. He was uncomfortable at the Ponderosa with these situations because the only one who could really cover his back was Frank; the two women were of no help. Frank was absent much of the time, so Logan was forced to deal with more than one unpleasant episode alone. He felt exposed.

One afternoon, a group of seven blacks, including two women, rented horses. The wranglers used the most spirited for cutting stock.

* Pseudonym

One of the men was mounted on Rhonda's horse and was unable to control him. Logan showed him how to handle the animal, saying he was accustomed to direction and responded readily, only if instructed properly. The man would hear none of it. The group rode off, but were back in less than half an hour, complaining about the horse.

Outside the office, the men confronted Frank and demanded a refund. For the first time, Logan noticed that one of them was carrying a gun. Frank explained repeatedly that there was no problem with the horse if he was properly handled. He would provide a different horse if that would make things right. The men wanted their money back and heated words were exchanged. Finally, Frank turned to Logan on the porch and said, "Get Bertha."

Logan reached inside the office and extracted a sawed-off shotgun Frank maintained for such situations. He moved so the men could see him brandishing the weapon. The blacks piled into their car and raised a cloud of dust as they spun around in a circle in the yard. The man with the gun stuck it out a window and discharged it into the air. That angered Frank, and he ran to the register for the handgun he kept there. When the car looped around to make another circle, Frank let off a volley that struck one of the car tires. The car limped out to the paved road and kept going.

There was another incident when a customer rode with his girl-friend, then returned and claimed he had lost his wallet in the desert. When he said he carried more than $1,000 in it, Logan did not believe him. Who would go riding with all of that money in their wallet? he thought.

Nevertheless, Frank had Logan and Rhonda saddle up and join in a search for the wallet. They covered the man's trail repeatedly, but had no luck finding the wallet. When at last they gave up, the customer hotly accused them of finding the wallet and keeping the money for themselves. Words were exchanged. Then the man jumped Frank. Logan pulled the customer off; Frank ran inside and grabbed Bertha. Logan and the man went face to face until Logan finished him off in a fair fight.

That's the way Logan liked to tell the stories at least. One time he had covered Frank's back, another time Frank had covered his. But Frank was not always there.

All things considered, Logan enjoyed working at the Ponderosa. Besides his salary, he made another $100 to $200 a month in tips. He had no expenses, since he slept and ate at the stables. He liked

Frank's wife and he enjoyed working with Rhonda, who had been around horses all of her life and more than carried her weight.

For Logan it was an idyllic time. The weather had cooled steadily since his arrival. During that fall, the daytime temperatures dropped from over one hundred degrees to the eighties and, by December, into the sixties. Though he knew he could not stay at the Ponderosa indefinitely, he thought this was about as good as life ever got.

He still needed that big score to reach Australia, but the need was less pressing at the Ponderosa, with the horses and the aroma of desert mesquite. He was content to continue like this for a long time.

Gillies received a break when California decided not to place a probation violation hold on him, since a hold would have required he complete his Arizona sentence without early release. Then he would have to be transported back to California in custody to account for his conviction. Instead, the California probation authorities decided to let him go. With luck he could continue breaking the law in Arizona rather than in California.

During Gillies's processing at the Arizona Department of Corrections in September 1980, he gave his first account of the crime that had landed him in prison. According to Gillies, Billy, the man he had robbed in Litchfield Park, had refused to loan him money, even though Gillies claimed he had lent Billy money a few days earlier. Gillies had called Billy a "dirty dog," then told him, "I should, bitch, slap you and take your money." He admitted stealing the money by force and then claimed that he had tried to return it. After that, he and Billy had made up. Then he sent Billy to buy sandwiches and beer.

After speaking to Gillies and reading his account of the crime, the intake officer commented, "Gillies doesn't seem to grasp the seriousness of this offense." Just a few weeks later, shortly after Thanksgiving, Gillies was transferred to a halfway house in Tucson from which he was to search for work in preparation for his parole. The state's Department of Vocational Rehabilitation provided him with $150 worth of clothes.

Gillies said he wanted employment as a wrangler where he would have room and board and could be with horses.

That Thanksgiving, Suzanne decided to pay her family in Saugus a surprise visit. Since moving to Scottsdale, she had been home half a dozen times. Suzanne called Donna to pick her up at the airport in Boston, then the sisters drove to the family home and surprised Suzanne's parents. She could only stay the four days. The girls attended the big Saugus High football game and found time to drive to Duxbury, where they had spent so many happy summers, for a walk on the beach.

That Saturday, Donna and Suzanne went shopping in Boston for the clothes Suzanne required for her new position. Suzanne was not comfortable in making the selection and relied on Donna's eye as she mixed and matched outfits. Suzanne was thrilled at her purchases. The two girls met their parents in Cambridge early that evening and ate at a Chinese restaurant.

Suzanne told her family that the company was planning to transfer her to upstate New York, so she would be only a few hours from home. She was looking forward to moving back east despite her love of the Southwest. It seemed to Louise that Suzanne had finished her time out west and was ready to move on with her life, surrounded by those she knew and loved best.

That night, there was an unofficial party at the Rossetti home, just like in the old days. Peter Jr. was engaged and planning to marry in the late spring. Suzanne's childhood friend, Debbie Crisafulli, was able to attend. Married now, Debbie was six months pregnant.

When Suzanne and Debbie had an opportunity to talk with each other and about Suzanne's father's illness, the subject turned to death. Suzanne told Debbie that she had thought about death during the long months of her father's illness and had decided that she was not afraid to die; it was something she had come to accept. Then they spoke of happier matters.

At one point during the visit, Peter Jr. took Suzanne aside to update her on her father's medical condition. Peter and Louise would be going to Arizona for their extended winter visit after Christmas, and he wanted to be certain that their father did not overexert himself, or dwell on death. It was important to keep his spirits up. Suzanne understood; she was just the person to keep her father happy.

Suzanne went to visit Joanie Saltzberg, her friend from college days, and to meet her husband. The women talked excitedly about Suzanne's life out west and the possibility that Joanie might be pregnant. There was a poignant moment when Suzanne told Joanie, "I'll never be a mother." Joanie assured her that she would in time; the right man would come along.

But Joanie was struck by the certainty with which Suzanne said it. It was as if she sensed that her life would be short and unfulfilled.

One morning during that visit, Suzanne was out jogging when Freddie Quinlan drove by. Freddie was working as a U.S. marshal. He stopped and, after they spoke for a few minutes, Suzanne invited him to come to the house, since she would be leaving again shortly for Arizona. They sat in the kitchen, where they had spent so much time together as children and teenagers, and talked emotionally for four hours. They wondered what had ever happened to them, and to their love. Suzanne told Freddie she would be home again in six months for Peter Jr.'s wedding, and that her company would soon be transferring her to New York. They would be able to renew their friendship and see each other again.

This was the first meaningful talk they had had since Freddie's wedding three and a half years earlier, and when they parted this time, Suzanne put back on her finger the friendship ring Freddie had given her in high school.

Donna drove Suzanne to the airport that Sunday. Farewells were always hard on the two sisters because they were so close, but this was an especially difficult one. Suzanne reminded her sister that she would be moving to New York and then they would see more of each other. Donna could tell, despite the reassuring words, that Suzanne really did not want to leave. The girls embraced and cried as they said good-bye.

Donna watched Suzanne board the plane until the last possible second. When she caught a view of her sister's face that final instant, she was struck with how sad Suzanne looked.

8
___.___

Wh99en the Arizona Department of Corrections computed Gillies's earliest parole date, it said that he could not be released prior to January 1981. Prison overcrowding was such that the staff sought every stratagem to release inmates; so it was decided to place Gillies into the work-furlough program, which would put him onto the streets earlier. On at least two occasions, Gillies was granted several days' leave for traveling to Phoenix to find work. In early December, he was transferred to a halfway house in Phoenix to expedite that search.

Gillies's attitude and lack of maturity were a problem for the staff at the halfway house. Within a week of his arrival, one officer recommended that Gillies have his pass to seek work rescinded because of his regular AWOL status and "his overall attitude about this program." However Gillies was allowed to continue as he was, and a few days later, Jerry Schneider hired him to work at the Weldon Riding Stable. Gillies completed the paperwork and submitted his program to the prison authorities for their required approval before he moved into the bunkhouse. In the meantime he was allowed to start working.

Parole Officer Almon King was assigned to investigate Gillies's proposed work-furlough program. King had already had unpleasant experiences with Gillies in the halfway house. One had occurred when Gillies declined to wash dishes when it was his turn, and another when Gillies logged in late. King had found Gillies to be highly manipulative, and did not trust him.

One night that December, King drove out to Weldon to look the place over and assess the people with whom Gillies was going to work and live. He found the bunkhouse to be decrepit and unsanitary. It was poorly lighted and stank of stale beer, cigarette butts, and soiled clothing.

One of the wranglers with a red bandanna around his neck packed a pistol on one hip and a knife on the other. He was especially filthy, though all of the men were unkempt and scraggly. Another squatted and repeatedly tossed a knife into the floor. A third openly smoked marijuana. According to the men, Gillies was walking a girl to her house.

King elected not to identify himself or his purpose in being there. He said, "My name is Al and I am a friend of Mr. Gillies." He struck up a conversation and was surprised when one of the men bragged that he had escaped from prison in New Mexico. After they talked for fifteen minutes, one of the wranglers suddenly asked, "Are you a cop?" Then he asked why King wanted to speak to Gillies. The parole officer hedged. King finally left before Gillies returned. He submitted a decidedly negative report.

Another parole officer was assigned to follow up. His report was better, though not by much. He wrote, "Three people share a bunkhouse. . . . The area is adjacent to the stable and not very clean. This area is barely adequate for client's needs." On December 22, 1980, King's superiors approved Gillies's release to live at Weldon Riding Stable.

At the Ponderosa Riding Stables, Logan had slipped back into chronic alcoholism, and it was increasingly difficult for him to conceal his constant drunkenness from Frank and the customers. Shortly before Christmas, Frank confronted Logan. At first, Logan denied the obvious, but finally said in effect, So what? He genuinely liked Frank, but the man was sticking his nose into Logan's business. Heated words were exchanged, and Logan told Frank to fuck off. Their relations were strained following this argument, especially since Logan continued to drink.

Between Christmas and New Year's Day, a senior employee of the parent company that owned the Ponderosa came down from Colorado to conduct a night ride for important people. As usual, Logan had been drinking steadily all day when he escorted the VIPs out into the desert to set up a steak fry. While Logan was working at the fire, the horses broke loose and scattered. The man from the home office was furious. He thought it was Logan's job to secure the horse line, and he blamed him for what had taken place.

The two men argued in front of the guests the company man wanted to impress. What is everyone supposed to do, he demanded, walk back? After the shouting, the noticeably intoxicated Logan retrieved one of the horses, then rounded up the rest. This was hardly a disaster in his mind. Maybe he quit, as he later claimed; probably he was fired. In any case, he gathered his belongings that night, sold his portable television set and other items to Karen's boyfriend, and left the Ponderosa on foot. He spent several days drinking and sleeping at a girl's house, but she made it clear he could not stay. In early January 1981, he called Jerry Schneider, who immediately offered Logan a job at Weldon. He would be paid $175 a month plus tips, and room and board.

Logan had never been to the Weldon stable before, and knew it only from Schneider's glowing descriptions. Logan bundled his possessions into a green garbage bag, dressed in his hat, Levi's, jacket and boots, and set out for Weldon on foot, carrying his racing saddle on his shoulder.

He hitched a ride to Van Buren Street but took a wrong turn, ending up out west by the freeway. Then he learned his destination was in the opposite direction. Hitching a series of rides along Van Buren, he came to the corner of East Fifty-second Street. The driver directed him south, down the street a short distance, to the Weldon Riding Stable. Logan hoofed it the rest of the way with a sense of anticipation.

As he approached Weldon, which lay just off to his right, he was dismayed. After Schneider's praise Logan could hardly believe what he was seeing. Where were you supposed to ride? Along the west side of Fifty-second Street was a well-developed neighborhood. Van Buren Street, just a few hundred yards to the south of the stables, was an old highway with businesses crowded along it. At the corner of Van Buren and Fifty-second Streets there was a U-Totem convenience store. There was a small motel across the street and the Pioneer Bar next to that. Just north of Weldon was a fenced National Guard facility, and within a stone's throw to the east across a patch of desert was a golf course. Where did people ride horses? This was in the middle of a city, for God's sake!

Schneider's operation was smaller than Logan recalled him saying. The office Schneider worked out of was rundown, but it was in good condition compared to the bunkhouse next to the stable. That was a wreck. Four wranglers were already living there in squalor. The men pointed to a broken bunk and told Logan that that was his. He asked about a shower, and they laughed. The water only ran half the time, and the shower rarely worked, even when there was water.

For Logan, this was like moving from Warren back to the Jeffries Project. He had returned to the slums. Only a few weeks earlier, everything had been breaking his way. He had a good place to live, a nice job, and money in his pocket. Now it was all gone and he was slipping backward.

He propped up his bunk, but knew at once he was never going to have a decent night's sleep in it. The other wranglers looked untrustworthy to him, and he would have to hide his few remaining valuables.

Logan knew, absolutely, as he finished off his final beer that night that he had to get to Australia, and for that he needed his big score.

The next morning the men were roused at 5:30. Schneider told Logan to join Gillies pitching hay for the horses. A New Mexican slowly drove the pickup truck as Logan and Gillies tossed the horses feed out the rear.

The two men had never met, though Logan recalled having seen Gillies once before, a week or two earlier when Schneider had been at the Ponderosa. Logan had observed a young cowboy sitting alone in Schneider's truck. That had been Gillies.

The two men talked as they worked in the morning darkness. Logan, at age twenty-seven, did not realize that Gillies, who was twenty years old, was so much younger than he was. Nor did he realize that Gillies was from California; he thought Gillies was an Arizona cowboy.

The previous night, Logan had taken the opportunity to really look at the other wranglers. He could live with what he thought to be their lack of honesty; he was not here to find friends, but none of the men looked trustworthy, none of them could be relied upon in his opinion, except for this one, Gillies.

The operation at Weldon was similar in some ways to the Ponderosa's, but it was also very different. From early morning until 5:00 in the afternoon, the five wranglers cared for the horses and tended the equipment, and saw to the customers. Wranglers did not escort

parties and there were no trail, breakfast, or dinner rides. These customers were looking to sit on a horse for an hour and ride around the
open desert area to the east and south of the stables. That meant there
was no meaningful opportunity to obtain tips. Worse, in talking to
the other men, Logan learned that Schneider had yet to pay anyone.
His practice was to promise money repeatedly until the man was fed
up and left. Then Schneider just hired someone else. That was what
the wranglers told Logan.

According to the men, Schneider also promised to clean and
repair the bunkhouse and plumbing facilities, but never did that either.
The men were fortunate if they showered once a week. Schneider did
buy basic food for them, but the cowboys had to cook it themselves
on a hot plate. There was nowhere adequate to wash dishes or to store
the food. Even the refrigerator did not work properly, and perishable
food spoiled quickly. The wranglers smelled of horses and the sour
stench of the bunkhouse.

Logan talked to Schneider, who told him he would take care of
the problems, not to be concerned. He promised that soon the two
of them would go north to round up horses, and Logan would make
big money breaking them.

After work, the five wranglers walked across the open desert,
passed a clapboard Baptist church, then went up a short street to Van
Buren and a beer and wine bar called the Homestead. The beer was
cheap, and the men played pinball and listened to country tunes to
pass the time. They were always broke and swapped money back and
forth. Sometimes they paid for drinks with pennies and nickels.

Down the street, beside the hotel at the corner of Van Buren
and Fifty-second streets, was the Pioneer Bar. There was a hitching
rail outside, and on occasion, when Schneider was away at night, the
men rode their horses over and hitched them to the wooden rail, just
like they had seen in the movies. The Pioneer served hard liquor and
was more expensive, so the men only went there when one of them
had money.

There was not much else to do at Weldon after the day's work
was finished. The men enjoyed the horses and would ride around on
them in the dark. Sometimes they ran a race and the winner would
brag about his horse and his horsemanship to the others.

Across the desert to the east of Weldon was the Papago Golf
Course and on the other side of it was the Phoenix City Zoo. Some
nights the men would slowly pass through the zoo to look at the

animals. The steady clatter of the horses' hooves echoed through the concrete walkways and off the animal cages. The security guards never questioned them, and the wranglers were careful not to cause any trouble, since Schneider would not tolerate any misconduct from his men. They also enjoyed seeing the animals and having this privileged access.

The wranglers were uneducated and occasionally they were troublemakers. One night, when they were lying around the bunkhouse, Logan dared one of them to fight Gillies. He taunted the pair as the others looked on, until finally Gillies attacked the wrangler, tossing him about the bunkhouse, knocking chairs over, and kicking the man when he was down. The wrangler did not fight back. He kept scooting away until he broke free, then ran for it.

Nothing about the altercation had been good-natured. There had been hostility in Gillies's eyes and he had meant to hurt the other man.

Gillies had befriended the clerk working at the U-Totem store up the street, and occasionally he talked the clerk into letting him shoplift a six-pack of beer. It was not much, but it was something.

Gillies and Logan spent more time with each other than with the others; one of the wranglers noticed the change that came over the men when they were together. He had always considered Gillies to be all right, but when Gillies was with Logan, he acted crazy. The two men just were not good for each other.

While working at the Ponderosa, Logan had met a girl who lived in nearby Tempe with a girlfriend. One of the girls was eighteen years of age, the other was seventeen. Now that he was closer to her at Weldon, Logan began seeing the girl more often. She and her friend both had babies and no men; they worked at the Motel 6 on Van Buren as housekeepers. After work, they would drive down to Weldon to see Logan, and he introduced them to Gillies. More than once the four would go to the girls' place in Tempe for sex. After one such trip, Gillies bragged about how great the girls were in bed and passed their address around to the wranglers with the suggestion that if any of them ever wanted to get laid they should just drop by unannounced.

But Logan's way with women entailed more than smooth talk. One day at Weldon, he roughed up a woman in view of the other men when she crossed him. He regularly called women "bitches," and Schneider cautioned him about using the word in front of the women customers.

Gillies had met a girl who rented a house just across Fifty-second Street. He was not really her boyfriend, but he dropped by steadily to have sex with her and sometimes took Logan along. Logan would drink her liquor, eye her valuables, and, when he had the money, buy drugs.

The men in the bunkhouse smoked marijuana constantly, and though Schneider forbade liquor on the premises, they hid bottles, as much from one another as from Schneider. When Logan had money, he would stumble back to his bunk from one of the bars and pass out, or he would lie there, sipping beer, until he passed out.

As the days and nights drifted by, Logan became increasingly desperate to do something about his situation. He sensed that if he continued to mark time, he would be arrested. He had to get to Australia, and soon.

9

Following her return from Saugus after the Thanksgiving holiday, Suzanne worked out vigorously in anticipation of another South Rim-to-North Rim hike across the Grand Canyon. She talked to Jo Ann Heckel about her trip home and how she missed her family and friends. More than once Suzanne had discussed her uncertainty about her life. This time she bragged about Donna, as usual, and told Jo Ann enthusiastically of the shopping trip in Boston. Jo Ann realized that Suzanne would not be with them much longer; clearly she was ready to return home.

During the Thanksgiving visit and by telephone in the following weeks, Donna and Suzanne had talked about one of their cousins living in Chicago. A man had broken into her place and raped her. It had been horrifying for their cousin and traumatic for the whole family. As a result, the sisters discussed what they would do if they were ever attacked. They agreed they had two choices: fight and try to break free, or yield and hope not to be hurt. It made no sense to either of them to continue fighting, especially if there was more than one man. Excessive resistance would only anger the assailant, who might very well be crazy, and could increase the risk of being killed. Suzanne told Donna that if it came down to it, she would do whatever was necessary in order to survive because in the end, that, was what really mattered. Donna agreed.

That Christmas, Jo Ann and Suzanne went together to Squaw

Peak to view the luminaries, a southwestern custom. Luminaries are small paper bags containing an inch of sand and a votive candle. They are laid along a path, and at night the candles are lighted. Each year, the trail up Squaw Peak is lined with them. Even from a short distance, the sight is inspiring; from far away, it is a vision.

Over the holidays, Suzanne's friend from college, Joanie Saltzberg, called to confirm that she was pregnant. Suzanne was thrilled, and the two chatted about names and plans for the child. Debbie Crisafulli's new baby was due that coming February. Debbie was going to call Suzanne after the birth, to tell her if she'd had a boy or a girl.

On January 6, 1981, Peter and Louise arrived for their winter visit in Arizona, with plane reservations to return to Saugus early on the morning of January 29.

During this winter visit, Suzanne and her mother had several opportunities to discuss her relationship with Eric Gregan. Suzanne said, "I never thought I would ever fall for a man who didn't have a college degree." She told her mother, "He's a carpenter. He works with his hands, but he thinks the world of me. He's very interested in me as a person. He enjoys backpacking, the things I do."

Suzanne asked if the family would object to her bringing Eric with her to Saugus for Peter Jr.'s wedding that coming May. Louise told her that it would be no problem.

Eric took Louise aside to talk about Suzanne. "Do you mind?" he stammered, "I was thinking . . ." Then he explained that he was considering asking Suzanne to accept his ring.

Louise said, "Oh, that's nice, Eric." But Eric had not acted on his intent by the time the visit came to an end.

While her parents were there, Suzanne kept Peter's spirits high, and everyone was feeling better about his prospects for full recovery. Whenever they visited, Suzanne's parents stayed in the first bedroom just at the top of the stairs. Because of the wiring and the placement of the bed, it was necessary to enter the room and turn the lamp on by hand. The light switch at the doorway controlled the outlet into which the clock radio was plugged. Everyone who lived in the condominium knew of the arrangement and was careful never to turn off the switch at the door.

Suzanne took her parents to work to show them off. Louise was talking to the manager when he said, "We don't expect to have Suzanne long."

"What do you mean?"

"She's scheduled for higher things." He told Louise that Suzanne would be promoted once again, and would be transferred to the corporate office in New York. Louise already knew about the transfer, but was happy to hear of the promotion. She was also pleased that her daughter was so well regarded by her boss.

On January 27, Logan and Gillies were told by Schneider to accompany a group of ten-year-old schoolgirls on a ride. Their parents had requested an escort. Logan and Gillies rode behind the group and then moved away to the crest of a gentle rise. They had stashed beer there, which they slowly drank as they sat on their horses and pretended to watch the girls.

Logan told Gillies that he was on the run from Michigan, where he had escaped from prison. He said his real name was not Mike Richardson, that he did not intend to stay in Phoenix much longer, and that he was planning to leave the country soon. To buy new identification and to finance his trip out of the country, he needed to steal big money.

What Logan did not tell Gillies was that he was planning to run to Australia. Logan had a contact through one of his brothers in Detroit who, for $500, could provide decent false identification, including a passport. Logan already had a passport photograph and earlier had called an airline to price a ticket. For the identification package, the airfare, and a little money at the other end, he figured the absolute minimum he required would be $2,000.

He told Gillies that he needed a partner and had selected Gillies for the role, if he was up to it. Logan did not know when the opportunity to commit a robbery would arise, but it had to be soon. He needed someone to cover his back and Gillies could expect to profit from it.

Gillies wanted to know about the timing because a local country-and-western station, KJJJ—which advertised as KJ—was planning a party at Weldon in two or three days that he wanted to attend.

Logan did not know when the robbery would be, but told Gillies to be ready at any time. Gillies agreed, and the men finished off their beer while the ten-year-olds played on their horses below them.

A road show of the Broadway hit *Dancin'* was scheduled to perform at Arizona State University in Tempe the Wednesday night of January 28. One of Suzanne's friends, a schoolteacher, bought four tickets to the show. She was bringing a friend to introduce to Suzanne and to Jo Ann Heckel, who was also planning to attend.

That Wednesday, Suzanne dropped off her Pinto at the Charlie Rossi Ford dealership to repair the brake cable, and picked it up later that day. Peter and Louise had reservations to leave from Sky Harbor Airport at 3:00 the next morning. Since Suzanne would be going out with friends, her parents decided to have dinner with Frances Chubinski early in the evening. Suzanne would be finished in Tempe around 10:00 that night. Peter planned to turn in his rented car, and from there Suzanne would pick up her parents and drive them to the airport.

Suzanne had told her boss that she would be late Thursday morning because she was planning to remain at the airport to see her parents onto the plane.

Wednesday morning, Suzanne dressed for the day and evening in a new outfit. She wore navy blue slacks with a matching vest, a cotton shirt with a flower print, and rather high-heeled pumps. She took along a handsome corduroy jacket for the evening chill. She also wore her ring with the blue star sapphire and a matching necklace.

She and Jo Ann were to meet at Monti's La Casa Vieja, an Arizona landmark, near the Mill Avenue bridge in old town Tempe. From there, they would take one car the short distance to Grady Gammage Auditorium, where they would meet the other women.

That same Wednesday morning, the wranglers at Weldon were angry with Schneider. They were tired of his promises and sick of not being paid. They discussed it heatedly and decided to steal drinking money from their employer for that night. Toward the end of the day, some of the wranglers distracted Schneider while Logan sneaked into the office and took $40. Two of the men walked up to the U-Totem and bought a cheap twelve-pack of beer, which they hid in the bunkhouse for later that night.

After Logan had confided in Gillies, Gillies told one of the wranglers that Logan was an escaped convict using an alias. He told the wrangler not to tell anyone about it.

At 6:00 that evening, Louise finished cleaning the condominium. As she and Peter left to meet with Frances and her husband, the five wranglers walked across the desert to the Homestead Bar to get drunk with what remained of the $40. Logan was wearing his dirty cowboy hat with the turned-down rim, a print shirt, Levi's, and boots. Gillies was dressed similarly and both men wore light jackets. Neither had shaved in several days and they had scraggly beards.

By 8:00 the wranglers were still fairly sober but completely broke. They decided to walk to the bunkhouse and finish off the twelve-pack, but when they arrived back, they were furious to find it missing. They concluded that Schneider had discovered they had taken his money, and had searched the bunkhouse and confiscated the beer.

Most of the men were discouraged and had drunk enough to settle in for the night. Gillies told Logan he thought he could talk the girl across the street into giving them money. They left together, telling the others they were going for cigarettes.

The pairing of these two men had been utterly random, yet each saw in the other what he had sought throughout his life. Gillies had the companion who nearly always went with him when he broke the law. Logan had a man he thought he could trust.

Of the two, Gillies was the more impetuous and quick-tempered. He was volatile and aggressive, more overtly manipulative, more self-indulgent. He was, simply put, self-centered and mean.

Logan was coldly calculating and premeditatedly manipulative, though a constant alcoholic haze diminished his effectiveness. He was capable of anything, but his primary motive was to get money.

Their size was nearly identical, but Gillies had the stronger physical presence. Though he would not admit it, Logan was a little intimidated by his new companion. Still, he believed he could control Gillies.

Shortly before 8:00 that night, the four women met in the Grady Gammage Auditorium parking lot and entered the theater together. *Dancin'* had no plot but was a series of dance routines, which Suzanne enjoyed. Afterward, Jo Ann visited with an usher who was the sister of a friend. She returned and the women continued talking until the crowd cleared. It was nearly 10:30.

They said good-bye in the parking lot. Jo Ann and Suzanne drove in her Pinto the short distance to Monti's, where they had left Jo Ann's car. Suzanne told Jo Ann that she was going into the restaurant to call her parents to make arrangements for meeting them. The two said good night. As Suzanne walked toward the restaurant, Jo Ann looked after her and called out again, "I'll see you tomorrow."

At the pay telephone in the restaurant, Suzanne called her parents at Frances's house. Peter answered, and they agreed to meet at the

Rodeway Inn, located near the airport at the corner of Twenty-Fourth Street and Buckeye Road. This was where Peter was to leave his rental car, but it was not a good part of town, so he was somewhat concerned. He told Suzanne that if she arrived at the Rodeway Inn ahead of them, she should lock her car and wait in the lobby. They would do the same if they arrived first. Suzanne understood and said she would see them there shortly.

Since she was closer than her parents to the Rodeway Inn, Suzanne called Eric Gregan at his nearby apartment and suggested she drop by to visit for a few minutes. Eric begged off, telling her that he had to be up early. They would see each other the next day.

With time to kill, Suzanne drove off from Monti's to meet her parents.

Across the street from Weldon, Gillies was upset to see the woman with another man. She was not his girl, but still he did not like the idea of her with someone else, or maybe he just wanted an excuse to be mad. He told her that he and Logan needed money. She did not have any to give him, she said. Gillies knew she owned a .22-caliber rifle, so he went to the closet and took it. The men also helped themselves to a plastic bag filled with marijuana and some pills. As the pair left, the woman screamed at both of them, demanding they give her rifle and dope back. Logan was not concerned about her calling the police, not with drugs in the house.

The men walked across the desert, passed the darkened Baptist church, and talked about ways to get money. They took the rifle into the Homestead Bar and tried to interest the bartender in the weapon, but he would have none of it. The men did not have a cent, so he sent them on their way. Gillies hid the rifle in the desert.

The men went across the street and down to the Motel 6, where the girls Logan knew worked. While Gillies talked to the one who was then working there, Logan went through her purse. Nothing.

Logan had always considered it a low-life crime to roll a drunk even though, in effect, that is what sent him to prison. He told Gillies that was their best bet. Who knew? They might get lucky and find one with real money. The men walked up Van Buren, then over to the Pioneer Bar. Logan had spotted a place where they could hide in the dark and wait.

It was cold that night. A winter front was moving through, and the temperature was in the low forties. The wind was restless, and the men were wearing only their light jackets. As traffic on Van Buren drove by, headlights cast light their way when the cars turned down a street. They spotted more than one police car.

After an hour of waiting, they had had enough. They walked around the bar, passed the motel on the corner, then crossed Fifty-Second Street to the U-Totem store. Gillies's clerk was on duty, so he went inside to see if he could get a free six-pack of beer. Logan waited outside and watched.

Gillies had no luck with his buddy. He told the clerk that he and his friend wanted to party but were broke. He argued, but the clerk refused. Gillies went to the service area and extracted a single bottle of beer. He told the clerk that at least he was going to take this, and the clerk let him.

Outside, Gillies and Logan sat on the curb and shared the bottle of beer. It was not quite 11:00 P.M. Gillies was very angry at the turn of events, and the more he talked, the angrier he became. He told Logan that what he ought to do was just go in there and take the money, that was what he should do.

Logan told him he was nuts. The clerk knew him and would inform the police. Besides, Van Buren was not exactly an empty street, anyone could just walk in. On top of that, they were on foot and, hell, they only lived just down the street. He was crazy to even think of such a thing.

Gillies said he was going to do it just the same. He was mad and he wanted money. The men stood up. Logan said there was no way he could stop him, but that he wanted no part of it. Gillies headed for the door.

At that moment, Suzanne Rossetti drove up in her Pinto. The most direct route from Monti's to the Rodeway Inn was this one. She could have taken Washington Street, but there was no store on it. The U-Totem was the first convenience store on the street, and it was located just before the seedier parts of Van Buren farther west.

Gillies watched her leave the car and enter the store. The men sat outside and discussed how much money she might be carrying. Suzanne bought a pack of chewing gum and appeared to be stalling for time.

When she finally came out, she discovered she had locked her keys in the car.

Suzanne went to the clerk and asked if he knew anything about getting into a locked car. He did not. She asked if he would come out and try to open it for her. "I'm sorry, lady," he said, "but I can't leave my register." Store policy.

Suzanne went back out to her Pinto and circled it, looking for some way in. Logan and Gillies watched her intently. Logan noticed how tiny she was, and how pretty she looked, dressed in matching blue vest and slacks. The men exchanged knowing glances and approached.

"Can we help?" Gillies asked.

PART FIVE

·

THE
SUPERSTITION
MOUNTAINS

"She was her father's baby.'
—Louise Rossetti

10

Suzanne looked up at the men, who each towered a foot over her, and flashed her broad grin. "I locked my keys in the car," she said.

Gillies and Logan were smiling back. Gillies moved slowly around the car, searching for a way into it. Logan noticed how clean Suzanne was. He liked to divide the people he met into those from the East Coast and those from the West. When he heard Suzanne's distinctive Boston accent, he had her pegged. He explained he was from Detroit, "You know, the car capital of the world."

Suzanne laughed and said, "Then you must know how to break into a car." He conceded he just might. Logan explained that they were wranglers who worked at a riding stable just down the street. His eyes fell to the purse she was holding, then he moved to the car.

Gillies suggested popping the window on the passenger side, just behind the door, and Suzanne told him to go ahead. If she did not leave soon she would be late in meeting her parents. The men entered the store and obtained a yellow-handled screwdriver from the clerk. Gillies worked on the window until the seal gave, then peeled it out of the frame. The window was now connected only by the propping mechanism. He unlocked the passenger door, then opened it, and reached across to unlock the driver's side.

Suzanne was noticeably relieved. She thanked the pair and asked if there was something she could do for them in return. When Logan suggested a six-pack of Budweiser beer, Suzanne went into the store to buy it. She came out shortly with the beer, which she handed to Logan, then went to the driver's side of the car to leave.

The men suggested she give them a ride just down the street to the bunkhouse. Suzanne did not give rides to strangers; certainly not when she was alone, and not to two men. She was also running late. Perhaps she did agree to give the ride; perhaps at this point, with one man behind her, she was intimidated into it, or perhaps one of them simply pushed her into the car while the other scooted in from the passenger side to hold her down as they quickly drove off. There was the screwdriver to press against her, to make sure she didn't cry out.

They traveled the three hundred yards to the stables. It was almost exactly 11:00 P.M., and Louise and Peter were just saying good night to Frances. Rather than taking the turn for the bunkhouse, they stopped in the desert where Gillies and Logan had watched the little girls play on their horses the previous day. As soon as the engine was cut, Gillies struck Suzanne without warning, two violent blows, his fist making a loud smack that startled Logan. Gillies tore at her clothes, then popped the door open, shoved Suzanne out, and lay his 185 pounds on her 100-pound frame as he pulled the cotton blouse above her breasts and ripped the bra apart.

Until then Suzanne had struggled, but now she was held pressed against the ground and could not break free. Gillies was pulling at her blue slacks and panties and quickly had them off. He fumbled his belt buckle open, pushed down his Levi's, and began raping her.

Logan had watched passively without saying a word or doing anything to interfere. Standing outside the car, he dumped the contents of Suzanne's purse onto the floorboards and fingered through it. He located $34 in cash, which he placed into his shirt pocket, then walked to the back of the Pinto, opened the rear hatch, and found Suzanne's camera and gym bag. As Gillies finished with the nearly naked Suzanne and rose from the ground, he told Logan to "get his." Instead, Logan told his partner what she had in the way of valuables.

They were only a short distance from the bunkhouse and no more than one hundred feet from a quiet road that ran to the golf course and Papago Park; they could be spotted at any moment. Logan held Suzanne fast while Gillies ripped one of her white towels into inch-wide strips. They made her slip her slacks back on without panties, then tied her hands and tossed her into the rear of the Pinto. They bound her hands to her feet and threw a blanket she kept in the car over her. Gillies took the wheel; Logan sat in the rear seat, with his left hand pressing down on Suzanne. He told her to keep her mouth shut, or things would get worse.

Gillies spun dirt as he hurried out of the desert to the paved road. He tuned the radio to rock 'n' roll, then turned the volume up as loud as it would go. Logan lit a joint, and the men passed it back and forth as they sped off.

Peter and Louise were just arriving at the Rodeway Inn at the southwest corner of Twenty-fourth Street and Buckeye Road. When they did not spot Suzanne, they locked the rental car and went inside to wait in the lobby. After a few minutes, Peter explained to the night clerk that they were waiting for their daughter.

Once Gillies and Logan finished the joint, the men drank the beer Suzanne had bought for them. Gillies was simply driving at random and when the beer was gone, they stopped for more. Logan handed Gillies some of Suzanne's money to buy the twelve-pack. They drove awhile, then stopped a second time for gas at a self-service station. Logan made certain Suzanne was fully covered with the blanket and kept careful watch. They decided to go to Suzanne's condominium to see what else they could steal.

At the Rodeway Inn, Peter and Louise were becoming anxious about Suzanne, since their daughter was known for her punctuality. It occurred to them that she might have had a flat tire, or perhaps car trouble, or even worse, had been involved in an accident.

Peter said to the clerk again, "I'm expecting my daughter." Then added, "She's late now." He asked if a young woman had been in before them, and the clerk said, "No." By midnight, they were seriously concerned that something was wrong.

At that time, Logan and Gillies, with Suzanne, pulled into the condo complex off Granite Reef Road in Scottsdale. Logan raised Suzanne's head so she could point out her place to them. Gillies selected a parking spot, pulled in, and went alone into the condominium.

Logan was still sitting as guard in the backseat. The car was suddenly quiet, with only the steady ticking of the engine as it cooled. On this winter weeknight, no one was about in the complex. Logan again told Suzanne to stay quiet, then opened a fresh beer, and sat thinking about the turn of events.

Logan's only concern now was that he not get caught. There had been no discussion about raping anyone and that had come as a surprise. Logan had been involved with the courts enough to know that of the two he was the less guilty. Technically, he was as guilty of rape as Gillies, but he knew if he made the right moves now, this instant, the fact that he had not raped the lady would count heavily in his favor. He could release her and expect lenient treatment. Or he could leave Suzanne and simply walk away.

The problem he faced, however, was in being a wanted fugitive. Even if he turned Suzanne loose and was not charged for Gillies's rape of her, he would still be shipped back to Michigan to serve the remainder of his fifteen-year sentence, plus whatever time they added on for his escape. Then there was this: The lady might have cash money in her place and he could not risk missing out on such a potential score.

So Logan sat, slowly sipping beer, for the ten minutes it took until Gillies came out and said it was clear inside. The men took Suzanne into her condominium.

Shortly after midnight, Peter called the Tempe Police Department. It occurred to him that Suzanne might never have made it out of Tempe. He explained his problem to the officer who was taking calls. There had been no reports of accidents and, no, they could not send someone to Monti's to check just because his daughter was an hour late for an appointment. No, Peter could not file a missing-person report, not for twenty-four hours. Probably their daughter had had a fight with her boyfriend and had gone off without telling anyone. Peter explained how that could not be the case, but the officer would not listen.

Peter called the hospitals. Nothing. He called the Tempe police back. Still nothing. Peter and Louise were becoming agitated, and Peter turned increasingly aggressive with each call.

Gillies took Suzanne upstairs into the first room off the stairwell, the one her parents used, and with less urgency, raped her again.

Downstairs, Logan tuned Suzanne's inexpensive stereo to rock 'n' roll and smoked weed as he searched for money or valuables. Instead of cash, he discovered Suzanne's ATM card. He thumbed it and wondered how much the lady kept in her account.

Outside the complex, one of the neighbors was walking her dog and noticed that Suzanne's Pinto was in the wrong parking space. That struck her as odd, since Suzanne had two spaces, both of them empty. The neighbor also heard loud music coming from the condominium, and that was even more peculiar because Suzanne was a quiet neighbor. Even when she had many friends over, there was never this kind of racket.

The neighbor wondered about it, but was not sufficiently disturbed by what she had heard and seen to call the police. When she went back to her place, she did nothing.

When Gillies finished with Suzanne, he called for Logan to come up to the bedroom. Logan told him about the ATM card; they grilled Suzanne on how much she kept in the bank, and learned it was just over $4,000. Logan made her tell him how the card worked, but was quickly confused by her instructions.

Indicating Suzanne, Gillies told Logan again that it was his turn. Logan understood that his continued refusal would stand as a rebuke of Gillies's conduct; until Logan actually raped Suzanne, he was not a part of the crime in Gillies's eyes. So he raped Suzanne, while Gillies was downstairs smoking weed and searching.

When Logan finished, he told Suzanne to dress. She pulled on her blue pants again without the panties, buttoned her cotton blouse over the torn bra, and put on her corduroy jacket. As they left the room, Suzanne turned off the wall switch and stopped the clock radio at 12:47 A.M.

Gillies had located Suzanne's collection of nearly two hundred silver dollars and filled a pillowcase with it, took a partially full bottle of Scotch from the cabinet above the refrigerator and the sleeping bag Suzanne had laid out for her Grand Canyon hike that weekend, plus a few odds and ends.

They were ready to leave. They could have left Suzanne tied up in her bedroom; instead, they took her out to the car and with Logan behind the wheel, drove off. They needed her to show them how to get the money out of the bank machine. It was now after 1:00 A.M.

* * *

At the Rodeway Inn, Peter was nearly panicked. He had called the Tempe Police Department at least a half dozen times, and the officer answering the telephone was becoming angry.

Louise called her sister Frances. "Is Suzie at your place?" she asked.

"No, she isn't."

"Well, she hasn't come here." Louise told Frances she felt something was wrong. Frances suggested that Suzanne might only have been detained. Louise was adamant. "No, something is wrong. I'm going back to the condo. It's not like Suzie to do this. She would have called." Frances could hear the suspicion in Louise's voice.

Peter called the Phoenix Police Department with the same questions, and received the same replies. He called the Scottsdale Police Department as well. Nothing. He asked, begged, Scottsdale to send an officer to the condominium to check for Suzanne or any sign of trouble. "We don't give that kind of service," was the response.

At 2:10 A.M., Gillies and Logan drove slowly by the Ugly Teller Machine at the Valley National Bank on East Apache Road in Tempe. They did not know that the machine was monitored by two cameras activated by motion, one of which snapped their picture. Eight minutes later they drove back to the teller machine and stopped. Logan was in the driver's seat, while Gillies kept an eye on Suzanne. Logan approached the machine with Suzanne's card, and the camera took his picture. In the background was the Pinto, containing Gillies and Suzanne, now sitting up.

Though Suzanne had told Logan her personal identification number and explained how to use the machine, he was still confused by it. He returned to the car and again she explained the procedure to him. Logan went back to the machine. He extracted $200, then tried the card another time, but it refused to dispense more in the amounts he attempted.

Back at the car, Logan and Gillies were furious. All of that money was just sitting there. It occurred to Logan that the card might work at another bank branch. They turned west and headed into Phoenix and at Twenty-fourth Street, drove north, searching for another Valley National Bank office.

• • •

Peter and Louise thought that perhaps, despite all of their careful plans, Suzanne had misunderstood and gone to the airport to wait for them there instead. They were afraid to leave the Rodeway Inn in case she suddenly arrived, or there was a telephone call for them. Because of Peter's medical condition, Louise would not be separated from him.

Around 2:30 A.M., Louise was standing at the entrance to the hotel, scanning the street for her daughter, when, coming from the south on Twenty-fourth Street, she thought she spotted Suzanne's car. She called out to Peter who was inside, "That looks like Suzanne's car!" But no, that couldn't be right. There were two scruffy-looking men in the car, and one of them was driving. "That can't be Suzie," Louise thought. "She wouldn't let anyone drive her car."

The Pinto drove quickly past and Louise decided she had been mistaken, it could not have been Suzanne. The girl with the two dirty men had looked so terribly sad, "like a lost soul."

Peter and Louise took a taxi to the airport and went to the boarding area at their gate to see if they could find Suzanne there.

Gillies and Logan stopped at another Ugly Teller shortly before 3:00 A.M. Logan tried for an additional two hundred dollars, but the machine declined to give it. Its limit was $250 in any twenty-four-hour period, running midnight to midnight. Gillies, back behind the wheel, began driving again at random, rock music blasting, while they finished the beer and started on the Scotch. Suzanne had been allowed to put on her running shoes, which she kept in the car. She was bound and lying down in the rear.

Logan was for heading immediately to California, pointing out that they would be there by early morning. Gillies said no, he had stuff at the bunkhouse he needed, and there was the party Friday night he planned to attend. He was adamant.

Logan began to think. Ever since he had escaped from prison, he had looked for that big score. A couple thousand dollars would see him to Australia. Now he held the ATM card that was the key to $4,000, but only at the rate of $250 a day. The money was there, he just needed the days to get it.

The lady was the problem. If they let her go, and even if Logan managed to get away, the bank account would be cut off to him. But if they did not turn her loose, over the next week or two, he could take all of her money.

Logan leaned forward in the seat and said to Gillies over the music, "What are we going to do with her?"

11

Peter and Louise imagined again and again that they saw Suzanne at the airport. Louise would spot a short young woman at a distance and say, "There she is!" with sudden relief that quickly turned to despair. No matter how often they thought they had seen her, ending the nightmare, it never happened. As the minutes passed, it became apparent to Peter that if they were going to see Suzanne again, he was going to have to find her.

He returned to the telephone and called the Phoenix police at least three times with no success. At 3:00 A.M., Peter told his wife, "Let's cancel our trip. I've got to find out where the kid is."

Peter called his son in Saugus. "Don't come," he said, "we've missed our flight."

Peter Jr. asked, "What's wrong?" His father said nothing was wrong, they had just missed the flight. Peter Jr. did not like the sound of his father's voice. His immediate concern was for his father's health, and he wondered if something of a medical nature had happened that they were not telling him.

Peter and Louise took a taxi to retrieve their rented car. The cabbie complained repeatedly about his rough night. Peter considered telling the man what a rough night was really all about.

With the car, they backtracked Suzanne's route, hoping they would spot the Pinto at any moment. They went to Monti's and then to Arizona State University. Nothing.

* * *

Logan repeatedly asked him what they were going to do with the woman; Gillies did not understand what he meant. At around the time Peter and Louise canceled their flight, Gillies finally comprehended Logan's intent.

Gillies drove east across Tempe, then through the Mormon settlement of Mesa, and along the two-lane highway toward Apache Junction at the foothills of the Superstition Mountains. At Apache Junction, a retirement and winter-visitor community for those unable to live in Sun City or Leisure World, Gillies turned north along the Apache Trail, officially designated as State Highway 88.

Shortly after the turn of the century, an old wagon trail along this way had been expanded into a dirt road that was used to haul supplies necessary to construct Roosevelt Dam on the Salt River. It was the water reservoir behind the dam which ended the floods that had stymied Phoenix's growth, and it provided a steady and cheap supply of irrigation water. The road was paved past the dam to Canyon Lake, and then to Tortilla Flat, a tourist attraction created with phony mining shacks and authentic mining implements. There had been a real settlement there at one time, but no longer.

Suzanne knew this country well. In her running shoes, she would need no more than a small opportunity to evade the men in the dark, if given the chance.

The booze and marijuana were gone. Gillies and Logan were tired and experiencing a mild depression after the alcohol and drugs. They had driven fifty miles since leaving Phoenix and still they were not in a totally remote area. First there had been Apache Junction, then the houses along the Apache Trail. Now they passed camping spots at the lakes and Tortilla Flat itself. Every time it looked as if they had found an isolated area, it proved to be close to people.

Beyond Tortilla Flat, signs of civilization finally vanished. Five miles later a sign read: PAVEMENT ENDS NEXT 22 MILES.

The road turned to dirt and beyond the car's headlights was darkness. Gillies slowed and picked his way cautiously around the sharp turns. At milepost 222, the road began a sharp descent down the face of Fish Creek Hill. Gillies turned the hairpin there and slowed dramatically. During another 125 yards, he pulled over to the right. He killed the engine and the music stopped. The two men climbed out of the car. They could see only blackness and heard the sound of their boots on the gravel.

It was even colder up here, a thousand feet higher than Phoenix. The wind was chilly and wet. The air came from down in the narrow canyon where the creek ran, and it smelled of mesquite and palo verde. The men shivered in their light jackets as they moved away from the car and peered over the edge of the road into the void below. Speaking in loud whispers, they discussed what to do next.

Of a like mind, Gillies and Logan walked to the car, opened the back door, and pulled Suzanne out. Gillies untied her legs and held her firmly in place.

Suzanne was disheveled and dirty. Her once-lustrous hair was matted, and contained twigs and burrs from the desert. The small amount of mascara she had applied hours ago was now smeared. Her skin was cut in several places, and she had a number of bruises. Her arms and legs were numb from being bound.

Suzanne said, "I guess you're going to kill me now."

Instead of answering, Gillies threw her on the road and pulled her pants off again. He pushed her arms up, unbuckled his Levi's, then raped her as she lay on the dirt road, while Logan stood at the side and watched. When Gillies finished, he straightened up and asked Logan if he wanted any. Logan dropped his pants and climbed on top of Suzanne while Gillies watched.

Afterward, Gillies untied her hands and yanked Suzanne by her arm, pulling her toward the edge of the road. "We're going for a hike," he said.

Suzanne pulled back. "I'm not going anywhere with you."

Gillies struck her in the face very hard. "Yes, you are," he said, jerking her arm, "you're going hiking."

When the trail had been turned into a narrow dirt road, the crew had blasted the face of the mountain at this point. The rocks spread in a large V down from where Gillies now stood.

There was a break in the guardrail and Gillies stood with one foot off the road. It was nearly 4:00 A.M., and it was very dark below. It looked as if the cliff fell for thousands of feet into an abyss. Suzanne was struggling and she pulled away from Gillies, but he held her wrist tight. Then Logan grabbed her from behind and pushed her toward the cliff, where the men locked eyes in mutual agreement.

Suzanne was begging them to stop, telling them over and over, no, no, no, don't, don't, but the two strong men pushed and dragged her until there was no earth below her, only space, and she was falling.

If the men had expected silence, or perhaps a long diminishing scream, they were disappointed. Almost as quickly as they threw Suzanne from the roadway, they heard the sound of her body striking, then moans coming from the darkness below.

Suzanne had fallen about forty feet and landed on nearly solid rock with the left side of her face and body. The force of the impact had knocked her left eye from its socket, and crushed the side of her face.

The men debated what to do. It was important to Logan that she not be found for a long time, preferably never. They located a flashlight in the car and slid down the loose rubble until they found Suzanne, groaning in agony.

Again the men debated what to do as they stood over her. Suzanne tried to rise, and Logan told her more than once to stay put. When she persisted, he shoved her hard back down on the rocks. She was bleeding heavily from her face. Suzanne said, "Let's go home and let me cook you a meal." Instead, the men argued over who was going to kill her. Suzanne begged them, "Leave me alone. I'm going to die anyway."

"You're damn right you are, bitch!" Gillies said.

They pulled her up as Logan said he was sorry, but this was the way it had to be. They pitched her down the cliff again, throwing her as hard as they could, thinking that the edge was just a few feet away. In fact, the first forty feet was the only cliff. The rest of the side of Fish Creek Hill was very steep but not vertical.

Suzanne fell twenty feet or so, and suffered more injuries. They could hear her moans. Gillies was angry. The men found her and they threw her a third time. Suzanne now lay, nearly unconscious, at the tip of the V of broken rock. The men slid down over the rocks to her, cursing at the effort, and the woman who would not die.

"Kill the bitch," Logan told Gillies. He was sitting down, almost beside her, breathing heavily.

Gillies picked up one of the rocks, big enough so that it took both hands to hold, and slammed it into the side of Suzanne's head. She was still breathing. He flew into a rage, striking her again, then again, shouting, "Whore! Bitch!" He struck her over and over, and between blows Suzanne was quivering. Blood flew off her shattered skull and struck Logan. The sound of her head being crushed was sickening. The blows were so forceful Logan was afraid one of them might injure him.

Finally, Gillies stopped, sucking in air, kneeling on the harsh rocks for what seemed a very long time.

The pair debated if Suzanne was dead. They could not just leave her here, exposed. They had no shovel, but it didn't matter because there was no dirt, just solid rock and the broken rubble from the road construction. Slowly, the pair gathered rocks and covered Suzanne. She lay on her back, with her legs unnaturally askew, one arm resting across her lower breast, the other to her side.

It was hard and treacherous work in the dark, even with the flashlight. Some of the rocks were so big both men had to lift them. They labored for over one hour, capping their effort by lifting one large rock together, and placing it squarely on top, as if its weight alone would hold the body fast. When at last they thought they were finished, Gillies saw Suzanne's hand sticking obscenely from under the mound they had created. He pushed it closer, and they gathered more rocks to cover it.

Exhausted from the raping, murder, and burial, they sat on Suzanne's grave and lit Marlboro cigarettes, the smoke of cowboys. They sat there a long time, discussing how hard she had been to kill, and what a bitch it had been to bury her. They talked a little about what they would do next, but mostly they sat in the dark on top of her grave in silence, smoking and gathering their strength for the climb up the steep mountain. When at last they were ready, they punched the last of the cigarettes out on the rocks over Suzanne, and started up the face of Fish Creek Hill.

At around this time, 5:00 A.M., as Peter and Louise entered Suzanne's condominium, Louise saw lights that had not been on earlier. As she entered the front door, she called out, "Suzanne!"

She looked into the living room and was shocked at what she saw. She and Peter quickly examined the condominium. Drawers were open; there was clutter everywhere. Upstairs, their bed was disheveled and drapes that were usually open were closed. They spotted the clock radio, stopped at 12:47, and knew at once that was a message from Suzanne to them.

Peter picked up the telephone and called the police. He wanted an officer to see this right now! This was proof that something sinister had taken place. First, the Tempe police said it was out of their jurisdiction, as did the Phoenix police. Scottsdale said the missing-person report was with Tempe and it was their case.

Peter argued that there was evidence of a break-in. The Scottsdale officer told him they could send an officer by after the shift change in an hour or two.

Peter was enraged. He was a man accustomed to solving problems and he was not used to accepting no for an answer. If the police had listened to him in the beginning, someone would already have been at the condominium. If they had listened, they would have put out an alert for her car. He was determined not to take any more of this runaround, and kept calling and calling.

Louise lifted from the carpet a troubling piece of aluminum foil with a peculiar burned residue. She spotted something else on the floor and picked it up. It was a piece of Zigzag paper.

Gillies and Logan slipped on the rubble and cursed. They had misjudged their destination and worked their way too far to one side. Gillies reached the road and stopped at the guardrail to breathe in air. Shortly, Logan joined him. They stayed there a few moments, then wearily walked along the dirt road to the Pinto.

There was nothing to say and nothing more to do. Gillies took the wheel and Logan sat beside him. The music roared out of the radio as Gillies drove off, heading without thought to the end of the Apache Trail, and the road that would take them to Globe, Arizona, and the main highway back to Phoenix. It was, in fact, better just to turn around, but these were urban cowboys, and neither man knew the country.

Logan leaned back in his seat and fell immediately to sleep.

12

At the Rodeway Inn and at the airport, Peter and Louise had not had telephone numbers for Suzanne's local friends. At the condominium Louise found Suzanne's address book, and they started making calls from there.

Peter reached Pug. "Do you know where Suzanne is?" he asked, after apologizing for waking him.

"No. Why?" Peter told him what had happened that night. "Something's not right, Pete," Pug said. "This is not like Suzanne. If she says she will be there, she will. Have you called the police?"

Peter explained about that and how futile his efforts had been. Peter hung up to telephone others, but called Pug back shortly. Pug could hear panic in his voice and decided to go to Suz's place and help.

Louise called Frances and her sister could detect fear in Louise's voice when she said, "I suspect foul play." She told Frances that liquor was missing, there was a piece of aluminum foil on the carpet that had been used to burn a drug, camping gear was askew, and some of it had been taken. Asked if the police had been notified, Louise said they claimed they could do nothing until Suzanne was missing for at least twenty-four hours.

Louise called Eric Gregan, who thought she was calling from Boston. "No, Suzanne never came for us," she told him.

Eric was immediately suspicious. "I don't know why she wouldn't.

119

Something must have happened." He rushed right over, and shortly others began arriving at the condominium as well.

Once Pug got there, Louise told him how Peter and she had found the place when they arrived earlier. "Something's not right," she told him. "Someone has been in this house."

Pug talked to Peter again about the police and their lack of action. Pug made two phone calls to Tempe headquarters and was angry at what he was hearing. At one point, he shouted into the telephone, "I am not going to let you go until you do something!" He told Peter they should go personally to the Tempe Police Department.

There, Peter faced the officer who had been ignoring his calls. The first thing the officer said was, "I've been hearing from you all night."

"Yes," Peter said, "and you're going to hear from me all day."

They exchanged harsh words. Finally, the officer threatened, "Watch out. I could have you arrested for being a disorderly person."

But Peter would not back off. By this time a new shift had arrived. Peter made enough of a ruckus that a detective came out to speak to him. When he heard the story, he agreed to go to the condominium to pick up a photograph of Suzanne. On their way back to Scottsdale from the police station, Pug and Peter searched for Suzanne's car. Nothing.

When the detective observed the condition of the condominium, he snapped a number of photographs. What kind of a person was Suzanne? What was she wearing? Pug told him that Suzanne was not the kind of person simply to wander off. Despite the officer's interest, Peter and Pug still found him hard to convince.

Peter explained that Suzanne's ATM card was missing. They had called Valley National Bank to learn if there was any activity on the account, but the bank had refused to release any information. The officer told them his department could have the bank flag the account for them. Finally, the detective circumvented the twenty-four-hour waiting period needed to investigate a missing person; he reported Suzanne's car as stolen. There was now an official police case, of sorts.

Suzanne had been dead for three hours.

Jo Ann Heckel, who had bade Suzanne farewell just the night before, was taking her morning shower when her roommate shouted there was a telephone call for her. It was Eric Gregan, wanting to know if Jo Ann knew where Suzanne was. Jo Ann, it turned out, was the last person known to have seen her. When Eric told Jo Ann that Suzanne had never met her parents, Jo Ann became very frightened. That was not the Suzanne she knew.

As Jo Ann drove to work, she went out of her way to check the parking lot at Monti's. At work, everyone had already heard the news, and a number of employees went to the condominium to try to help.

Suzanne's friends conducted searches themselves, rather than depend on the police. They speculated as to where her car might be found and formed search parties only to return, tired and crestfallen, reporting no success. They searched the Papago golf course and the zoo near the Weldon Riding Stable. They even drove by the U-Totem store on the corner. They searched at Monti's and the Arizona State University campus. Pug and others walked the condominium complex, stopping everyone they encountered, knocking on doors, asking if anyone had seen or heard anything that would help.

Logan and Gillies were hungry and pulled into the all-night truck stop in Globe at dawn. They both ordered eggs and bacon with hashbrowns and toast, and smoked a pack of cigarettes. Their dirty, torn clothes were speckled with blood. They paid for breakfast with the silver dollars they had loaded into their pockets. Then they put ten dollars worth of gas into the car, again counting out the heavy coins like in a western movie. Logan argued for pushing on to California; the possessions Gillies wanted from the bunkhouse were simply not worth the risk. The longer they had the car, the hotter it became. What mattered was making distance. They could use the ATM card in California as easily as in Arizona.

Gillies was unconcerned and not persuaded by Logan. He wanted his things, and he wanted to attend the country radio station party the next night. Liquor stores were open, so they bought two twelve-packs of beer and drove west toward Phoenix. By 10:00 A.M., hungry again, they stopped at a restaurant near the downtown area. Logan had a hamburger and fries while he tried to convince Gillies that they needed to continue to California. But Gillies was adamant about obtaining his few belongings and hanging around for the party. This made no sense to Logan, but Gillies shrugged off his arguments. They were staying. They paid for the meal with more silver coins.

Gillies decided that he wanted to see a girl he knew named

Connie Parks* who lived in Litchfield Park. Gillies stayed in the car while Logan knocked on the door. Connie had known Gillies since the previous May and had dated him a few times after he was released from prison. Just that week, she had told him she did not want to see him anymore.

Connie had never seen the blue Pinto station wagon before, and Gillies coming by like this was very unusual. She went out to the car with Logan and observed boxes and articles in the backseat that did not seem appropriate for the men. There was a woman's shoe, a small backpack, a sleeping bag.

Gillies wanted her to go with them to the nearby White Tank Mountains Park, presumably to smoke weed and have sex. She said she did not want to go and instead told Gillies she was having money trouble. She had written several bad checks and needed $60 to cover them. Gillies said that was no problem and climbed out of the car. He reached into his Levi's and pulled out cash. He peeled off $60 and handed it over, telling her he had over $3,500. He looked at Logan and said, laughing, "Didn't we have a good time and a lot of fun in the Superstition Mountains?"

Logan laughed. "Yes, we did."

Connie asked where the car came from, and Gillies said he was leasing it. Then he asked again if she wanted to go with them to the park, and again she refused. The pair told her they were going anyway and drove off.

Once again Logan tried to convince Gillies that they should leave town. They had the ATM card, they had the cash, they had the car. If they stuck around another day, they risked being caught. Someone was going to miss the lady.

Gillies would not hear of it. All week the wranglers had been talking about the big party, and he was going, his mind was made up.

They left the park and headed by a different route toward Phoenix. Passing through Sun City, the men stopped at a store where Gillies bought a new jacket for himself. Logan bought pants, a western shirt, and a jacket. They had lunch and drove toward the Black Canyon Freeway in west Phoenix. At Metrocenter, a large shopping mall, Logan tried Suzanne's ATM card six times in four minutes, but received only $45. The men went to a western store where they each bought new cowboy boots. Gillies selected a new Bailey straw cowboy

* Pseudonym

hat. With the new pants, shirt, and boots, Logan was very pleased. He already had a cowboy hat that he liked.

In central Phoenix, Gillies went to visit his parole officer, but found she was attending a meeting. While they waited elsewhere, the men discarded their dirty clothes, then planned the story they would tell others about the previous night.

After 1:00 P.M., Gillies returned to the parole office. He had seen his PO for the first time on January 6, and this was their second meeting. He told her that he had paid off outstanding fines for old traffic tickets, and he reported that he was still working at Weldon.

As Gillies left, the parole officer wrote on her contact sheet, "No problems to report."

Peter continued looking for his daughter. Upwards of fifty people were in and out of the condominium in Scottsdale during that day. Groups searched everywhere, only to return with nothing positive to report. When they were not making calls to check on Suzanne, the telephone would ring immediately from someone wanting to know if she had been found.

It had been an exhausting and sleepless night for both Peter and Louise. Peter had been subjected to enough stress to kill him and Louise was very concerned; he had recently been taken off most of his heart medication.

They stayed close to each other during the day. Others could see them crying spontaneously, but if anyone approached, there was a quick smile for them through the tears. Everyone tried to talk of other things, but there was only one issue that concerned them. At times, one of Suzanne's friends would go up to Louise or to Peter to express his or her feelings. There would be hugs, then suddenly everyone would start crying again.

Frances had gone to work after her sister talked to her, but she worried about Suzanne all day. She called the condominium several times, but the telephone was always busy. Shortly after work she reached Louise. No one heard from Suzanne, and Louise confessed that she was beginning to fear the worst; she did not know what to think anymore. Frances asked if there was anything she could do, and Louise told her that everything that could be done was being done. Frances made plans to come by that weekend.

Peter was experiencing an accelerated heartbeat. He and Louise rushed to Scottsdale Memorial Hospital, where Peter explained his medical condition and what had been taking place. The doctor gave him a sedative and restored his prescription. By 6:00 P.M., Peter was back at the condominium and tried to sleep for an hour.

It was apparent that Peter was nearing the breaking point. His own doctor and medical records were all in Saugus. Louise and Peter decided that he would return on the 3:00 A.M., Boston flight. Louise would stay on until Suzanne was found.

After dark, around 7:30 P.M., Logan and Gillies drove up to Weldon. One of the wranglers was surprised to see them in a car and walked up to the pair. "Where'd you get the car?" he asked.

Gillies said they had been to Globe and a lady had hired them. She had given them $2,000 with which to buy fenceposts and ranching items for her place there.

The wrangler peered into the car. He could see panty hose and high-heeled shoes, funny things for these two to have, but shrugged it off. Logan and Gillies stood by the car, and as they bragged about their good fortune, the first wrangler noticed the men were now wearing new boots.

Logan and Gillies left after an hour and went to the dog track not too far away to spend their newfound money. They had bad luck with the betting, however, and just after midnight went to see a girl Logan knew near the Ponderosa. At 3:30 A.M., they extracted another $250 from an Ugly Teller Machine on South Central Avenue, then, finally, slept.

At 3:00 A.M., Peter Rossetti was seated in the plane bound for Boston. Later, when Peter Jr. arrived at the airport to pick him up, he spotted his father standing alone in the cold waiting for him. As soon as Peter was in the car, before he had said a word, he started crying. Peter Jr. asked, "Where's Mom? What's wrong?"

Peter said, "Suzie's missing." As he blurted the story out, his son reassured him. Then he considered the situation. Clearly, he was going to have to make decisions for the family. Louise had remained in Arizona and something would have to be done about that. Back in Saugus, Peter Jr. asked his fiancée, Geri, and others to come over. He called Donna. "You've got to come home right away," he said.

"What's the matter?" she asked. "Is it Dad?"

"No, it's Suzanne. She's missing."

That Wednesday night, Donna had tried to call her sister in

Scottsdale with no luck. Hearing these words, she believed that Suzanne was dead. She hurried over to her father's office.

When Donna arrived, her father looked dreadful. The telephones were ringing and someone was talking to Louise or one of Suzanne's friends in Arizona continuously. There had been no progress.

Peter Jr. knew that if he left for Arizona, his father would be in the office that very day trying to run the business, and his health could not stand it. There was absolutely no question that someone had to go to Phoenix; Louise had to be in Saugus with their father.

Donna agreed to leave that weekend, although she did not think she was emotionally strong enough or capable of doing what was required. Friends offered to go with her, but she declined. However, when her boyfriend, Robert,* a sensitive medical student she had been seeing for five years, asked if she wanted him to go out with her, she accepted and thanked him.

Late that Friday morning, Gillies and Logan drove back to Weldon. They were already drinking, and more than a little drunk. All the wranglers had heard about the new job and gathered around, wanting to know more.

Schneider had also heard the talk and was peeved that his two men had been absent when they should have been working. He had been transporting horses from his place to south Phoenix and had seen the pair in the Pinto twice the previous day. Once, Gillies had honked the car's horn and waved wildly at Schneider, who was coming from the opposite direction.

Schneider did not care for Gillies much. In the short time Gillies had been with him, the stable owner had seen him knock a much smaller man, hardly more than a boy, off his feet and threaten him over a trivial matter. He had not liked it. His opinion of Logan was no better. He knew Logan had been fired from the Ponderosa for being a drunk, and he did not trust him. Schneider came out of the office to learn what was going on, and what these men, who had no money, were doing with a car.

Gillies and Logan smelled of the liquor they had been drinking. They said they were quitting their jobs to work for a lady who had a spread in Globe. Schneider wanted to know how they had met her.

* Pseudonym

They said they had helped her break into her car after she locked her keys in it up the street at the U-Totem. They had gotten along well. She had bought them beer for their help, then suggested they join her at her place in Scottsdale, where they spent the night. She gave them money to buy new clothes and to buy fencing posts and other things she needed. They were to be at their new jobs by Monday.

Logan pulled a wad of bills from his pocket, which he claimed was $2,500, traveling money that this woman had given them.

The whole story sounded fishy to Schneider. First, this was not the kind of vehicle any rancher used on a spread. Second, he knew all of the ranchers near Globe and there was no woman among them. He eyed the men in their new clothes, observed their bravado, and wondered what they had done.

Schneider told the pair they would have to clear out if they were quitting. He did not allow men to hang around the place if they were not working for him. Before noon, the pair had driven off.

Louise was grasping at straws by this point. When someone mentioned that they had heard of a psychic who worked with the police to locate missing persons, she asked for the person's telephone number. Around noon on Friday, Louise called the woman, named Joan, * at her home in Indianapolis. When Louise explained what she wanted, Joan was willing to do what she could. Though she often found it useful to touch objects owned by the missing person, that was not absolutely necessary. She had often worked by telephone in the past.

Joan said to Louise, "It's not easy to find either people or things," and cautioned her not to get her hopes up. After they spoke for a few minutes, Joan said that she must first meditate and that she would call when she was ready.

In Indianapolis Joan cleared her mind of interference. She prayed for a time, then took out a Bible. In a technique she often used, she let the book fall open where it would. She lowered her eyes and they locked on a verse. She read a passage from Psalm 121.

In speaking to Louise, the situation had sounded to her as if Suzanne had run away. Now she could visualize Suzanne in a car with two angry men. She thought, "Why did you do that?"

Joan called back and spoke to Louise. She began by describing Suzanne correctly without ever having seen her. Then Joan said, "I

---

* Joan has asked that her last name not be used. All other details are accurate.

get the sign: 'I will lift up mine eyes unto the hills . . .' Does that mean anything to you?"

"Yes, it does," Louise said. "Suzanne climbed Squaw Peak every night after work." She told her that her daughter also often hiked in the mountains, and that she had been planning a trip to the Grand Canyon that weekend.

As Joan spoke, the scene of the abduction and of the murder came to her as if she were in the center of it, though her orientation was disjointed. She could see three people driving by old buildings, like mine shacks, and an unpaved road in the mountains, but there was no snow. She could smell dirt; suddenly it came to her with conviction. Joan told Louise, "She's been kidnapped by two men and raped. I also see two figures, the number eighty-eight. Does that mean anything?" Louise could think of nothing at the moment.

Joan knew now that Suzanne was dead. "Oh my God," she thought, "how sad for the family." She had no wish to disturb them with her vision of what had occurred, and she hesitated to utter the words because she could be wrong. The men, she knew, had both been in prison. One was the leader; the other was weaker, but very mean.

She felt so terribly sad for the poor girl. She knew the men would be caught and that the body would be found. She did not say all of this, not yet. The family was suffering enough.

"Keep me informed as to what is happening," she asked. So often people contacted her when they were desperate, but never told her the outcome, and it was very hard on her.

13

Though Peter Rossetti continued to hound the police by telephone from Saugus, the case was not receiving much priority. He also called the Scottsdale and Phoenix police departments, neither of which had started an investigation. Talking to an officer in Phoenix, Peter demanded, "What are you going to do?"

"Well," the officer said, "we're going to get a plane."

"How many planes have you got?"

"We have one police plane."

Peter considered that ludicrous. A city the size of Phoenix with one police airplane? "Hell," he said, "you can't do anything with a hundred and sixty men. What the hell can you do with one plane?"

The conversation deteriorated from there, ending in a heated exchange.

A Tempe detective arrived at the condominium and spoke with Louise, Jo Ann Heckel, and Eric Gregan. They related what little they knew, information the detectives already possessed. Louise had located the Charlie Rossi Ford repair receipt because the police had wanted the Pinto's license plate number. She handed this to the officer, who then dusted for fingerprints above the stove in the area where the bottle of Scotch had been taken, but no prints were lifted.

• • •

That Friday, Pug called a friend and explained the situation to him. The friend was a pilot who owned a two-seater Cessna. They contacted Sky Harbor Airport and received permission to fly at a very low altitude along the bed of the Salt River. This was the most likely place Suzanne's car would have been abandoned, since increasingly it did not look as if the police could locate it on routine patrol. They also overflew areas of Tempe and the open areas surrounding the airport. Nothing.

The searches by Suzanne's friends had become systematic. Pug and others, including many from the Arizona Mountaineering Club, divided the city and nearby areas into zones, and organized teams to search them—the focus was on her car with its distinctive luggage rack. If they found the car, they would have a starting point from which to look for Suzanne. Their biggest fear was that she was injured and in desperate need of help. Pug thought that perhaps Suzanne had been involved in a car accident in an isolated area, and was unconscious. He even thought she might have been kidnapped.

Joan called later that day, and Louise had her speak to Pug, who was just back from the airport. Pug was surprised when he was handed the telephone. He did not believe in psychics and wanted no part of this.

"Do you have a map in front of you?" Joan asked. Pug took one from the collection they had for the searches and spread it out. "Now I want you to follow my directions." She told him to place his finger on the map.

"Okay," he said.

She had him move his finger in an ever-greater circle, then told him to stop. "You're close."

"What?" he asked, startled.

"You're close," Joan repeated. "Under the letter"—she named a letter of the alphabet that was near his finger—"is where she is."

Pug looked closely now at his finger. It was on the Apache Trail, State Highway 88, in the Superstition Mountains.

"I don't know where that is," Joan said, "but Suzanne is there."

Pug told Louise what the psychic had told him, and she repeated it to the police, who elected to disregard the information.

Late that Friday afternoon, Logan and Gillies went to the Campus Cleaners in Tempe near the university. Inside, Gillies asked the owner,

Sarah Kokat, how much it would cost to do his laundry. The man looked filthy to her. She quoted him a price.

"Well, we just left a place which was a nickel cheaper," Gillies said.

"That's my price," she said. "I'm sorry."

Gillies asked if they could do their own laundry, and she told them they could. Logan loitered outside with the Pinto station wagon, but Kokat could not get a clear view of him. Even when the men moved into the Laundromat, Logan stayed out of sight. Gillies brought two pairs of pants over to her and asked to have them altered. She measured his leg and told him the pants would not be ready until Monday. He did not know the Weldon telephone number but told her the name of the stable where he worked.

When Kokat prepared to leave work at 6:00 P.M., the men were still at the Laundromat, which remained open for self-service until later that night. As she was tossing out the day's trash, she spotted towels and recalled that earlier she had observed the men cleaning out their car here—some things they threw in the trashcan, others they just threw on the ground.

She dumped her trash on top of theirs and left for the day. Later, her husband took the trash container and pitched its contents into the dumpster in the alley for city collection.

FBI agent Gary Reid returned from an assignment on one of Arizona's many Indian reservations late that day. When he arrived home, his wife said, "There's a problem. Suzanne is missing." When she told him what had happened, Reid instantly feared that Suzanne was dead. If she had been involved in a car accident, it would have been located by this time, and if she had been abducted and raped, she would likely already have been released. There was a remote possibility that she was being held hostage, but that struck him as highly improbable. He and his wife drove to the Rossetti condominium at once.

Jo Ann Heckel and a co-worker also drove to the condominium after work. All that day Jo Ann had felt sick to her stomach, a feeling that persisted as Louise told them what was taking place. Louise was especially frustrated because none of the police departments were willing to take charge of the case. They were caught up in a jurisdictional dispute.

Reid and his wife consoled Louise and the many friends gathered in the condominium, Reid being careful not to express his fears. After he had learned all he could, he contacted the Tempe police detective assigned to the missing-person case. The detective told him that he understood his concern. "Although it's not on the books as suspicious," the officer said, "I am working it as an abduction."

That night, Reid went through the complex, knocking on doors, identifying himself, and asking for any information that would help. He learned absolutely nothing of use.

Schneider and his wranglers were all at the Friday night party for country radio station KJ. Gillies and Logan had gone to the dog track earlier in the evening, and then driven up to Weldon in Suzanne's car after 10:00 P.M., when the festivities were in full swing.

One of the station's disk jockeys was playing records in the barn, which had been cleaned and set up as a dance hall. At this time, fifteen guests were dancing and drinking. Others were still arriving and the crowd swelled. Gillies and Logan were decked out in their new finery. Logan had borrowed Gillies's new Bailey cowboy hat with a white feather in the headband for the occasion. Logan had cash, Suzanne's card in his pocket, and was feeling better about not having left for California. He was planning to enjoy himself.

Gillies and Logan had been drinking all day and were inebriated when they arrived. The men split up at once, though Logan kept a close eye on his partner. Logan met a man about his age named Curly,* and Curly's pretty twenty-year-old wife. The three of them hit it off, and he spent most of his time in their company.

Across the dance floor, Gillies was thoroughly smashed and was bragging loudly about all the money he had. When one of the wranglers asked about it, Gillies said that he and Logan had been to the dog and horse tracks and had won it there. Later, the wrangler said he was going for more beer because they were out, and Gillies reached into his pocket, flashed bills, and said the wrangler did not have to spend his money because he had plenty. He was buying for everyone. Gillies went off with him and returned with two cases of beer.

The drunker Gillies got, the wilder he became. Throughout the night, he approached people and, under one pretext or another, persuaded them to hand him the keys to their vehicle. Then he took the car and raced it into the open desert, spinning wheelies and driving

*Pseudonym

it fast over the small hills. He continued until either he was stopped, or the vehicle became stuck, and people were starting to complain about it. Logan did not like the fact that Gillies was drawing attention to himself.

Finally, when no one would lend him a car, the drunken Gillies took Suzanne's Pinto and raced it around until it became stuck as well. He kept calling out for Logan, who refused help, but others pulled the Pinto free. Twice now, Logan had noticed policemen drive slowly by the party.

Logan said to himself as Gillies struggled with the car, "That's it for you." He approached Curly and his pretty wife, and suggested that the three of them leave. That was fine since it was getting late. They told everybody they were going for more beer. Logan took the time to borrow the last of Gillies's money to pay for it.

Curly owned an old four-wheel drive International Scout that had been spray-painted in camouflage. Logan sat in the rear seat and did not look back as they drove off shortly after midnight.

Around 1:00 A.M., someone drove up to the stable and spun his tires in a slow U, then sped off. This angered Schneider, who jumped into his truck to give chase. Others piled into their cars too. Gillies raced after them in Suzanne's Pinto. Cutting across the open desert at high speed, Gillies jumped over a little rise, then bottomed out on a rock. The Pinto came to a stop with the front end damaged as well as the undercarriage. Gillies asked for help, and the men towed the inoperative Pinto back to the stable.

When Gillies realized that Logan had not come back, he flew into a rage and stomped around the barn complaining that Logan had stolen all his money. In a loud, drunken slur, he said he was going to find Logan and kill him.

Schneider reminded Gillies that he had to clear out. Gillies said he couldn't now that his car was broken. He told Schneider he would repair it and leave as soon as he could to find Logan and settle things. Gillies joined another man and, with two young women, drove off in their car for a cowboy breakfast of steak and eggs now that the party was over.

PART SIX
∎
HACKWORTH

"Fuck you, Hackworth!"
—Jesse James Gillies

14

Logan handed Curly some of Suzanne's money to pay for the two twelve-packs of beer they bought. The three of them drove around the city drinking. Logan told Curly to stop at one of the Ugly Teller Machines, where, after three attempts, he extracted $250.

Logan was not a man accustomed to such niceties as ATM cards, but in his few lucid moments, he had given these machines some thought. He looked closely at the glass above the device and reasoned that there was a two-way mirror that contained a camera. He was not certain, but he suspected each time he used the ATM card, the machine was snapping his picture. Well, there was nothing to be done about it now.

Logan was hungry and suggested breakfast, on him. They went to the all-night Carrows restaurant on Seventh Street in Phoenix. Afterward, Curly's wife complained that she had to go home to their baby. The men dropped her off, drove off in the truck, and continued drinking.

By the time they ran out of beer, the liquor stores were closed. Curly explained this wasn't a problem because he knew a "nigger" in south Phoenix who was a bootlegger. He directed Logan to a ramshackle house on East Buckeye, not far from the Rodeway Inn. Logan waited in the truck while Curly bought the beer. After that, they drove and drank until Logan passed out.

. . .

Within hours of Peter's arrival in Saugus, there was a steady
procession of concerned visitors to the Rossetti home.

Carolyn Peters's father was now the Saugus chief of police. He
received a telephone call from the police in Arizona and confirmed
to them that Suzanne came from a reputable family and was known
to be reliable. His daughter was Suzanne's friend, for God's sake!

Donna made arrangements to miss work the following week and
booked her flight to Phoenix for late Saturday night. Before she left,
she said good-bye to her father. "Don't worry, Dad," she told him as
they hugged tightly, "we'll bring her back."

In Scottsdale the searches continued. Word of the psychic spread,
and people asked one another whether or not they believed her. Maybe
Suzanne had been kidnapped and was being held against her will.
Maybe she had been tied up and abandoned somewhere. Maybe she
was seriously hurt and dying. These were matters discussed in whispers.

Joan called once or twice on Saturday, but there was no progress
to report and she had nothing further to contribute. There was a sense
of urgency as Suzanne's friends continued hunting for her car. Another
friend of hers rented an airplane on Saturday and repeated the search
Pug had performed the day before. They found nothing.

At dawn after the KJ party, the wranglers dragged themselves
out of bed for their usual chores. The horses had to be fed and tended
no matter how hung over anyone felt. Gillies was still furious with
Logan and cursed him as he worked. He did not know what he was
going to do. Here Logan had taken off with the money that nice lady
had given them with which to buy fencing posts and now it was all
gone. The car she had loaned them was broken. Gillies did not know
what he was going to do.

At midmorning, one of the wranglers suggested that Gillies should
just call the lady and tell her what had happened. She would understand that it had not been his fault. The suggestion sobered Gillies.

Schneider asked what the problem was. "Is the car hot?" he
demanded.

Gillies smiled and said the car was not stolen, that this was "no
big deal."

Schneider said, "Don't you think you ought to call the lady the
car belongs to and tell her that her car is broke down?"

Gillies said he would call the lady, but later. First, he had to repair the Pinto so he could take it back to her. That was the reasonable thing to do.

Schneider told Gillies once again that since he had quit work at Weldon, he was to pack his gear and clear out. Gillies said, "Okay, as soon as I get the car running."

After doing their immediate chores, a few of the wranglers helped Gillies and succeeded in getting the Pinto to run. Gillies loaded his possessions from the bunkhouse and at 1:00 P.M. drove off, announcing that he was taking the car back to the lady rancher in Globe, and goddam that Logan anyway.

That morning, Logan awoke on the floor of someone's living room. He was fully clothed and had no idea where he was. He lay there looking around and could hear a couple talking quietly in the kitchen. Then he remembered. "I want beer," he called out from the floor with a grin. Curly said they had drunk it all the night before. Logan pushed himself up from the floor and asked about the nearest convenience store. Curly offered a ride, but Logan said no, he wanted to walk and clear his head.

He headed south down a major street. After three quarters of a mile, Logan reached Van Buren and a store where he bought three twelve-packs of beer with the last of Suzanne's silver dollars. On the way back, he veered one block off the main drag to keep out of sight. He had drunk two beers by the time he reached the apartment, his usual morning pick-me-up. As he walked through the door, he shouted, "Let's party!"

While Curly and his wife ate breakfast, they talked about what they might do. Logan suggested they go to Turf Paradise in northwest Phoenix, the horseracing track for the city. Curly and his wife liked the idea, but were broke. Logan told them that it was no problem, the day would be his treat.

It occurred to Logan that he might run into someone at the track he knew who would provide him a ride to California. At the same time, he would bet what he had and hope for a big score that would give him the $2,000 he needed.

Two hours after he left Weldon, Gillies came walking back. He said the car had stopped running just a mile away, near the zoo. He told the men that he had called the lady who owned it, and she told

him this was no problem, she had insurance. He asked Schneider if
he could sleep over until Monday, when he could have the car taken
care of, and Schneider agreed. Two of the wranglers drove him over
to the zoo in a pickup, and watched while Gillies unloaded his gear.
There were a number of tickets from the dog tracks and Gillies just
tossed these on the ground. One of the men worked on the car for a
while, but had no luck.

Back at the stable, Gillies used the telephone to try to locate
Logan. He contacted Frank at the Ponderosa and told him that Logan
had stolen his money. If Frank heard from or saw Logan, would he
give him a call? Gillies really needed that money bad.

On Saturday night, Schneider was leaving for one of his periodic
horse-buying trips in northern Arizona and hitched his trailer to his
truck in preparation. Then he went into the office and called Crime
Stop, the Phoenix Police Department emergency number. He had
asked one of the wranglers earlier to write down the license plate number of the Pinto. This was the same man Gillies had told that Logan was
an escaped convict, and the wrangler had informed Schneider.

Schneider gave the police the license plate number, the location
of the car, and Gillies's name. He told them he thought the car was
stolen. He also said that Gillies had been hanging out with a man
who might be an escaped convict, Mike Richardson. That done, he
climbed into the truck and left for Winslow.

At the racetrack, Logan spotted several men he remembered from
the circuit, but they were not people he could approach. When he
had no luck with the horses, Curly drove Logan to a nearby Ugly
Teller, where he attempted three times to extract various amounts of
money. They dropped off Curly's wife and drove to Rhonda's sister
Karen's place. She and her friends were celebrating Saturday night.
When Logan displayed his money roll, Karen asked where it had come
from. He told her his grandfather had passed away and left him money.

What was he going to tell her? he thought. That he killed a
woman for it?

They sent out for pizza and beer, and Logan told Karen to call
a girlfriend of hers, a rail-skinny woman with an acne-scarred face
who kept a methamphetamine lab in her house. Logan did lines of
the speed she brought as he partied. There was an unlimited quantity,
so when the rush ended, Logan would inhale another line. At

10:00 P.M., Curly said he had to leave. Logan told him to wait while he bought dope, and then announced he was ready.

He did not want to sleep at Curly's again and said to leave him on East Van Buren at one of the many cheap motels there. But when Curly left, Logan was still wired from the speed, so he telephoned for a cab to take him out on the town. The cabbie was twenty years older than Logan, but he found her attractive. He told her to take them somewhere if she wanted to drink, and she could join him. She would keep the meter running and the evening would be on him.

The cabbie took him to a series of bars on North Central in Phoenix, but at 1:00 A.M. when they closed, Logan was still high from the speed he had been inhaling in the rest rooms. Back at the motel, he told the cabbie to radio others that he was holding a card game in his room. Logan ran a stud poker game with no more than six players at a time. Logan preferred to play stud because he believed he could count the cards and gain an edge. He won this night.

Ten cabbies showed up and soon the party got out of hand. When others staying at the motel complained, the manager called and told Logan to shut down the party or he would call the police. The man's Arabic accent was so thick that Logan had a hard time understanding what he was saying with all the noise in his room. When he heard the word "police," he shouted at the cabbies to clear out.

It was dawn by this time. With the party over, Logan could stay, but he was afraid the manager would call the police anyway. He told his cabbie to take him to another East Van Buren motel. As they were riding, he asked if she owned a car. Then he said he would pay her $1,000 to drive him to California. She laughed at the thought before realizing he was serious. She said she had three children at home and could not leave on the spur of the moment, but she could arrange it in two or three days. Logan told her he had money, not time.

He paid her off at the motel and lay down inside the new room. He was able to sleep only three hours that morning, what with all the beer and speed in his system.

Logan could have taken a bus or, for that matter, simply have taken a short drive to Sky Harbor Airport and flown to Los Angeles. He did not consider either of these options; he was fixated on driving to California.

· · ·

That Saturday night, Gillies joined one of the wranglers and attended a rodeo dance with him. Without money Gillies had a quiet night, and the pair were back at the bunkhouse by 10:00 P.M. for bed. Early that Sunday morning, a large group showed up for a trail ride before breakfast. After that, Gillies walked into the desert toward Van Buren and dug around in the brush until he found the .22 rifle he had stolen the previous Wednesday. He brought it back to the stables and started target shooting with it. Guns were not uncommon at Weldon, but no one actually shot them inside the city limits, so the wranglers stood around watching, wondering just what Gillies was up to.

Soon a Phoenix police car arrived to check a report of someone firing shots. Gillies was shaken and ran into the bunkhouse. He pulled over one of the wranglers and said, "You don't even know me. I'm not here." The wrangler nodded his head and watched as Gillies squirmed under his bunk. That seemed to him an overreaction, but he shrugged it off.

On Sunday morning, Donna arrived in Phoenix accompanied by her boyfriend, Robert. Louise told her about Joan, the psychic, and what Joan had said about Suzanne. After seeing the state her mother and the others were in, Donna asked that a priest be summoned. One from Suzanne's parish arrived almost at once. He stayed, prayed with everyone, and told them he would be available at any time if they needed him. Over the next several days he was a frequent visitor.

In her adult life, Donna had not been as active in her church as she was while growing up. She had never faced a disaster like this, and it brought all of her thoughts of religion and God into question. How could God let this happen? she thought. This is not the God she knew and had been raised to love. When she considered the plight of her mother and father, she became increasingly bitter and angry.

Pug and the others told her what they had been doing to find Suzanne, but Donna wanted to see for herself. She was taken to the different locations where the search had been concentrated.

Back at the condominium, Donna was now in charge, as her mother was clearly distraught. More than once, Pug looked over at mother and daughter and saw Donna holding Louise. Both would be crying. Finally, they booked Louise on a flight to Boston for very early

Tuesday morning. Now the questions and decisions went to Donna, as did the lion's share of telephone calls.

Gary Reid had never met Donna previously and was at once impressed with her. She was obviously a Rossetti in her loving and caring manner. As he watched her handle this crisis, he was also taken with her emotional strength and ability to see things as they were, and act accordingly. She was holding together under the strain and devoted herself to the others, who were not taking matters as well.

Eric Gregan had been fired from his job for not reporting to work while he was searching for Suzanne. He told Reid about Suzanne's telephone call to him just before she left Monti's for the Rodeway Inn, and blamed himself for what had happened. Reid explained that no one could have anticipated what had occurred, but Eric continued to blame himself and became increasingly distraught.

Not everyone at Suzanne's condominium was actively involved in trying to help. Many were stunned into inaction, numbed by apprehension and uncertainty; for every person offering consolation, there was another in need of it. Food was constantly arriving and being prepared. The mood was of a wake, with some pretense of normalcy.

At every moment, Donna felt herself unable to handle what needed doing, yet she did it. For all of the doubts she suffered, others saw Donna as the rock, practical and steady. Increasingly, people were drawn to her for solace and comfort.

From time to time, Donna slipped quietly into an upstairs bedroom where Robert would join her and hold her while she sobbed. After a bit, she went back out and resumed her obligation.

In Saugus the burden had fallen on Peter Jr. He was closely monitoring his father's physical condition, speaking to Donna in Arizona, and handling the endless stream of concerned family and friends, all the while trying to keep the family business operating. He had great faith in Suzanne's ability to deal with adversity and spoke to Gary Reid a number of times for updates, since Reid was in frequent contact with the police. "Whatever happened," Peter Jr. thought, "she'll get out of it."

Pug had not met Reid before this weekend. Though he was a law-enforcement officer, Reid was obviously moved by Suzanne's disappearance. The two spoke in private at one point, and Pug asked for Reid's professional assessment. Reid told him it did not look good.

"What do you mean?" Pug asked, taken aback.

The longer the disappearance lasts, Reid said, the less likely it is that Suzanne is still alive. Pug was desperately clinging to hope and was sobered by the FBI agent's observation.

Many people at the condominium were turning to Reid for direction, a phenomenon he found particularly frustrating. He was able to speak directly with the officers involved, and provide the most current information to friends and family. But this was a local case and the local police were best qualified to handle it. Because of the mystique surrounding the FBI, the average citizen overestimated the Bureau's ability to deal with crimes. The family and friends at the condominium considered Reid an expert and they believed that somehow he would bring Suzanne safely back. How he wished he could.

Before noon on Sunday, Logan took a taxi to Curly's. He had considered his situation and decided that he would pay Curly to drive him to California. Curly liked the idea just fine, but his truck would not start that morning. Curly had been fretting over what he was going to do about it, since he was broke and did not have a job.

Logan told him his problem was solved. He would have the truck towed to a shop, pay for the repairs, and hire Curly to drive him to California. Curly was ecstatic, much too appreciative to ask questions, something on which Logan was banking.

Logan peeled off bills, which he handed to Curly so he could start repairs. After the mechanic checked the engine, he announced it would cost $700 and take two days. Logan was not pleased about the delay, but he told Curly to go ahead; he could wait two days.

Now that Logan had a definite plan for leaving Phoenix, he was relieved. Soon he had to call his brother for an identification packet, but there was plenty of time for that; what he needed now was more money.

At Weldon, Gillies unsaddled horses and told the wrangler beside him he had something important to say. He said that things were not as he and Logan had said they were. On Wednesday night, they had helped a lady who had locked her keys in her car, that much was true, but she did not own any ranch and did not offer them a job. She had bought them a six-pack of beer and given them a ride. Logan had grabbed her from the backseat, and the two of them had sort of raped her right out there in the desert. Afterward, they stole money and credit cards from her purse.

Logan had driven them to the Superstitions and told the lady she had to climb down a cliff. When she tried, Logan pushed her off with his foot. The two of them climbed down to see if she was still alive. While she begged them to leave her alone, Logan sneaked up behind the lady and bashed her head in with a rock. Gillies did not know what to do, so he helped Logan cover the body with rocks.

As he told this remarkable story to the wrangler, Gillies was smiling and the wrangler did not know what to make of it. Gillies cautioned him not to tell anyone and asked for a ride back to the Pinto so he could pick up more of his belongings.

The psychic, Joan, called the condominium again on Sunday and spoke to Louise. Joan said her sense that Suzanne was dead was absolute by this time. She also said that the men would be caught and her daughter's body recovered. Joan told her how terribly sorry she was.

Louise spoke to her sister Frances shortly after the call. Frances could tell that she was upset by what the psychic had related, and was trying to come to terms with the idea that her baby was dead. Until now, it had not occurred to Frances or Louise that Suzanne might have been kidnapped and murdered. This made it very real.

Frances began to wear a yellow ribbon. The Iranian hostages had been released earlier that week, and her friends thought she was wearing it for them. Frances did not correct the impression because she could not bear to speak of her far more personal tragedy.

Logan took a taxi to the dog track Sunday evening. Along the way, he told the cabbie to stop at a hamburger stand where he offered to buy her lunch, which she did not accept. This cabbie was even older than the one from the previous night, but possessed a better sense of humor. After eating, Logan told her to pull into a Valley National Bank branch, where he took $250 from Suzanne's account. At Twenty-fourth Street and Van Buren he pulled into the Kon Tiki Hotel, where Suzanne and her friends from the Burn Treatment Skin Bank had so often eaten lunch. He rented a room to have a place to stay later that night.

At the dog track he attempted the same deal with this cabbie as he had with the other one the night before. She would leave the meter running and join him. Though she appeared interested, Logan sensed that she was afraid he would run out on the fare. When she turned down the offer, he paid her off.

In an early race he won $300. He walked around the betting area drinking beer and bragging about the money he had won, flashing it for people to see. Two men, who appeared to be regulars, befriended him and gave him a tip on a trifecta. Logan won. He bought drinks for his new friends and let everyone within earshot know he was a winner. Periodically, he went into the rest room and snorted white-powder speed. He bet the second tip and won on it as well. He bet individual races and his string of luck continued. When the track closed, Logan was holding $1,700.

At last, he had enough money to repair the truck, drive to California, and buy his identification packet. With the money he could pull from Suzanne's account, there would be enough to take him to Australia by the end of the week. Life was finally breaking his way.

Logan had made such a spectacle of himself earlier, bragging about his winnings, he was afraid to leave the racing grounds. In the men's room, he shut himself in a stall and stashed most of the bills around his ankles inside his new cowboy boots. Then he went to the payout window and requested a security guard to escort him off the track. He stood outside with a plainclothesman, probably an off-duty Phoenix police officer, and waited for his cab. The cabbie was the one from the previous night.

He announced he was a winner, and they were going to party. They spent the rest of the night working through the bars along East Van Buren. By the time the bars closed and she drove Logan to the Kon Tiki, he owed her $100.

Freddie Quinlan's wife read in the local newspaper that Suzanne was missing. She told Freddie, who read the article with extreme apprehension. Since becoming a deputy U.S. marshal, he had seen behavior in men he had never imagined possible, and he was struck by the thought that something terrible had happened to Suzanne. He called the U.S. Marshal's office in Phoenix and asked his fellow deputy marshals there to find out what was really going on. Then he called Carolyn Peters to inform her that Suzanne was reported missing and to ask if she had heard from her.

Carolyn had not heard from Suzanne and for a time thought that her friend was backpacking and had neglected to tell anyone where she was.

Logan was still wired from speed when he called the new wrangler at the Ponderosa. She was named Victoria* and had an English accent he loved. She picked him up in her van, and as they went for dinner, he considered paying her to drive to California that night. When he asked about the condition of her vehicle, Victoria told him she was having trouble with it, so he never made the suggestion.

They ate lobster, then he suggested they go to his room. Victoria was attractive enough, but more than a little overweight. He snorted more speed, which he shared with her. They sat naked on the bed and drank beer with the television blaring.

Logan telephoned his brother to order the identification packet and confirmed that the price was $500. His brother still worked the tracks in Michigan and asked Logan if he knew of a certain type of horse for sale out there in Arizona. Logan did not, but said he would check it out for him. He called the Ponderosa, and Frank said he would locate one. Logan left him his telephone number at the Kon Tiki.

Victoria was eager to have sex and Logan wanted to oblige, but was unable to perform. She was worked up and very angry when he could not satisfy her. Between the speed and alcohol and lack of sleep, Logan could not attain an erection sufficient to take care of her.

She stayed angry until they both passed out.

Early that Sunday evening, a Phoenix police officer spotted the Pinto parked at the zoo. A detective phoned Gary Reid. Reid had cleared his involvement in the case with the Phoenix Bureau's weekend supervisor, but his request to open a formal federal investigation had been denied. At the zoo, he stayed out of the way, since he did not want to contaminate any evidence that might be used in court. This was still a local investigation, and he was present only as a courtesy.

It was cold and moonless that night. The Tempe detective and the identification technician were checking the car by flashlight. They were careful not to touch anything needlessly and were concerned about not soiling evidence. In the dark, this was hard not to do.

* Pseudonym

"At least there is no blood," Reid thought. That indicated that Suzanne had not been murdered in the car. Reid recalled how just a few weeks earlier he and his wife had run with Suzanne in this very place.

The Tempe detective checked the undercarriage, and the car appeared to be inoperative. He searched for clues as to where the car had been recently driven, but the desert brush attached there was found everywhere in the state.

There were a large number of items in the Pinto, and once the Tempe detective gained entry, he slowly inventoried and impounded them. There was a woman's bracelet, hairbrush, and comb; dog track racing tickets; a blue backpack; a woman's jogging shorts and matching shirt.

The detective observed that the driver's seat was fully back, not in the driving position Suzanne would have used. Then he found a high-heeled shoe shoved all the way down in a panty hose leg. He did not know what to make of it.

Reid was bothered by several of the items. Suzanne's athletic bra was especially unsettling. Also, the heel of the shoe had been pressed through the nylon of the hose, which struck Reid as completely alien to Suzanne and was the most chilling discovery of the night. His sense that the worst had happened to her intensified.

Then the detective picked up a laundry receipt with the name "Chess Gillees," written on it. Dated after Suzanne's disappearance, it was the first real lead in the case.

The Tempe detective instructed the identification technician to join him in dusting the car for fingerprints. It was difficult work under these conditions. Whenever they were close enough to observe a print, their breath would fog over the surface. They worked slowly, but at best this examination was cursory. Finally, the Pinto was towed to the Tempe Police Department impound lot.

Reid told Donna that Suzanne's car had been located. A number of the searchers—including Donna—had been to that very place and had not seen the car. It indicated that someone had been using the Pinto after Suzanne was reported missing.

Local television coverage of the disappearance was starting now that the cameras had activity to film. Donna was cautioned not to watch the news accounts, as they could be very traumatic.

A deflated mood permeated the condominium, and the volunteer efforts of Suzanne's friends were reduced. Robert screened more and more telephone calls for Donna, who was bracing herself for confirmation of Suzanne's death. Her main concern was for her parents and the impact this news was going to have on them.

Now that Gillies had started talking about Suzanne's murder, he took increased pleasure in retelling it. He related to another wrangler the same story he had told the day before, adding that he had been sick to his stomach when Suzanne's head had cracked open. This time he laughed out loud repeatedly and snickered as if he were telling an obscene joke. Gillies smiled enthusiastically as he spoke and said the woman was dark-haired and very pretty. He bragged that she had an absolutely great body, rock hard. Gillies told the wrangler that Suzanne had been murdered because he and Logan were afraid she would report them for having raped her.

He pulled a department store credit card from his pocket with a woman's name on it. Gillies said he had tried to buy clothes with the card, but the clerk had told him he was not authorized to sign on the account. He also took the wrangler over to the bunkhouse and showed him Suzanne's brown camera case and equipment. The cowboy hardly knew what to make of all this.

A short time later Gillies persuaded one of the men to drive him to Tempe, where he attempted to locate Logan at the apartment of the two girls they knew. When he couldn't find Logan, he told the wrangler solemnly that he was going to kill Logan when he did finally track him down.

15

On Monday morning Victoria stomped up to Logan's room at the Kon Tiki to tell him her goddam van would not start. Logan called a cab, saying she could take care of the van after work. Once she was on her way, he called Curly to check the progress on his truck. Curly angered Logan when he told him that the mechanic had reported the Scout would not be ready for three days. Logan told Curly to borrow transportation and pick him up.

After Curly arrived, they drove to a bar on Van Buren, where Logan had sometimes hustled pool with mixed results. The men passed the day sucking beer from long-necked bottles and shooting pool. As the day progressed, Logan began winning.

Shortly after 8:00 that morning, Tempe Police Detective Mike Palmer was informed that the missing Pinto had been discovered by the Phoenix police. The detective who had been working the missing-person report was off that day, and Palmer was instructed to locate Suzanne Rossetti now that they had some definite information. At age twenty-eight, Palmer was the youngest homicide detective in the state, and at least one deputy county attorney considered him to be the finest. Palmer was a Tempe native and had been on the force for seven years.

First Palmer went to examine the evidence. He had worked Missing Persons before becoming Tempe's only homicide detective, and

148

now decided that Suzanne was dead. It was possible she was being held, or had been tied up and left somewhere, but he did not believe it.

He called Sarah Kokat at Campus Cleaners and asked her about the receipt found in the car. Sarah told him that two dirty men had come into her place the previous Thursday. She described one as six feet tall and weighing 200 pounds, the other as five feet ten inches and weighing 180 pounds. The man named Chess had left two pairs of pants for alteration and was to pick them up that Monday, but had not done so yet.

Palmer asked Kokat what kind of car they had been driving, and she told him a light-colored Pinto station wagon. She said Chess had worked at a riding stable, but she could not remember its name. She thought it started with a W.

Palmer contacted Officer Dennis Fender to assist him. Fender was also a native of Tempe whom Palmer had known since childhood. He worked narcotic stakeouts as a plainclothesman. Palmer told Fender to put Campus Cleaners under surveillance; the two men might come by to claim the pants.

Palmer drove to the police department's impound lot to see the car for himself, arriving at 9:30. The first thing that caught his eye was the desert brush stuck to the underside of the front license plate frame. He knew the car had been seized at the zoo near Papago Park and that the open desert areas beside the park had identical brush. So did most of Arizona. But when the car had been damaged and rendered inoperable, it had probably occurred right there.

Palmer checked the Pinto's mileage from the Charlie Rossi Ford repair receipt that Louise had given the Tempe police against the mileage now on the odometer, and he noted the car had been driven 498 miles. Palmer had known about Weldon Riding Stable all his life, and it was the first place that had come to mind when Sarah Kokat told him the name of the stable started with a W. He knew Weldon was located right by the zoo.

He bent down and took a close look at the car's brake pedal and found it caked with dry mud. Then he removed two strands of white hair, which he suspected would test later as being from a horse. He scraped samples of the mud from the pedal, and from three other places in the car. If it came down to searching for a body, he knew the soil samples could possibly pinpoint the area for them.

Back at the police department, Palmer located his sergeant and told him what he had learned. Then the two men drove in an un-

marked car to Papago Park. Palmer intended to search the desert area
for signs a car had been plowing cross-country through the brush. It
occurred to him that Suzanne just might have been left tied up in one
of the gullies there. This was a popular area, but stranger things had
happened.

Or maybe they would find her body.

Early Monday morning, Gillies saddled a horse at the stable. One
of the wranglers asked, "Where are you going?"

Gillies said, to check on the Pinto. A short time later, he returned
in a sober mood. Asked about the car, he said it wasn't there any
longer.

On Monday, Gary Reid told his regular supervisor that it would
be impossible to carry out his normal duties as long as Suzanne was
missing. Reid requested permission to continue working on the investigation, on his own time if necessary. He was told to do what he
thought necessary. If it came down to it, Reid's supervisor said, his
own squad would open a federal case in support.

Tempe Police Officer Dennis Fender contacted Sarah Kokat and
her husband at Campus Cleaners. Gary Reid joined them, but remained in the background. Fender informed Sarah that he was staking
out the place. She told him that when the two men had cleaned out
their Pinto in the back, they had dumped items in the trash can and
on the ground.

Fender and Reid were especially interested in the towels she
mentioned. Sarah, her husband, and the two officers went to check
the dumpster. The city had not yet collected the trash, so Sarah's
husband reached in and retrieved the torn towels he had tossed there.

Reid realized the purpose of the strips of cloth at once. They had
been used to tie up Suzanne. Maybe, he thought, the abductors had
left her bound.

After being informed that Suzanne's car had been recovered in
bad condition, Donna telephoned her brother in Saugus. "Be ready
for bad news," she told him. Donna was certain more tragedy would
follow. Then she called Father Creed, saying the family would need
him for the next few days. Peter Jr. had also contacted Father Creed,
as well as Peter Sr.'s doctor to determine what possible impact further

bad word could have on his father. He was not encouraged by the doctor's answer.

Reid joined Fender in the stakeout at Campus Cleaners in hopes the two men would return. Fellow FBI agents were aware of what was taking place, and, one by one, they checked in with him over the radio. They were taking care of other matters nearby, and could be with him at a moment's notice once he notified them. Suddenly, it seemed, every active Bureau case in the greater Phoenix area was centered at the Campus Cleaners. Reid was moved by the concern of his fellow agents and their willingness to go out of their way for him, and he was deeply appreciative.

When Palmer and his sergeant arrived at Papago Park, they took their unmarked police car and drove it like a four-wheel drive vehicle, working back and forth across the desert, in and out of gullies, searching for signs of Suzanne. As they worked their way toward Weldon, Palmer spotted men riding horseback, exercising the animals, trotting them back and forth like jockeys before a race. He stopped the car, and the officers climbed out, then motioned for the riders to talk. They were obviously cowboys in their worn western clothes and nasal twang; all except one, Gillies, who struck Palmer as looking more like a longshoreman with his black ski cap.

The sergeant spoke to Gillies, inquiring about a hayride. Gillies did not believe the man actually cared about such matters. "If you're really interested in a hayride," he said from atop his horse, "then go into the office." They could help him. Instead, Palmer and his sergeant climbed back into their car and drove off.

Palmer had noticed that besides his clothes, Gillies did not have a distinctive western accent. There was a manner about him, a shifty-eyed look, Palmer had seen many times before in interrogation rooms, in court, in jails. Palmer said to his sergeant, only half in jest, "That was probably the guy who did it."

Gillies watched the car leave, then told the man beside him, "That was a cop." The wrangler asked how he knew. "I just do," Gillies said.

Palmer received Fender's call to go to Campus Cleaners. First he dropped off his sergeant and arrived there at 10:35 A.M. He examined the three strips of towel taken from the dumpster, and noting they were virtually identical to the larger torn towel removed from the car. It was obvious that Suzanne had been tied up. He asked Sarah if the stable the man mentioned could be Weldon, and she exclaimed, "That's it!"

Palmer told Fender to resume the stakeout. Early that afternoon, Palmer returned to the impound lot for another look at the car. He could sense that he was close to making an arrest. Slowly, he went through the Pinto again. Stuffed beside the driver's seat and the transmission hump was a credit card holder that contained the license of Suzanne Rossetti. Under the passenger floormat was a yellow screwdriver.

Then up under the driver's seat, he discovered something that struck him as odd. He picked up a cheap, gold-colored coin marked "Gospel." It looked as if it had been stamped from an arcade novelty machine. Inscribed across the back was: "Jesus Christ came into the world to save sinners." He fingered it momentarily, then slipped it into an evidence envelope.

He also found two trifecta tickets dated January 31; a small tool kit, fresh tissue paper, a Hallmark card, Camel filter cigarette stubs, an Acme door key, a woman's compact, and Zigzag papers.

Finished with the interior, Palmer stood back a short distance and scrutinized the car carefully, searching for something he had overlooked. His eyes kept returning to the right rear window, and he asked himself, "What's wrong with the window?" He looked closely and realized that it had been removed from the seal and set back in place but not fully installed. He examined it closely and there, visible to his naked eye, were two latent fingerprints. He dusted them, lifted the prints with tape, then placed them on two cards that he marked and secured.

That day in Saugus, Peter Rossetti called a Tempe police officer to request an update. The officer told him that his daughter's Pinto had been recovered at the Phoenix City Zoo in Papago Park.

"That car wasn't at Papago Park Thursday morning because I scoured that area," Peter told him.

"Well, the night man spotted it last night. They thought it belonged to somebody at the zoo."

"Do you mean to tell me something as hot as that with a registration number wasn't on the police list?"

"We can't keep everybody on the list," the officer told him, unaware that the car had been on the hot list.

"What was in it?" Peter asked.

"Her pocketbook and her shoes," the officer said.

"I don't like the sound of that."

At 5:00 P.M., Mike Palmer drove to see Dennis Fender at Campus Cleaners, since the daylong stakeout had proved futile. Palmer decided to press matters and instructed Fender to call Weldon. On the telephone, Fender asked if a Chess Gillies worked there. No, was the answer, but they had a Jess Gillies. Fender asked to speak to him. A few minutes later Gillies was on the line. Fender said that he was calling from Campus Cleaners, Gillies's pants were ready. When was he planning to pick them up?

Gillies told the policeman he had forgotten all about those pants, and if it was all right, he would pick them up the next day.

Palmer impounded the towels and other items retrieved from the dumpster, thanked the Kokats, and returned to the station. He was satisfied that he had enough to arrest Gillies for possession of a stolen vehicle. It was a standard police ploy to take the suspect into custody on the first significant charge discovered while the larger investigation continued. Who knew? The suspect might confess.

Palmer put together a team of three others, including Fender, and told them they were going to arrest Gillies at Weldon.

By dusk Monday, work had come to an end at the stable. Before it was fully dark, the wranglers saddled their favorite horses for a race. There was an improvised oval course to the south of the stable that they used for such contests. It was all very informal and usually ended in arguments about what was fair and who beat whom.

As the line of four Tempe police cars turned the corner of Van Buren at the U-Totem and headed north up Fifty-second Street, the wranglers were poised for a sprint from the south end of the stable area heading north toward the bunkhouse. Gillies could see the line of cars with their headlights, and urged the others to start the race. Suddenly, the horses broke and the cowboys hooted and hollered as they ran all out for the finish line, galloping headlong, parallel to, and then past, the four police cars.

Palmer looked out the window as the horses thundered beyond

them and muttered, "Ah shit." This was going to be like the Old
West. Though Weldon was located in the city and housing developments were quite close by, there was open country favorable to a
horseman evading cars. The golf course and its surrounding terrain
were nearby, and there was an expanse of desert in Papago Park beyond
it. The Salt River bed was not that distant, located just south of Van
Buren. There were pockets of thick growth and stands of mesquite
trees. If Gillies broke into any of these areas, the policemen in their
cars were not likely to catch him.

The procession of vehicles turned off the road into the stable
area. All of the horsemen, except for one, rode up to see them. Palmer
climbed out of his car and announced that they were looking for
Gillies. One of the wranglers stood up in his stirrups and pointed to
the lone rider about one hundred yards to the north. Palmer could
see Gillies staring straight at him, eyeing him suspiciously, as his mount
eased away. When the wrangler pointed at him, Gillies whipped the
flank of his horse with the bridle strap, crouched over, and tore off,
heading dead west.

The policemen piled into their cars and took off in pursuit across
the desert. The wranglers on horseback shouted, then with a hoot
and lots of yells, followed in the cars' dust.

Palmer radioed for assistance and within a short time, fifteen
police vehicles were combing the area. He established a command
center at the stable and positioned officers along Van Buren to prevent
Gillies from reaching the riverbed.

The wranglers, excited from the chase, streamed all around. The
Phoenix police helicopter joined in the search. It was dark now, so
they had to work slowly back and forth over the area.

One of the wranglers told Palmer that Gillies hung out with
another man named Mike Richardson. Richardson had not been
around for a few days and the cowboy figured he was now working at
the Ponderosa. Palmer called the Ponderosa and learned that Richardson had not worked there for the last month.

The police had lost sight of Gillies when he ran out of open
desert and turned his horse down an alleyway in a housing develop-
ment. For an hour, the officers searched with no luck. It was incredible
that with such a commitment of manpower, Gillies could have simply
vanished. Then Palmer called off the search. One of the detectives
left his card in case Gillies returned. Palmer, using a plan, had the
officers make a show of driving off and soon the stable was quiet again.

The wranglers did not know what to make of the situation. Their instinctive loyalties were to Gillies, and they had no idea what the police wanted with him. One of them figured it was over the earlier shooting episode; another thought maybe they were after him for a traffic warrant. Shortly, a wrangler spotted Gillies squatting down beside his horse, which he had maneuvered between a house and a camping van. He rode up to tell Gillies he ought to come on back to the stable. Gillies climbed on his horse and followed him.

The cowboys asked Gillies what this was all about. He dismounted and went into the barn, telling them he had to hide. The wranglers were disposed to help him, and they dug a hole in the haystack up in the loft over the office. One of them brought Suzanne's sleeping bag and Gillies shoved it into the hole, then crawled in. The wranglers moved boxes and feed sacks so Gillies could not be seen. All the wranglers gathered down below asked him again what this was all about.

"We killed somebody," Gillies finally said, his voice falling from the darkness above. Two of the men had already heard the story, but to the others this was a thunderbolt.

"When?" one of the men asked.

"A few days ago." Gillies laughed.

"How did you do it?"

Gillies told his story now for the third time. He and Logan had been out that Wednesday night and were at the U-Totem, when this lady locked herself out of her car. They helped her break into the car and she bought them beer, then offered them a ride for their assistance. They told her to detour at the stable, then, just over there, they raped her.

"We tied her up and threw her in the backseat," Gillies told the men. He said they went to her condominium and stole her sleeping bag, her camera, and other things. They found an ATM card and other credit cards, then made her tell them how to take money out of her bank machine. She had over $4,000, but they could get only $250 a day.

"We drove her out to the Superstition Mountains," Gillies said, where Logan pushed the lady over the side of a cliff. They were not certain she was dead, so they climbed down and found her still breathing. Logan struck her with a rock, then picked up other rocks and threw them at the lady, hitting her on the head. It was awful, he said.

"I didn't bury her or nothing," Gillies said from the loft to the

men in the dark below him. "I didn't touch her. The only time I
touched her was when I picked up her hand and scooted it close to
her and buried it up with rocks."

Once again, as he related the story, Gillies laughed almost continuously, not with embarrassment or nervousness, but as if he were
telling an indecent joke. Often he would break into outright laughter.
All of the men were troubled by the story; more than one did not
believe it. They left him hiding in the haystack and went into the
bunkhouse to talk.

At 7:30 P.M., Gillies crawled out of hiding long enough to make
a telephone call from the office. He took the detective's card, called
the Tempe Police Department, and left a message that got to Palmer
later that night.

By 10:00 P.M., Palmer had checked state criminal records and
received the name of Jesse James Gillies, an inmate on release from
the state prison. The wranglers had told Palmer that their Gillies had
come from prison, and Palmer was satisfied he had identified his man.

He believed that once the police made a show of leaving the
stable, it was likely Gillies would return to Weldon. With Fender,
Palmer drove back to Weldon with their car lights extinguished. They
stopped a distance away and approached quietly on foot. Palmer asked
a wrangler standing outside for Gillies. The wrangler said they had
just missed him. Gillies had come back all right, but he had left ten
minutes earlier.

One of the wranglers who believed Gillies's story walked up the
street to the U-Totem, where he called the Phoenix Police Department
and told the answering officer what he had heard. Then he came back
and let the others know what he had done. The wranglers ate dinner and looked repeatedly out the dirty windows of the bunkhouse for
cop cars.

At 11:00, Jerry Schneider drove up in his truck, pulling the horse
trailer. Usually, the men came out to see if he needed any help, but
tonight only one of the wranglers approached him. Schneider could
tell he was upset over something. "What's the matter?" he asked.

The wrangler said that Gillies had informed the men that he and
Logan had killed a woman. Then Gillies came out of hiding and told
Schneider that he had to talk to him in the office. Schneider con-

sidered that but did not like the sound of it. The wranglers knew he carried plenty of cash on these buying trips. He told Gillies to go into the bunkhouse, he would be in shortly to talk to him. Once Gillies was out of sight, Schneider went alone into his office and locked his money away.

As Schneider entered the bunkhouse, all of the wranglers except Gillies cleared out. The two men sat down. Gillies began by saying he had a long story to tell. He said that he was in serious trouble, that his conscience had been bothering him, and he needed to get this off his chest. He and Logan had been involved in a murder. Now, for the fourth time, Gillies launched into his story.

As it unfolded, Schneider listened with keen interest, though the story sounded to him like a fantasy. He had trouble taking it in, it was so horrible and shocking, but little by little he came to accept what he was hearing as the truth.

Schneider had many shortcomings as a man. He often preferred a good lie to the honest truth. He was fond of conning and manipulating others. He cheated people and frequently bragged about it. He had been dishonest in his horse dealings.

But he was a man of the West, and fancied himself a man of honor when it came to women. He might lie to get a pretty thing into the sack, but slap a woman around or, for God's sake, kill a woman, that went beyond the pale. Decent men, cowboys, treated ladies with respect.

Gillies told him the car was stolen, just as Schneider had suspected. He and Logan had picked the lady up at the U-Totem. She had locked herself out of her car on the way to take her parents to the airport to make a plane to Boston. They had helped her and then driven back toward the stable. They gave her phony directions, causing her to drive in circles. She told them she had to get to the airport, could she drop them off? Logan reached over the seat and grabbed her. "You're not going anywhere," he said.

Then Gillies told Schneider, "I guess we kind of raped her. The bitch wouldn't shut up. She just kept talking," he said. He said they went to her place and robbed her. Gillies said he had to find Logan because he needed his share of that money. He was visibly angry because Logan had taken all the money they had stolen from the woman. As Gillies related the story, the other wranglers wandered in and out of the bunkhouse, pausing to listen to different parts of it.

Though Gillies was nervous as he talked, he also snickered and there was a smirk on his face that troubled Schneider. From time to time, as Gillies described the details, he broke into a giggle.

Schneider finally asked, "Why did you kill her?"

"She refused to forget it," Gillies said. "She kept telling us that when she got loose she had us by the balls."

Gillies looked frightened when he had finished. He told Schneider that he needed his help to leave the state because Logan had taken the money.

Schneider nodded his head and said he understood. "Jess," he told him, "I am going to try to help you. I am going to call my attorney and you stay right here till I get back. You are in a bad mess."

Schneider drove off, straight to his father-in-law's house not far away in Scottsdale, and called a detective he knew. The policeman told him to call the homicide detail of the Phoenix Police Department. Phoenix directed Schneider to contact the Tempe police, who were handling the missing-person report. He told Tempe what he had just heard from Gillies.

By now, Palmer was exhausted and uncertain they would be able to arrest Gillies that night. He sent two officers to meet with Schneider, then drove home to sleep.

The two detectives met with the Weldon owner not far from the zoo. As far as Schneider knew, he said, Gillies was now asleep at the stable. One of the officers climbed into Schneider's truck and lay on the floorboards so he would not be observed as they drove to Weldon. The other officer followed some distance back with his headlights off. It was just after midnight.

When they stopped outside the bunkhouse, the officer bolted from the truck and, with Schneider right behind him, barged into the darkened bunkhouse with a drawn gun shouting, "Freeze! Police!"

One of the drowsy wranglers raised his head from his bunk. "He's sleeping in the haystack," he told them, in a hole he had dug there covered by grain sacks and boxes.

The other officer was out of his vehicle and, inside the barn, the two officers identified themselves and demanded that Gillies come out. Schneider suddenly pulled out a gun he carried. The two officers climbed up to Gillies and tried pulling him out of the sleeping bag with no success as Gillies fought them off. Finally, they dragged both Gillies and the bag out of the hay.

Schneider spotted a pitchfork at hand, so he moved close to

Gillies and pointed his gun straight at his face. The officers then pulled Gillies out of the sleeping bag and cuffed him. The other wranglers were waiting outside as they took him away.

Palmer was summoned from his home when the arrest was made. He was standing outside the bunkhouse, talking to one of the other officers a short time later when objects started flying out the door and landing all around him. The wranglers had finally decided that Gillies was a murderer. Palmer asked what they were doing.

"That's his crap!" one of them shouted from inside. "We want it the hell out of here!"

"Hold it," Palmer said. "Stop!" An officer would be back with a search warrant, and they did not want anything disturbed. He told the wranglers to go to bed, then posted an officer to be certain everything was left undisturbed.

16

At 1:15 A.M. on Tuesday, Phoenix homicide detective Jack Hackworth received a call at home from his sergeant telling him that a murder suspect was in custody. Hackworth was assigned to interrogate the man at once.

Sometime during Monday, Tempe police had notified Phoenix that it appeared their missing-person case had become a homicide. The victim had apparently been abducted in Phoenix, and when an arrest was made, Tempe would turn the investigation over to them.

Hackworth had been a Phoenix policeman for seventeen years, having worked a short time as an officer in Kansas and in Prescott, Arizona. He was a native of Kansas and still retained a mild midwestern accent. He was of average build and wore metal-framed glasses. His most striking feature was white hair, which he wore combed nearly straight back. It had abruptly turned white when he was thirty, and for a time there was a single ribbon of dark hair like a part, which women found attractive. He had a reluctant smile and a wry wit those who first met him frequently mistook as sarcasm.

Hackworth had been a patrol officer for a few years, a night detective, and had worked the robbery detail, sex crimes, and assaults. He had most enjoyed the robbery detail because of the adrenaline rush that went with the chase when they closed in on armed suspects, but he liked solving homicides almost as much. He was more than satisfied

160

with his life because he had looked forward to every single day of work for all of those seventeen years.

When Hackworth arrived at the Phoenix Police Department downtown, Gillies was already in an interrogation room. Palmer had briefed a sergeant on what he had learned that day. Hackworth knew Gillies was a murder suspect and was reported to have made damaging statements about his involvement.

Hackworth went in to interview the suspect alone. Gillies had received his Miranda warnings from the Tempe officers, but Hackworth repeated them anyway. Then he told him he was a murder suspect.

"I don't know what you're talking about," Gillies said. "I never murdered anyone. What's this all about?" Gillies was very nervous. In Hackworth's experience most murder suspects were.

Under questioning, Gillies said he was on work furlough from the state prison and was employed as a wrangler at Weldon Riding Stable. Hackworth told him it had been reported that he and another man had kidnapped a woman and murdered her in the mountains.

"I think I know what you're talking about," Gillies said finally. "However, I had nothing to do with that."

Gillies said that a man he knew as Mike Richardson, an escapee from prison in Michigan, worked with him at Weldon. Asked for a description, Gillies said that when he had last seen this Richardson, he had been wearing a Levi's jacket, jeans, new boots, and Gillies's brand-new cowboy hat.

Gillies told the detective that if he wanted to find Richardson, he should contact these two girls who lived in Tempe, they would know where he was. Or he should contact Frank, who ran the Ponderosa Riding Stables. Gillies himself wanted to find Richardson because he had stolen $100 from him, and he had already called Frank looking for him.

Gillies explained that he had been with a girlfriend, Connie Parks, in Litchfield Park, and could have had nothing to do with any kidnapping or murder. Gillies related that on Saturday, about 4:30 in the morning, Richardson had awakened him and suggested breakfast. He told Gillies to bring his clothes and they would do their laundry after eating, and the two of them took off. Richardson was driving a light blue Pinto that Gillies had never seen before. Hackworth asked where Richardson had obtained the car.

Gillies said, "A woman who had a ranch in the Globe area was going to hire us to work on her ranch and she had loaned him the car." After breakfast, they started drinking and continued drinking all that day. Hackworth asked if this had taken place at 4:30 A.M. on Friday instead of on Saturday.

Gillies said there had been a party at Weldon on Friday night for KJ radio, then he suddenly stopped. When Gillies spoke next, he said he no longer cared to pursue the conversation. This was a heavy charge they were trying to lay on him, and he wanted to talk to a lawyer.

Hackworth went out of the room to obtain a plain white letter envelope and a Polaroid camera. Back in the room, he told Gillies he was going to take samples of his pubic hair and photograph him. Gillies was not pleased at this. Hackworth had him drop his pants and shorts, and told him to pluck hairs from both sides. "Reach down and get a good sample," he directed. After these were placed in the envelope, Hackworth told Gillies to lift his testicles and pluck hair from there as well. Gillies did not like it, but he complied.

Hackworth had first been introduced to obtaining pubic-hair samples when he was a sex crimes detective and he noticed suspects really hated pulling the hair from their testicles. So, one night at home, Hackworth had pulled one of his own to see what it was like. It hurt like hell.

With the samples collected, Hackworth laid the envelope aside, told Gillies to put his pants back on, and snapped two photographs of him, one profile and one straight on. As he was ready to leave, Gillies asked, "What do they do to you in Arizona when they put you to death?"

Hackworth said the penalty for murder in Arizona was death.

"I know that," Gillies said, "but how do they put you to death?"

"Gas chamber."

Gillies looked up and said in a loud voice, "All that just for killing that bitch?"

Hackworth left the room and wrote his notes from the interview. Gillies was formally booked into the Maricopa County Jail a few blocks away on charges of homicide, kidnapping, and sexual assault. During processing, he told one of the detention officers that he was going to kill himself, and so was placed on a suicide watch.

•　•　•

One of the detectives working homicide with Hackworth was a longtime personal friend, George Klettlinger. The pair had worked one year in burglary, five years as a team with the robbery detail, and had been together on the homicide squad for the last year and a half. They had formed a close bond over the years.

At this time in Phoenix, there was a single homicide detail in the police department, and only veteran detectives with established track records worked on it. As each case was received, the sergeant assigned it on a rotating basis to one of the homicide detectives. At any given time each detective was case agent for at least one killing, on rare occasions for two. They assigned the other officers to do legwork as required, depending on the status of the murder for which they were case agents. This meant Hackworth was Klettlinger's boss on this case. Next week, the roles would be reversed. He told Klettlinger to prepare a search warrant for Weldon Riding Stable.

Palmer had come down to the Phoenix Police Department after posting his man at the bunkhouse. He was exhausted; the high that had sustained him was spent. Though he understood that the case must now be turned over to the Phoenix police, he still felt cheated. Since 8:00 that morning, this case had clicked, each step leading to the next, culminating in an arrest of one of the suspects. He wanted to see it through.

Instead, he sat with Klettlinger and dictated the information required for the search warrant. Then, his role complete, he drove home, emotionally drained, and went to sleep.

Hackworth immediately dispatched several homicide detectives to take statements from Schneider and the wranglers. This process lasted throughout the very early morning hours. The detectives briefed him on what they learned as they finished each interview.

At 4:00 A.M., Deputy County Attorney Jeffrey Hotham was awakened from a deep sleep by the Phoenix Police Department informing him that they had a homicide suspect in custody and were in pursuit of a second. The victim's name was Suzanne Rossetti, and a missing-person report had been filed on her. The suspect in custody had made incriminating statements to others suggesting she had been kidnapped, raped, and murdered. They did not have a body and were not certain of the date of the killing. Hotham's presence was not requested at this time, since they did not have a murder scene, and questioning was proceeding. He would be advised. Hotham thanked the caller and went back to sleep.

At 5:00 A.M., Hackworth called Pug Willis at his home, having learned that he was a close friend of the missing woman. Hearing that Hackworth was from the homicide detail, Pug asked if Suzanne was definitely the victim of murder. Hackworth related to him what he understood Gillies had told the wranglers, plus a little of what Gillies had told him. Pug said he would break the news to the family.

That Tuesday morning, Schneider arrived at work and was angry when he saw the wranglers had not started their chores. "Why haven't you put the hay out yet?" he demanded.

One of the men came up to him and said, "Look here what I found. This was wedged in the hay." The man was holding a gray shirt that Schneider recognized as belonging to Gillies. His ex-employee had often used the heavy shirt like a jacket. Schneider reached out for it and grabbed the pocket as he took it. He could feel something hard.

"What is that?" Schneider reached into the pocket and pulled out a brown Broadway department store credit card in the name of Suzanne Rossetti. "Look here," he said.

Another wrangler told Schneider that they had started tossing the hay as usual earlier, and had found something funny. They handed over a small pair of women's panties. The men understood that a policeman was coming by later with a search warrant. Schneider said they would turn this stuff over, then he told the men to get the horses fed.

Before leaving the Kon Tiki Hotel on Tuesday, Logan went down to the front office and reregistered with a different clerk. He still had the key from his first room, just in case, and now had paid for another night in a second room.

He returned to the bar on Van Buren with Curly, drank beer, and hustled pool. The Scout was to be repaired on Thursday, and Logan would then leave for California. That morning, he hit Suzanne's bank account for $250, then tried again in the afternoon with no success. He returned to the bar with its smell of beer and tobacco smoke, and the steady clacking of the balls on the green felt table.

• • •

At three o'clock Tuesday morning, Donna Rossetti saw Louise off at Sky Harbor Airport. She was concerned that her mother be with her father. Not long after Donna returned to the condominium, Pug arrived and told her what he had learned from Hackworth. Donna called Peter Jr. while her mother was still en route. Pug was standing nearby, drained of all emotion, and watched the morning sunlight streaming in the window as Donna spoke quietly on the telephone. She told Peter Jr. that the police had made an arrest and the man had bragged that he had kidnapped, raped, and murdered Suzanne, then buried her in the desert. She told him that she believed Suzanne was dead, but because of the circumstances, Suzanne might never be found. Their parents had to be informed.

When she finished the call, Donna began crying softly. Eric Gregan, Gary Reid, and Pug all broke down under the weight of their grief.

Peter Sr. was already at the airport to meet his wife. Father Creed, the family attorney, and other close friends of the family had been summoned by Peter Jr. to the company office, where they waited for Peter and Louise. Peter Jr. called for an ambulance to be kept just out of sight in the parking lot across the street.

When Peter and Louise walked into the office, they were greeted by a somber gathering. Peter Jr. told them that Donna had called. An arrest had been made, and it appeared nearly certain that Suzanne had been kidnapped, raped, and murdered. According to the police, she had been buried somewhere in the desert and they could not be certain Suzanne would ever be found.

His parents broke into tears and were joined by everyone else in the room. Peter Jr. was watching the tragic scene as if they all were acting a part. Ever since his father had arrived in Saugus, the situation had been like one continuous wake, with no end in sight. He watched his father closely, fearing that at any moment he would collapse and CPR would have to be administered.

Peter Jr. could not believe that his sister was really dead. His father said that they must have the body of Suzanne back for burial. Peter Jr. agreed; until they had Suzanne home, they would never know for certain that she was dead.

Word spread throughout Saugus that the nightmare was true. Suzanne Rossetti had been murdered.

• • •

That morning at his office, Jeff Hotham was formally assigned the case. Not much later Jack Hackworth called him for a briefing. For the past six years, Hotham had served as a prosecuting attorney and since 1979 had been a member of the Major Felony Bureau, which prosecuted the most serious crimes committed in Maricopa County. In the twenty-seven felony trials Hotham had prosecuted, only one man had not been convicted. Hotham had a string of nine first-degree murder convictions, with seven death penalties imposed, the most for any prosecutor in the state.

Hackworth informed him that they were searching for the body in the usual places and that friends of the victim were planning to assist. Hackworth said that he hoped this was just a situation where the suspect in custody had a big mouth, but he did not think so.

At this point in his career, Hotham believed he was accustomed to the nature of murder, having seen it in many forms. This case, however, was different. As the details were presented, Hotham was struck by the utter depravity of the crime.

Much of what Hackworth told Hotham was encouraging, but without a body, and with Gillies refusing to talk, he had almost nothing on which to base a prosecution. The situation was that only the killer, or killers, knew where the woman was located.

Hotham was more than a little relieved that Hackworth was working this case. The prosecutors of the Major Felony Bureau worked frequently with the homicide detectives of the various police departments in Maricopa County, and he had learned whom he could trust. In Hotham's experience, the detectives assigned to the homicide squad of the Phoenix Police Department were the best, but they had different areas in which they excelled. Some were good at working a crime scene, while others were better at questioning suspects. Still others made the best witnesses on the stand. In the case of Hackworth, he had a knack for persuading suspects to talk.

Hotham had watched the detective operate and was impressed with the manner in which Hackworth appealed to a suspect's sense of fair play and decency, often in cases where Hotham doubted the suspect possessed either. If the killer could be touched, Hackworth found a way to do it.

It was a sight to behold as the white-haired detective with the mild Kansas drawl quietly posed his questions and listened patiently to the answers. Never hostile, never aggressive, he was relentless, and ever so polite. Even the hardest of men found themselves saying things that were later heard repeated in court as their defense attorneys squirmed in their chairs.

Over the next several hours, Hotham conducted research and spoke to other veterans in his office about the missing body. He learned that in the history of Arizona, no one had ever been convicted of murder in the absence of the body of the deceased.

Hotham understood the difficulty he faced in convincing all twelve jurors beyond a reasonable doubt that there had been a murder when he could not produce a body. Then he had to prove that this man had committed it. An added legal concern was that without the body, Hotham could not use in a trial the statements Gillies had made to the wranglers. Obtaining a conviction was a nearly impossible task.

When he received a call from Peter Jr., Hotham had very little to tell him beyond what was already known. Peter Jr. emphasized that the family needed Suzanne's body because until they had her back, there would always be doubt. They had to know, and Suzanne deserved a Christian burial. Hotham said he understood and would do his best.

About 10:00 A.M, Tuesday morning, Klettlinger arrived at Weldon with his search warrant. The wranglers handed over the shirt, credit card, and panties, all of which he bagged and marked. In the bunkhouse and outside on the ground, he seized Suzanne's camera bag, her sleeping bag, and other items. Then he returned with them to the police department.

Later that morning, Gary Reid called Hackworth, saying that he was a friend of Suzanne's. He told him his interest was personal because his office had not opened an investigation, but his supervisor was aware of his involvement and Reid wanted to do whatever he could.

Hackworth told Reid about this man, Mike Richardson, who was supposed to be an escaped convict. Could he contact Michigan and obtain a list of all escapees matching his race, age, and description? Reid could, and twenty minutes later called back with a list of four escapees. Photographs were on their way.

Because Hackworth had reason to think Suzanne's Valley National Bank account had been used after she was reported missing, he asked the head of bank security for the videotapes taken of these transactions. That afternoon, the two men watched the tapes together.

Hackworth saw the Pinto drive by the camera, then return a few minutes later. Two men were apparent in the car, even at a distance, and in one sequence he could see a young woman. He watched Logan use the machine and could spot Gillies in the background.

Periodically, he stopped the tape and snapped black-and-white Polaroids of the television monitor; he took nearly a dozen of the most incriminating views. He asked the head of security for the similar tapes from other branches, and wanted to be informed once the bank had them available.

Hackworth drove to the Scottsdale condominium to speak to Donna. One of the standard procedures of the homicide detail was that only the case agent dealt with the family. After talking to Gillies, Hackworth had no doubts that Suzanne was dead. There was always the possibility of a miracle, but he was not expecting one in this case. Because Pug had broken the news to the family, they faced the fact of their loved one's loss more gently. It had been for this reason that Hackworth had called him.

The detective found the condominium filled with people, bright, well dressed, and professional-looking. Hackworth was not college educated and was always mildly embarrassed by what he believed to be his country accent.

He was introduced to Donna, who said she and her sister had discussed what they would do if they were ever raped, and she was confident that Suzanne had given the men no reason to kill her. Then she took Hackworth upstairs and told him about the clock. Clearly, the victim in this case was a bright, savvy woman, Hackworth thought.

It seemed to him the men had murdered Suzanne simply because they wanted to. According to what Gillies had told the wranglers, the woman had given them a ride. That meant they had a pretty good defense against a rape charge. It would have been their word against hers. They had robbed her at the car and had taken everything of value from the condominium. There was only one reason to keep the woman with them—the desire to kill her.

Hackworth did not believe in capital punishment, and had never once attended the sentencing of a single murderer he had arrested. It was his belief that murderers did not consider the likelihood of capture and were not deterred by the possibility of execution. With thousands of them on death rows all over the country and a single execution every few months, it was apparent they would never be killed as fast as they were sentenced. Hackworth was content to let them serve the rest of their lives in prison.

He was also influenced by the fact that he had liked many of the murderers he had met over the years. They were often decent people who experienced genuine remorse over what they had done. In half the cases he had worked, the victims had been nasty people who were not missed. How did you separate those cases from cases like this one? In his view, you did not.

But sentencing was not his concern at the moment. His priorities were to catch the other killer, and locate the victim's body.

Detectives contacted Frank at the Ponderosa, and he gave them Logan's hotel and room number. They called Hackworth early that Tuesday evening with word that Logan was staying at the Kon Tiki Hotel at Twenty-fourth Street and Van Buren. Three detectives with backup were dispatched to place room 307 under observation.

Logan was talking to Curly about leaving the bar with their winnings. They were seated in a booth, drinking from bottles of beer beside the pool tables where they had played all that day. Several black hookers came in, all cheap perfume and loud talk, and tried to interest the men in a party.

Logan figured the whores were sent in to get them outside to be rolled. He placed $50 into the palm of one of the women and handed her the key to the room he had slept in the previous night. He told her and her friends to go there and wait, he and his buddy would be along any moment and they would really party. He doubted the women would actually go to the room, but he reasoned they had the fifty bucks and would settle for that.

About half an hour later, another black entered the bar. He walked up to Logan and offered to sell him dope. Logan decided this was one of the whore's pimps checking them out. The man had marijuana so Logan bought ten dollars' worth. When the pimp went outside, Logan said to Curly, "I just did that to prevent trouble."

Curly said he was not concerned about trouble. He reached behind him and pulled out a huge automatic pistol from the back of his pants.

"I guess you aren't," Logan said with a laugh.

Since Curly had the hardware, Logan was no longer worried and told the bartender to call them a cab. When the cabbie arrived, he had Curly escort him outside. Logan was drunk enough, however, to go looking for trouble. He abruptly told the cabbie to take off, they did not need him after all. The cabbie was angry, so Curly paid him off from their pool winnings.

Logan told Curly to shadow him from his borrowed truck. Logan would stroll down Van Buren to the Kon Tiki. If the "niggers" made any trouble, he said Curly could just kill them.

Curly liked that and climbed into the truck, as Logan walked slowly toward his hotel, soliciting trouble.

Donna spoke to Pug, and other friends of Suzanne, and said they should begin planning a memorial service. They had to face the reality of her death. Tragic as it was, her body might never be recovered. There should be something to remember her by, a release for the anguish and suffering so many who knew her were experiencing.

Friends embraced the project. The Franciscan Fathers were contacted, and the rotunda at Suzanne's church was reserved for that Thursday when a Mass would be celebrated.

Logan's attempt to provoke a confrontation turned out to be a bust. Filled with beer and walking with numb legs, Logan reached the Kon Tiki without incident. He told Curly through the window of the truck how disappointed he was and that he would see Curly the next day.

Logan was confused as to where his room was located and went to the fourth floor. He was already out of the elevator and walking down the hallway when he looked at his room key and realized his error. He went back to the elevator and rode down to the third floor. It was 9:20 P.M.

Just as he reached into his pocket for the key to his room, the police sprang out from surrounding rooms. They gave him no chance to escape or to resist; he was down on the floor and in handcuffs within seconds. He was patted for weapons and hustled into a nearby room. There were so many cops, Logan was concerned about what they had in mind. But very shortly after that he was in the back of a marked police car and being driven to main headquarters, where he was placed in an interview room.

No one had said anything to him about charges, but he knew at once that Gillies had turned him in. Logan was chastising himself;

he should have been long gone by now, not hanging around the dog track or shooting pool. He could not believe he had been so stupid.

This moment he had a more immediate concern. In the cursory search for weapons at the time of his arrest, the officers had missed the two marijuana cigarettes in his shirt pocket. With his cuffed hands, he fumbled them out and sucked them onto his lips. He was fumbling with a book of matches and was about to light them, when he heard the door open. He spat out the cigarettes out and placed his boot over them as a uniformed policeman stepped in to stand guard.

After a few minutes, Logan asked if he could have a cigarette. The officer said he could if he had his own, where were they? With his chin Logan pointed down at his shirt pockets. As the officer reached for the left pocket, Logan quickly said, no, they were in the other one. By now the officer had removed a Valley National Bank ATM card bearing the name of Suzanne M. Rossetti.

"Who is this?" the officer asked.

"Who? Susan?" Logan said.

"Who's this girl on this credit card?"

"She's an ex-girlfriend," Logan replied.

"Does she know you have her card?"

"Yes, she does."

The officer looked at the card, then at Logan. "This card is not reported lost or stolen, is it?"

"No," Logan said, "it is not."

The uniformed officer went outside. A few moments later, the door opened again and in stepped a man with all-white hair wearing a neutral expression on his face.

17

"**W**hat's your name?" Hackworth asked, after repeating Logan's rights to him.

"I'm Mike Richardson from Lansing, Michigan," Logan said. "Why have I been arrested?"

Hackworth told him that he was under arrest for kidnapping, sexual assault, and murder.

"I don't know what you're talking about. I was just walking into my room when these two officers jumped me and arrested me."

Hackworth told him that he knew his real name was not Mike Richardson, though he suspected that the Mike part might be correct. He said there was an extensive investigation going on. "We've arrested Jess Gillies." Gillies had made a statement about the crime and had implicated him.

Logan said he still did not know what Hackworth was talking about.

Hackworth pulled Suzanne's ATM card from his pocket and showed it to Logan. "Do you know who this lady is?" he asked.

"That's my girlfriend," Logan said. "Susan."

Hackworth asked if he knew where she was at this time. Logan shook his head and said he did not.

In his soft voice, Hackworth told Logan that this woman had been murdered and her body was someplace near the Superstition

Mountains. He said he thought that he and Gillies were responsible for what had happened to her.

Logan was more than a little nervous. "Maybe Jesse knows something about it, but I don't know anything," he said, "and I didn't take part in it." Logan concluded by saying he did not think he wanted to talk to Hackworth any longer.

The detective stepped outside for five minutes and poured two cups of coffee. He took these back into the interview room. He handed Logan a cup, and the two of them sipped coffee for a moment. Hackworth said he did not believe Logan was a compassionate person. Clearly, Logan had no respect whatsoever for the parents of that poor girl, nor for their feelings about their daughter's body being left in the desert.

This was a standard approach that Hackworth had used many times in the past with good results. Often at the time of arrest, murderers experienced genuine remorse for their conduct as well as a large measure of self-pity. He was not seeing any remorse in Logan, though there was a full dose of self-pity, but he thought the approach was worth the effort.

Logan considered this for a moment, then said, "I'll tell you exactly what happened."

Logan said that at 10:00 P.M. the previous Wednesday night he and Gillies had been broke after spending what little money they had between them. They had had drinks and tried to find a drunk to roll, but had no luck. At the U-Totem, the lady had driven up and locked her keys in her car. After they had helped her out, she bought them beer and offered a ride. Just south of the stables Gillies had struck her on the face and throat at least twice, then pushed her out of the car and raped her.

"I was so shocked I just stood there," Logan said. After he was finished, Gillies had put the lady back into the car and drove off. Logan was left just standing there in the desert, dumbfounded.

Hackworth appeared to consider this, then told him that he did not think Logan was telling the truth.

"Well," Logan said, "Jess took a towel or something out of the car and tied her up, and we put her in the back of the station wagon. We then checked her purse for money, credit cards, and anything else and found twenty-nine dollars—no, correct me on that. There was an extra five dollars—thirty-four dollars because we didn't see the first five until he counted it."

He said they drove around for a while. They had her address and went to her condominium, but only for ten or fifteen minutes. Then Logan said, "I got a little bit."

Hackworth asked what he meant by that.

"I had sex with her."

"Was it consensual?"

"I don't know what you mean."

"Did she ask to have sex with you?"

"No, she didn't want to." Logan said they used the ATM card in Scottsdale to get money. They bought some beer and then drove to the Superstition Mountains.

"Did the lady say anything?" Hackworth asked.

"No, she didn't say a word."

"Was she crying, or making threats, or trying to get away?"

"No, she wasn't saying anything."

"Was she gagged?"

"No, she was just tied up with towels." Logan said they drove a long way before the road turned to dirt. Gillies got out, cut the cloth from her arms and legs, then told her that she was going to go hiking with him.

Logan told the detective she said, "I'm not going anywhere with you."

"Yes, you're going hiking," Logan said Gillies told her. Then Gillies walked a ways down a cliff, came back up and grabbed the lady by the arm and jerked her off the cliff, but she did not fall very far. The two of them went down, and Logan could see she was bleeding over her left eye. Gillies called her a bitch and a whore.

"Did she say anything at this time?" Hackworth asked.

"Let's go home and let me cook you a meal." Gillies called her all kinds of names; then he picked up a rock and started crushing her head in with it. Logan said he asked Gillies, "What are you doing?"

"She was going to turn us in," Gillies told him. "We have to do something with her."

"What did you do?" Hackworth asked Logan.

"I just stood there froze and didn't know what to do and Jess had to slap me two times in the face before I got my senses." Then the two of them buried her. They drove across the dam at Roosevelt Lake, went to Globe, and bought $10 worth of gas after daybreak. Back in Phoenix, they used the ATM card to obtain more money, got drunk, and lost it all at the dog track.

Hackworth asked, "Can you draw a map where the victim was left?"

"I don't know. I've never been there before in my life. I've only been in Phoenix about three months, but I think I can show you if you want me to."

Yes, Hackworth told him, he would like for Logan to show him.

PART SEVEN
HOTHAM

"Suzanne Rossetti had some rights too: She had the right to live."

—*Jeffrey Hotham*

18

Hackworth and his sergeant escorted Logan to an unmarked police car and retraced the route from Tempe that Logan claimed to recall. It was 12:30 A.M.

As they drove, Hackworth kept Logan in the mood to cooperate by maintaining a constant, innocuous conversation with him. It was important Hackworth not press him because then the suspect might balk, but it was equally important for Logan not to be left in silence and permitted to become morose. The two policemen shot the bull with each other and chatted with Logan in a friendly manner. They stopped for coffee and a sandwich, and Hackworth saw to it Logan smoked a steady supply of cigarettes.

Logan had no trouble pointing out the major street intersections he and Gillies had taken, and after an hour they were on State Highway 88 heading toward Tortilla Flat. Nothing was easy after that. Logan could not remember how far he and Gillies had driven, and in the dark tonight it all looked the same to him.

Once they were beyond Canyon Lake, Logan would call out, "This looks like it!" and the men would pile out of the car only to have their prisoner shake his head and tell them the location was not quite right.

Hackworth believed that Logan was genuinely trying to help them. He was just a city boy unaccustomed to the country and had never been out this way before, except the one time. It was dark and each turn in the road looked the same as the last to him.

What Hackworth did not believe was Logan's story. So far, all he had heard was one side. Gillies would have a version, and Hackworth doubted very much if the two would agree.

Having talked to the two men, Hackworth was convinced that Logan was the sharper of the pair and was certainly the most convise. Logan understood that giving help like this could make a difference in his case, while Gillies did not have a clue. He was too busy acting the tough guy.

Finally, they reached the hairpin turn at the crest of Fish Creek Hill at milepost 222. There was a change in his voice when Logan said he was certain they were quite close.

The police car crept down the dirt road as Logan peered out the window, searching for the place where he and Gillies had stopped. When they drove by milepost 223, he told them that they had gone too far.

Up the road, Logan selected a spot and told them he thought they had raped the lady right here. The detectives climbed out of the car, walked to the edge of the road, and peered over. Hackworth could understand how Gillies and Logan had thought throwing the woman off this ledge would kill her. It certainly looked as if a body would fall hundreds, possibly thousands, of feet, and that would have been the end of their problem. He decided they had been thinking of those coyote and roadrunner cartoons where the coyote is thrown off the mesa and his cry dwindles away until he hits the ground with a *poof*.

But this had been real life, not make-believe. A flesh-and-blood woman had not fallen as far as that, then men had climbed down and stoned her to death, with blood pouring out on the harsh rocks while she experienced excruciating pain and then died after terrible long minutes of genuine terror.

It was apparent Logan could not be certain this was actually the location, and the two detectives realized they could do nothing in the treacherous terrain in the dark. They returned to Phoenix, and at 5:45 A.M., Logan was booked for murder, kidnapping, sexual assault, and escape from prison.

Shortly after dawn on Wednesday, Klettlinger left Phoenix in the police helicopter to conduct a search for the burial site. He had not been with Hackworth and their sergeant a few hours earlier and therefore did not know that Logan had pinpointed an area beside Fish Creek Canyon. Klettlinger was working from the information developed the previous day, and he was under the impression that the two killers had turned to the right at Apache Junction, driven through Florence Junction, then on toward Globe. On the contrary, they had turned left into more rugged country.

From Apache Junction out, the terrain below the helicopter was flat desert, thick with saguaro cacti, sagebrush, and mesquite trees. Klettlinger's working theory was that the desert ground would readily reveal a new gravesite. He and the pilot searched both sides of the highway for a high cliff from which the men could have thrown the victim, but they had no success. Finally, the mountains beyond Superior became so prominent, Klettlinger decided the men would surely have done it before reaching here.

Flying toward Phoenix, Klettlinger was informed that the actual location was on State Highway 88 at Fish Creek Hill and instructed the pilot to divert. They flew along the foothills of the Superstition Mountains, across Canyon Lake, then up the mountain road until they spotted several cars lined at the top of Fish Creek Hill.

Slowly, he and the pilot moved across the face of the mountain, hunting for signs of a grave. Often the road was above them. When they flew high enough, the terrain appeared flat and Klettlinger could not detect distinguishing marks. When they flew low enough to spot a disturbed area, the field of vision was so restricted they could not cover any area of significance. The only place they could land the helicopter was on the other side of the canyon on the dirt road a distance away.

Hackworth and other detectives had come straight from booking Logan to resume the search in daylight. One of the standard techniques for uncovering a body in such a location was to rely on smell. Suzanne had been dead for six days, and Hackworth thought there would be a noticeable odor by this time. He drove, and then walked, up and down the dirt road, testing the wind with his nose but detected nothing. He finally reasoned that it was too cold in the mountains for significant decomposition to have occurred. If Logan was correct, Suzanne lay on the north side of the mountain, an area that was receiving less than a half hour of direct sunlight a day at this time of year.

Hackworth and the other officers formed a line at the most likely place from milepost 222 and tried to work their way straight down the steep slope so that every foot of the area was in someone's observation. They had on their city shoes and cursed as they ruined them. The plan sounded good in theory but did not work in practice. The terrain was so precipitous and treacherous it was impossible to hold a straight line. Men were slipping and falling regularly. The detectives inevitably veered left or right because the going became impossible, leaving large gaps between them.

Worse was the lack of soil; the whole area was rock scattered around jagged boulders. It was impossible to spot any place of disturbance because the entire location looked disturbed. There were water cuts and rises, short cliffs and vast stretches of broken rock, all with the same gray appearance. There was no sign any human had set foot here, ever.

The television helicopters soon arrived and circled above, shooting footage for the evening news. As word spread, sightseers drove slowly by, and the officers wasted valuable time telling them to move along. Finally, Hackworth requested that two uniformed deputies handle the traffic situation.

Members of the Arizona Mountaineering Club came out to help. While well equipped for the effort and in good physical condition, they simply had no idea what they were searching for. Hackworth did not appreciate their efforts as he watched them moving skillfully across the face of the mountain, because he believed they were inadvertently destroying evidence that might be crucial to his investigation, but he could not find it in himself to tell them to stop.

The club members were acting in the final, desperate hope that Logan was mistaken. They were telling themselves that Suzanne was only seriously injured and in urgent need of their help.

At thirty years of age, Jeffrey Hotham possessed tall dark good looks that routinely attracted the attention of women. He was always meticulously attired in a city known for casual dress and was soft-spoken with a ready, warm smile. As was the case with the young Turks in the Major Felony Bureau, Hotham believed he was making a difference.

The dozen bright young attorneys of the Major Felony Bureau were the cream of the County Attorney's office, and knew it. They had a reputation for competence, for going the extra mile, and, most of all, for obtaining convictions and maximum sentences. It was a reputation they relished. Most of them were married, as was Hotham, and they often socialized together.

Peter Jr.'s call the previous day was just one of the many conflicting interests Hotham juggled. The families of the deceased were always demanding, though Hotham sympathized with the anguish they experienced; he heard it in every conversation with them. But building a case, making the hard decisions that go into convicting a killer, allows precious little time for compassion or, for that matter, any emotion. Killers went to prison, or to death row in the state prison, because prosecutors like Hotham assembled cases that accomplished the job, not because they coddled the families, or sought vengeance for them, or despised the killers.

His was the business of justice, and the families of the murdered rarely understood, or even cared, about that. They wanted the body of their loved ones returned and the son-of-a-bitch who did it, dead.

The Major Felony Bureau was a busy operation, but in the midst of the frenzy of the office, it was Hotham who remained collected. From the moment he entered his office until he left at the end of the day, the telephone rang continually. Defense lawyers and other prosecutors, police officers and prospective witnesses were in and out constantly. Amid all this, he prepared summaries, plotted strategy or made an appearance in court. Hotham never became flustered or short-tempered. He was first, and always, a gentleman, performing a demanding and emotionally exhausting state function. And though Hotham was shocked at the circumstances of Suzanne's murder, she was just one of several important cases on which he was working.

During Wednesday, he was informed that the second suspect, one Michael David Logan, was in custody and that attempts were under way to locate Suzanne's body.

Hotham spoke with Peter Rossetti Sr., by phone, as well as with Gary Reid. Suzanne's father was highly emotional as he repeated what his son had said the day before. He conveyed to Hotham the family's very deep feelings that his daughter's body be found and Suzanne be granted peace in death.

Hotham had formed what he believed was an accurate picture of the character of the victim and was especially impressed with the cohesiveness the family was demonstrating. This was not something he encountered very often in these situations. Because of the professionalism of his office, Hotham struggled to maintain his distance. He had learned that if he involved himself emotionally with a case, he would be consumed by passion and could make injudicious decisions. He was able to let the anger and rage boil inside until he could use it to his advantage during the trial.

Usually, such objectivity required only his customary effort, but in this case, as he listened to Peter, he was finding it very tough going.

Acting on his legal concerns and the desire of the family, at 4:30 that Wednesday afternoon Hotham called Maricopa County Deputy Public Defender Richard Mesh at his office. They were personally acquainted, having been adversaries on a number of occasions. Hotham told Mesh that he been informed by the Public Defender's office that Mesh was the attorney for Jesse James Gillies. Until this moment, Mesh had never heard of his client but the first two names caught his attention at once.

"I want to tell you a little about the case," Hotham said, "since time is of the essence." He related the basic facts of the situation as he had learned them. He said he understood that Logan was blaming Gillies as the actual killer, while Gillies's statements to the wranglers made Logan out to be the principal killer. This was going to be a finger-pointing case.

Hotham said it was essential that the missing woman be located, if for no other reason than to provide her with a Christian burial. He said if Gillies would lead them to the body, and if Mesh could convince Hotham that his client was not the one who had wielded the rock that killed Suzanne—he would not ask for the death penalty.

Hotham was personally offended by plea bargaining, but was compelled to face the reality of it every day. Though the elected County Attorney campaigned on the promise he would oppose plea bargaining and officially pressured prosecutors to take everything to trial, the reality of the heavy caseload was to bargain.

Without a file, Mesh went straight to the nearby county jail to meet with Gillies.

There is a competitiveness between criminal trial attorneys that is palpable. They are the high-wire act of the justice system, with the lives of clients hanging in the balance, risking either incarceration or execution. Each trial attorney is convinced he is the best and will rarely acknowledge committing a tactical error in a case. Professional reputations ride on outcomes. And everyone keeps score.

Hotham was not surprised that Gillies's defense had been assigned to Mesh, since he was one of the two or three heavy hitters at the

Public Defender's office. Mesh had won a startling number of recent acquittals.

At 6:30 that evening, Mesh telephoned Hotham and said he could not make a deal with him regarding his client. He would, however, call Hotham the following morning. He wanted to let Gillies sleep on their conversation and was planning to meet with him again early the next day.

Hotham was not surprised. The accused rarely admitted their guilt during their first contact with an appointed counsel. It was often necessary for a public defender to visit the client more than once to explain the hard practicality of plea negotiations.

In Gillies's case, there was very little time to ponder the offer. Gillies might not understand that, but Mesh did.

Police abandoned the search at dusk, and that night the atmosphere at the Rossettis' Scottsdale condominium was extremely somber. Following the frustration of the day's search and the certainty with which the police accepted Suzanne's death, her friends were coming to terms with reality.

After his initial anger at the police inaction, Pug had come to respect the dedication Hackworth and the others were bringing to their job. It was apparent to him that the men were moved by what had happened and that they were trying hard to locate Suzanne. The memorial service was scheduled for the following night, heightening the sense that Suzanne, truly, was dead.

Pug had been briefly interviewed by a local television station concerning a project he was working on. But when Suzanne's friends turned in to the evening news to watch him, they saw vivid pictures taken from a helicopter of policemen searching on the rocky side of Fish Creek Hill for her body. Donna was stunned and visibly shaken, in such a state of shock she could not compose herself long enough to turn off the set.

Then the station flashed the mug shots of Gillies and Logan; two hardened faces, dirty, unshaven, with scraggly hair, staring like death straight ahead.

"Oh my God," she thought. She had never wanted to see what the men looked like, and here they were, just as despicable as she had imagined. When the program was over, she fell apart.

• • •

Before dawn on Thursday morning, one week following Suzanne's murder, Klettlinger was at the Phoenix Police Department K-9 pound. His sergeant had come up with the idea that a police dog could be of assistance in the mountain search.

Klettlinger was not so certain. These dogs were not bloodhounds and had not been formally trained to locate bodies. They were used for sniffing out drugs and for personal defense. He watched the German shepherd climb into his car, then drove the K-9 officer and his dog out to Fish Creek Hill.

Mesh met again with Gillies at 7:00 A.M. Thursday to discuss the case and Hotham's plea-bargaining offer. At his office, Mesh telephoned Hotham and said he could not help him with locating the body. Mesh understood that Logan had been assisting the police, and if he was successful, it was Logan who would receive the benefit of the offer to spare him the death penalty. But there was nothing to be done about it; his client had made his decision.

Unaware of this exchange, Hackworth figured that if Logan could not do the job for them of locating Suzanne's body, then maybe Gillies would like another chance. He went into the detention area of the jail and had a guard awaken Gillies.

Hackworth told the prisoner that he had him cold, and if Gillies was man enough, he would not leave the poor woman to the elements and would tell them where she was. Gillies told him to do it on his own if he thought he could, then shouted when Hackworth was out of sight, "Fuck you, Hackworth!" He called out that he would help the detective later if he felt like it. Right now he was sleeping.

Hackworth, who rarely became emotionally involved, was developing a real dislike for Gillies.

Hackworth roused Logan from his jail bunk and asked if he was interested in trying to find the woman's body during daylight. Logan was. While he was being driven back to the scene, the car formed part of a long caravan of vehicles, and it appeared to Logan as if all the cops wanted in on this search. At noon, they stopped at the Tortilla Flat restaurant to feed Logan; then the procession drove to milepost 222 near the hairpin turn at the top of Fish Creek Hill.

Over a dozen officers were present, including the sheriff's deputies needed to handle the anticipated traffic. These were the same deputies who regularly patrolled the area. Today, the city officers were decked out in rugged hunting boots and worn Levi's. They were sore and frustrated that they had been unable to locate the body the previous day.

From the rear of the police car Logan voiced confidence that the body was in this vicinity. After looking around, he said she should be no more than twenty-five yards off the roadway under a pile of rocks they had used to cover her. This was consistent with the version of events he had related, since he never mentioned the two additional times they had tried to toss Suzanne off what they believed was a nearby cliff.

Logan told them that it had taken more than an hour to bury her, so the mound should be pretty big. He said one of her feet had been sticking out from under the rocks and they had covered it up as well. He went on to say that when he and Gillies first arrived, they had looked over the side of the road. Then they had cut the bonds on her legs and pulled her from the rear of the Pinto.

Hackworth asked what the two of them had been discussing as they looked over the edge of the cliff, before they went back and pulled the girl from the car. Logan refused to answer.

Hackworth left Logan to another officer and joined in the search. Sweat was soon running down Hackworth's back under his shirt, and he was wheezing and sucking air. He watched the K-9 officer pamper his dog, moving him ever so carefully from place to place. The dog would sniff around, but nothing attracted his interest. He was carefully handled, but it was hard going for an animal accustomed to the luxury of a pound. After a short time, the K-9 officer told the sergeant that the dog was becoming tired. If he kept this up, he would hurt his paws on the sharp rocks and get sick. The sergeant sent the dog back into town.

Hackworth and Klettlinger swore when they heard that. The effort was too tough for a dog, but the detectives could run up and down this goddam canyon all day long. They finally knew where they stood with the brass.

The television crews were back with their helicopters and cameras as well. Hackworth was angry. He felt that this was turning into a circus. One of the pilot-reporters with a television station was known for his ego. In one previous case, he landed his helicopter in the desert before Hackworth had finished working the crime scene. The wind from the copter's blades had blown away anything that was not nailed down, including some of the evidence. Hackworth had shouted at the hotshot, telling him to get the hell out. The pilot complained to the newspaper, which ran an article accusing the police of trying to suppress evidence in the investigation. So Hackworth wished the television helicopters would take their pictures and get out of the way.

Logan was never taken out of the police car. In daylight the area was as new to him as if he had never been there before. It had looked entirely different under the blanket of night. The driver eased the car up and down the road, but Logan could give no more information than he had previously.

The search this second day was much the same as before, only with increased helicopter and tourist interest. The detectives were cut and bruised from climbing up and down the side of the mountain, and they had strained ligaments and aching muscles. Hackworth was beginning to wonder if it was possible to locate the gravesite in this terrain, even with Logan's information.

At 3:30 that afternoon, the two sheriff's deputies were smoking cigarettes, leaning forward against the guard railing while they slowly scrutinized the terrain below them. Cars regularly went off the road here, and they marked the wrecks with paint so that the more recent cars were quickly apparent to them. Two weeks earlier, they had pulled a body out of such a car and spent considerable time at this location.

These men were also accustomed to the contours of the desert. They spent every workday out in the open, and any irregularities here quickly caught their attention.

One of the deputies spotted something and pointed. "That mound doesn't look too natural to me, does it to you?" he asked.

The other agreed. "No, let's go look."

The pair worked slowly down toward what they had seen, then suddenly stopped. Sticking out from under a pile of large rocks was a human foot. The deputies went up the slope to their car and put out a call.

At 3:45, Hackworth heard the call over the radio and drove the short distance to the scene. He looked where the deputies pointed, but could see nothing but rock. He continued looking and finally, over one hundred yards down the mountain, saw a tiny mound in the loose rock. He was impressed that these men had actually spotted it from the road, the disturbance in the terrain was so minute.

The officer with Logan drove to the site. When he saw the officers pointing and looking down over the edge, Logan said, "I wasn't too far off, was I?" After a few minutes, Hackworth had him returned to jail.

Now that the body was located, Hackworth wanted no mistakes. There was no need to rush after death; they had plenty of time to do this right.

The more he considered the crime, the angrier Hackworth became. Gillies and Logan had held Suzanne for hours. Whatever they had wanted from her, they had taken. Alone, they might not have had the nerve to kill her, but together they had. Each of the men had goaded the other, and together they had brutally murdered the woman because she was small and helpless, and because they had the power to do it, and for no other reason.

He wanted them convicted; he wanted it very badly.

The first person Hackworth sent down the slope was the iden-tification technician with his camera. The officers remained near the road and watched him work slowly toward the site, snapping nearly three rolls of photographs as he went.

Klettlinger approached the scene and could not believe they had missed the grave during their search. He personally had passed within twenty yards of the mound and had not spotted it. This rock pile appeared no different from hundreds of others that had been formed naturally.

Behind the technician, Hackworth and Klettlinger eased their way down the side of the mountain, searching for signs of evidence. It took a while, but finally the technician was at the grave, with the detectives close behind. The technician called back, "She's here for sure. I can see her foot." He snapped a photograph. When on top of the site, he took more pictures until he was finished and Hackworth approached alone. Hackworth noticed that the ground was not flat. The mound was nearly at a forty-five degree angle, not at all what he had expected.

Six feet away from the mound, he saw blood. Squatting down, he could see human hair scattered about in a manner that suggested rodents and insects had accessed the body. When he moved closer, he could see cigarette stubs on top of the grave and stopped to consider their meaning. The men had sat on her grave and stubbed out those cigarettes on top of it because they were assholes, that's why. It was clear enough.

Hackworth looked up the hill to the road 125 yards away. The way Logan had told it, Suzanne had been thrown from the ledge, then murdered where she fell. That was the reason the search had concentrated closer to the roadway. But Logan's version was clearly impossible. After the short forty-foot fall, the mountain sloped off at an angle. Suzanne had not been thrown to this location from the road. She had been dragged or tossed here after the first fall.

The rocks used to cover her were surprisingly large. Above the body he looked straight down and through the rocks, quite clearly, he could see the dark blue of Suzanne's new slacks.

He and Klettlinger worked very slowly. From time to time, Hackworth directed the technician to take more photographs. The cigarette butts were placed into plastic bags and marked. Hairs were lifted, bagged, and marked. There were fewer signs of violence, and considerably less blood, than Hackworth had anticipated from Logan's description of the killing. Animals and insects had done their work.

With Klettlinger's help, they lifted rocks from the body. Periodically, they stopped and Hackworth had additional photographs taken. More than one rock was large enough that it required both detectives to lift it. One placed nearly over Suzanne's chest was so huge they grunted and strained to remove it.

When at last the body was uncovered, Suzanne lay cupped by the other rocks as if in a cradle. Hackworth had seen brutal murder before and had witnessed hundreds of autopsies. This devastation was not the worst he had seen, only the most memorable. Though the sight was grotesque, on one side of her face, the beauty of the woman was still evident. It was not difficult to see Suzanne as she had been when she was alive.

He examined her closely and carefully removed the last of the rocks. As nightfall approached, Hackworth had a body bag brought down the slope.

Over the years, Hackworth had come to believe that he was the guardian of the deceased's final hours on earth. No matter how good, or for that matter how evil, the dead had been, he believed it was his duty to preserve their dignity for this last period of their existence. Once a body was turned over to the medical examiner for autopsy, all semblance of humanity vanished.

Working just with his friend Klettlinger, he carefully eased Suzanne into the body bag. This young woman, hardly more than a girl, had arrived raped and brutalized to this place, then had been slain in an especially heinous and depraved way. Her arrival had been in pain and terror; he wanted her departure to be with respect and grace. Once it was closed, it required four detectives well over an hour to carry and pull her up the slope to the road. On the roadway, an ambulance waited and the attendants slipped Suzanne into the rear. With the headlights on now that it was dark, they drove her back to the city and away from the quiet of the desert.

19

That Thursday afternoon, Donna received word that Suzanne's body had been located and she experienced a sense of release. Peter Jr. had been unable to function at work and had just arrived at his parents' house when Donna called with the news. He told Louise, who was standing beside him, and she broke into tears.

Carolyn Peters's father, the Saugus chief of police, drove to where she was teaching and took her home. He said that he had been informed that Suzanne was dead and her body had been recovered. Carolyn began sobbing.

That same Thursday, Connie Parks received a telephone call from Gillies in jail. He told her that what she was reading in the newspaper was not true, he was innocent. He said that Logan did it, but did not tell her exactly what it was Logan had done. Gillies told her Logan had stolen $3,500 of his money from the glove compartment of the Pinto and taken off. He wanted her to believe him.

Connie thought this over, then called the Phoenix Police Department and spoke to one of the homicide detectives. She told him she was a former girlfriend of Gillies's and had seen him and his friend, Mike, the previous Thursday. They told her they had quit their job at Weldon. Then Gillies loaned her $60, which she needed badly. They said they were going to the White Tank Mountains, but she saw them later at the grocery store. She did not know what the police could do with this information, but wanted them to have it.

Throughout Thursday, Suzanne's friends had been arriving from out of state for that evening's memorial service at La Casa de Paz y Bien, and the condominium in Scottsdale was filled with mourners. They had come from Texas, California, and as far away as Ohio.

Pug picked up the telephone and called Joan in Indianapolis. He told the psychic that Suzanne was dead, and that her body had been recovered in the Superstition Mountains off State Highway 88. Two men had kidnapped, raped, and murdered her. They were both in jail.

There was a long silence, and then the single whispered word "Damn."

Jo Ann Heckel and a number of employees from the Burn Treatment Skin Bank drove to their manager's home and watched the news on television before leaving for the service. They saw the helicopters and search teams with the dog on the side of the mountain. Jo Ann recalled that she and Suzanne had hiked in that area and camped at Canyon Lake.

When the time came, they drove to the condominium, where Jo Ann met Donna for the first time. The strain on Donna was obvious, but she was holding herself together for the service. When plans for it had first been made, someone had suggested displaying photographs of Suzanne. One was her smiling, with a scarf in her hair, seated on her bicycle at the youth center. Another showed Suzanne, dressed in shorts and a heavy man's shirt, standing in her hiking gear between two walls of granite. The third was a close-up of her smiling face.

At the Casa, every seat in the rotunda was taken and friends stood along the walls into the hallway. The three photographs had been enlarged and were displayed in front by the stained-glass wall. Someone had thought to gather desert flowers, which Suzanne had loved, and had decorated the altar with them.

Donna told those attending that Suzanne would have wanted this to be a happy occasion. "Suz would not have wanted people sitting and crying," she told them. They were to make this a celebration of life.

The Franciscan Father spoke of life and of loving, of the memory of Suz. Sounds of sobbing marked his every pause. Following the homily, friends played James Taylor's "You Can Close Your Eyes."

Then in prayer:

Blessed are You, Lord of Life, who gave us Suzanne as a gift.
Blessed are You, Lord of Life, who has called Suzanne from
    this life to yourself.

Pug rose and passionately read "Come On, Let's Live!" by Everett Wentworth Hill. Then slides of Suzanne backpacking, laughing and playing were shown as the Judy Collins version of "In My Life" was played.

A friend rose to read a letter Peter Jr. had written for them. "I am not the one to tell any of you how to deal with this event," he wrote, "but I hope you will consider what I have to say. I would like this gathering, as would my family, to be a celebration. Suzie loved life. . . . She will always be with me in my mind. I hope that each of you can find some comfort in the fact that as long as you keep the memories of her that you have, whether it is a little sister, or as a friend, she will never be gone from our lives. The sum total of anyone is the memories and the friends. . . . My family and I want to thank everyone for all that you have done for Suzie."

When the service ended, Willie Nelson's high-pitched, nasal voice filled the rotunda as he sang "On the Road Again." It was the song by which many of them remembered Suzanne. Pug and others had wanted to end the service on a positive note. Instead, the cheery song of the traveler brought Suzanne's personality back, and those who had stopped crying were suddenly overcome with emotion. The mourners in the line were sobbing as they extended sympathy to Donna and filed from the room.

When Donna returned to the condominium, Suzanne's friends were gathered for an open house to console one another. Hackworth had already arrived and was sitting at the bar beside the kitchen. Donna joined him.

"As we told you," he said gently, "we have found a woman's body. She had some jewelry on her. Can you describe your sister's for us?"

She told him the pieces she knew Suzanne owned. The ones the police had found were a match.

Hackworth then described a birthmark on the leg of the body they had located, and other specific physical features. They were all matches for Suzanne.

"Do I have to identify her?" Donna asked, terrified that she might be required to go to the mortuary and see Suzanne's body.

"No," Hackworth said, "but we want you to be comfortable this is your sister."

Donna said she was satisfied in light of all that had happened, the jewelry and identifying physical features. When the detective left, the family and friends turned to the task of mourning.

Hackworth went home and slept for the first time in seventy-two hours.

Early Friday, Deputy Chief Medical Examiner Thomas B. Jarvis began the autopsy of Suzanne Rossetti. Also present were Jeff Hotham and Jack Hackworth. Until now, Hotham had been responsible for the prosecution of thirteen homicides. During his military service he had seen the bodies of men killed in combat. From that experience and previous autopsies, he believed he had developed a certain measure of toughness against the sight of violent death. Hotham was completely unprepared when the body bag was unzipped. He had never before seen a body in such a state and was shocked. Rising from the open body bag was the cloying smell of death.

The procedure called for the medical examiner to dictate his notes as he worked. Certain routine samples were always taken for testing. Whenever the doctor found something that appeared related to the death, it was called to the attention of the case agent. Dr. Jarvis and Hackworth worked as a practiced team and requested what additional samples and photographs should be taken.

The medical examiner noted the damage caused by animals done to Suzanne, established the presence of semen in her vagina and the absence of alcohol in her blood, and recorded the various lacerations, cuts, and concussions she had suffered. An overhead shot was taken of her chest because a line of blood ran between her breasts. This indicated she had stood, or been stood, erect after she was bleeding from the head.

Suzanne was rolled onto her side and a full-length photograph

taken of her. She looked as if she were resting, and even with the
visible bruising, she had the appearance of a fit and lovely woman,
except for her demolished head. All of the brutality that night, all of
the savagery, had been directed there—to smash her life.

It is the nature of medical examiners never to acknowledge a
mistake and as a consequence, they rarely commit themselves to an
opinion until they are certain beyond any doubt. Because of that,
Hotham and Hackworth were stunned when Jarvis dictated with pre-
cision that Suzanne Rossetti had died some time *after* she had been
buried.

Hackworth considered the implications of this determination.
While those bastards had covered her with rocks, she was still alive.
Only after she had been buried had Suzanne finally choked to death
in her own blood. Hotham could tell that Hackworth was as shaken
as he was by this revelation.

When the autopsy ended after two hours, Hotham was struggling
to control the hatred he felt for the killers. As he stepped out into
the air of the city and tried to clear his lungs of the smell of Suzanne's
death, he was also overwhelmed by a sense of utter sadness.

Following the autopsy, Hackworth returned to the condominium
accompanied by two identification technicians. Donna was very angry
and said she just could not believe that anyone could do something
like this. Suzanne had done nothing wrong; this should not have
happened to her.

"Why are they allowed to be alive?" she demanded.

"There is nothing we can do about that," Hackworth said. "At
least two more are off the streets. You've got to realize these are not
human beings we are dealing with," he said emphatically. "This is
the scum of the earth. They don't think like you and me. They are
not like us, and there is no logical way you can perceive what goes
on in their minds."

Hackworth asked to take fingerprints from the condominium.
She agreed, but then immediately became irritated at the request. She
had not been in Phoenix when the Tempe police officers dusted
previously.

"Where were you days ago?" she wanted to know. There had
been as many as fifty people at a time in the condominium, upwards
of one hundred had been in and out, what could they expect to find
at this late date?

He explained it was necessary, there were places to check that had probably not been contaminated. He asked everyone to remain downstairs while the bedrooms and bathroom were checked. In the midst of the investigation there had been no time to do this thoroughly. Hackworth knew that Tempe police had dusted in the most likely areas with no results.

Donna left for Saugus late Saturday with Robert, arriving Sunday morning. She did not know how she could have survived this ordeal without him. When she arrived home, her family asked her to tell them everything that had taken place in Arizona. As she talked, all of them were crying. Getting through this was the worst part of the ordeal.

Pug, Eric Gregan, Jo Ann Heckel, and other friends decided to attend the funeral. They flew to Saugus on Sunday, and were invited to stay at the Rossetti home. By coincidence, they took the flight that transported Suzanne's casket.

The blue casket was placed in the first room on the right of the main entrance to the funeral home, which was located just around the corner from the Rossetti residence. The Saugus florist had located desert flowers and skeleton cacti, which adorned the top of the casket. Pug had brought the three enlarged photographs used at the memorial service.

Before the start of the wake, Donna walked to the funeral home and went alone into the room that held her sister. She stood beside the casket for a time with her thoughts. She wished it had been she who had died; it would not have been so bad. If she could, she thought, she would trade places with Suzanne in an instant. She did not think her loss would be so devastating for the family.

Freddie Quinlan picked up Carolyn Peters from the school where she taught. They arrived at 2:00 P.M., since Carolyn also wanted some time ahead of the crowds. Freddie was beside himself with grief and was clutching her hand as they went into the funeral home.

Shortly before 7:00 P.M., Peter, Louise, and Peter Jr. went to the funeral home. Donna's father had always been the rock of the family, the man who remained calm and saw to it that matters were taken care of. Donna felt she had to be strong for him now and did not know if she could manage it. "Oh, Suz," she prayed as she stood beside her father, "help me through this."

The family gathered at the casket, and the line of mourners began to enter. The town of Saugus had never witnessed such an occasion. It was snowing that night, a steady fall of heavy white flakes against the black sky. The line extended down the street, then continued to grow until it wrapped around the block.

At 10:00 P.M., the wake ended. The family was exhausted and numbed from the experience, and somehow that night passed.

In Phoenix, Hotham's first hurdle was the grand jury. In Maricopa County each grand jury was taken from the voter rolls, was convened for three months, and met twice a week for daylong sessions. There were two prosecutors assigned to present cases, but those with the Major Felony Bureau made their own presentations. On the second day of Suzanne's wake, February 10, 1981, Hotham had scheduled one hour for his presentation. Hackworth was his only witness.

The mood in the grand jury chamber was somber and dignified. After an indictment, a transcript of the proceedings was provided to the defense counsel. He had the right to argue that the prosecutor had abused his discretion with the grand jury, and judges were receptive to such arguments. As a consequence, prosecutors in Arizona tended not to engage in the types of abusive practices for which the grand jury system elsewhere was sometimes known.

Hotham presented a straightforward case through Hackworth's testimony. There were no questions from the grand jury, and they were finished within the hour. The jury handed up indictments against both Logan and Gillies that afternoon by unanimous vote. The pair were indicted for first-degree murder, sexual assault, kidnapping, aggravated robbery, and first-degree computer fraud.

Suzanne had been dead for thirteen days.

The second day of the wake in Saugus began at 2:00 in the afternoon and ran until 10:00 P.M. Again the family stood and received the condolences of their friends. When Peter learned that a television station would cover the funeral, he asked them not to and they complied.

The line at the funeral home extended nearly to the Cliftondale Square rotary. The quiet crowd stood in the intermittent snow and shuffled slowly toward the building. Inside, the family members spelled one another with short periods of rest at home.

The family wanted something written by Suzanne on the funeral program. In her personal journal, scrawled in her hand, occupying a single page to itself, they found these words, "It's nice to be important, but it's more important to be nice." It characterized Suzanne perfectly and was placed in the program, along with a verse from Isaiah, "See! I will not forget you. . . . I have carved you in the palm of my hand."

Wednesday morning, the casket was taken by the family to St. Margaret's for the funeral service. A priest from Suzanne's childhood had come to help officiate. Father Creed returned from his new parish as well. Altogether five priests, each of whom had known Suzanne, jointly conducted the service.

Debby Crisafulli was in her ninth month of pregnancy, and her family had expressed concern about her attending the service. Eric Gregan, who was overcome with grief, filled the church with his loud sobbing as the gentle strains of the Ave Maria were sung. Carolyn Peters managed to hold her composure until Father Creed, in his homily, referred to "Suz," then she broke into tears. Their religion teacher from high school rose to sing, and as her clear voice filled the church with the words from "In My Life," Freddie, who was clutching Carolyn's hand, experienced it as an unexpected and very personal message. Carolyn was sobbing and tears streamed down Freddie's face.

So many were crammed into the church that a crowd stood outside, and others were forced to sit in cars. The entire Saugus City Police Department was present for traffic control, and Chief Peters had arranged for the state police to man their headquarters in the absence of the usual force. The central portion of Saugus was closed, and cars were double-parked, allowing just a single lane down the middle of the street for the procession.

The snow fell sporadically. The road was slush and the ground soggy. From St. Margaret's, the casket was borne to the hearse. A lone police car, its red light flashing overhead with a steady click, led the solemn procession around the block, then along the two-mile road to the Riverside Cemetery.

As the car in which Carolyn rode turned the corner, she saw a policeman who had known her and Suzanne since they were children standing in the snow in his heavy coat, directing the funeral cortege. She was struck by the sight of the tears that glistened on his cheeks as the car passed.

When the hearse turned into the graveyard, the last car had yet to leave St. Margaret's. People gathered in a massive crowd that filled the aged cemetery as the final words were pronounced over the coffin. Peter Sr. suddenly threw himself on the casket, sobbing. Louise,

Donna, and Peter Jr. lovingly lifted him away, then the coffin was slowly lowered into the grave. Each member of the family tossed a single crimson rose after it.

And finally, it was done. The crowd moved slowly back to their cars, and the Rossetti family returned home and began the task of living again.

20

Deputy Public Defender Richard Mesh was no novice. He was so good and so experienced, it was unlikely an accused criminal could have hired better counsel.

During the last two years, Mesh had tried twenty-four cases. Two trials ended in hung juries. Three cases were dismissed on legal issues he raised, and successfully argued once the jury was selected. One defendant was found guilty of a lesser offense. Another client who was found guilty had his verdict reversed on appeal and was acquitted following the second trial. Twelve times Mesh had emerged with outright acquittals for the defendants.

Only five of his clients were convicted.

Never had a client of his been sentenced to death. Not without reason had he earned a reputation among his peers for excellence, and because of that Hotham was preparing his case with special diligence.

Mesh had practiced law since 1969. For two years, he had been a prosecuting attorney with Maricopa County, and in fifteen trials had won fourteen convictions. In the other case, the jury had found the defendant mentally incompetent. Mesh switched to the Public Defender's office for six months, expecting to go into private practice from there. Instead, he was recruited to teach trial practice at the Arizona State University Law School, then, in 1976, he returned to the Public Defender's office. He was in private practice for two years, and in May 1980, rejoined the Public Defender's office.

Mesh was six feet tall, and weighed 185 pounds; he had dark hair and wore metal-rimmed glasses. He was a flamboyant, loquacious litigator with a relish for the combat of trial. He spoke in even, measured tones.

He was one of the senior public defenders and maintained under his wing an entourage of devoted fledgling lawyers. Within the office, the major cases were staffed and argued. It was valuable experience for the young attorneys as Mesh and the two other most successful defenders explained their approaches and demonstrated how to win.

When Mesh was assigned a new murder case, there was a sense of excitement among the troops. Mesh was just the man to show a newcomer how to secure an acquittal in a seemingly hopeless case.

"It's you against the world," he often reminded the other lawyers, "and sometimes your client works with you."

In a killing, he taught, there were many levels of guilt, from Murder One to involuntary manslaughter. If your client is guilty, of what is he guilty? Victory is measured by more than acquittals.

"It is a hard job," Mesh reminded the new lawyers. There were prosecutors who recognized the job the public defender had to do, like Hotham who was a gentleman and a man of his word. Others could not believe any decent person would represent those charged with horrible crimes, and treated defense counsel accordingly.

The defenders knew that some clients, and their acts, were despicable, but it was still their responsibility to defend them. They could accept the accused's story, or, once in a great while, believe it. Believing in a client was a luxury to be relished when it crossed one's path.

Defendants intuitively sensed this. A public defender faced the two-pronged reasoning of the guilty client charged with a heinous crime: First, the accused did not think his appointed lawyer could defend him without believing him innocent, so he lied. Second, the accused believed that if his lawyer thought he had committed horrible deeds, he would never act to get him off, so he lied.

From this jailhouse logic came the public defender's creed: "A client is someone who lies to his lawyer, and tells the truth to everyone else."

It was, Mesh taught his flock, the role of the defender to hold the State to its constitutional responsibility of providing the accused with a fair trial. Philosophically, Mesh considered himself to be the fail-safe man, the one individual standing between a reprehensible client who is guaranteed the presumption of innocence, and the injustice of an improper prosecution. He did not have to like his defendants—they were not his personal friends—but he did have to respect the process, and their right to it.

Personally, from what Mesh knew of the case at this point, he considered Hotham's offer to be a hell of a deal and wished Gillies would accept it. Too often, by the time a client understood what he was facing, the opportunity for cutting a deal had passed and Mesh feared that might be the situation here. Still, he was an optimist and knew the trial, if it ever took place, was months away.

The murder case of Jesse James Gillies and Michael David Logan, officially identified as CR117615, was assigned to Maricopa County Superior Court Judge Stephen H. Scott. Scott was that rarity in Phoenix, a native, and had served as a United States attorney in the Organized Crime and Racketeering Section before going into private practice in 1973. Six years later, he was appointed to the bench.

Scott was known as a judges' judge. He was measured and scrupulously evenhanded in his dealings with the attorneys who appeared before him. Both Hotham and Mesh had argued in his court countless times. They had high regard for him, and Scott held them in esteem as well. This was a busy year for the judges in Maricopa County, and Scott was disposed to move cases along in order to prevent the accumulation of a backlog. Arizona's Speedy Trial Act called for early trial of the accused, especially if he was incarcerated.

Scott had just been transferred from the civil to the criminal court calendar, and this would be his first murder trial.

An inmate at the county jail named Ronald Winkle, who was pending extradition to Florida, contacted the Public Defender's office, saying he had information in which they might be interested. An investigator interviewed him on February 11.

Winkle said that he had been Logan's cellmate for two or three days, and they had discussed his case while they were together. He said Logan had told him that when he helped the lady break into her car, Gillies had knocked her purse over and Logan had spotted a thick wad of money in it. Logan said to himself that somehow he was going to get his hands on that money.

She offered them a ride and, by the time they reached the golf course, she was demonstrating a liking for Gillies, which made Logan jealous. Then Gillies suddenly raped her, tied her up, and they drove to her condominium.

The second time Logan told the story, it came out another way, according to Winkle. The two had met the lady, helped her out, and she had bought them beer. She took a liking to Gillies, and they went to her condominium to party. Gillies and the lady went upstairs and Logan fell asleep.

The next morning, she wanted to cook them a meal but did not have food. Logan left with her, drove to the desert, bashed her head in with rocks, and threw her off a cliff. He stole her belongings, then went to the condominium, where he told Gillies she was searching for work. But later, he admitted to Gillies he had killed the lady. They used her ATM card to take $250 a day from her bank account.

Winkle claimed that in addition to these two versions of the events, Logan had talked in his sleep. He had muttered that Gillies had nothing to do with the killing, that he did not even know the location of the body.

The investigator prepared a report of the interview and forwarded it to Mesh.

On February 26, Mesh and Hotham appeared before Judge Scott to argue Mesh's motion to have Ronald Winkle deposed prior to his extradition. Mesh wanted to preserve Winkle's testimony, since he would likely be out of state by the time of Gillies's trial. Scott ruled that if and when Mesh could demonstrate that Winkle would not be available for the trial, and that his testimony was relevant, they would consider a deposition. In the meantime, the motion was denied.

On March 8, 1981, Connie Parks called the Phoenix homicide detail once again and spoke to Hackworth. She related her previous story, but added that she believed that the $60 Gillies gave her was money he had stolen from that dead woman.

She recalled that the two men had said something that made sense only after Connie read of the murder. Gillies had turned to Logan and said, "Didn't we have a good time and a lot of fun in the Superstition Mountains?" He had laughed like it was a joke or something. Logan had replied, "Yes, we did."

She reported that Gillies had telephoned her twice and written twice since his arrest. He claimed that a former girlfriend was traveling to Phoenix to hire a lawyer, and would sue the state for $10 million for defaming him. When Connie asked Gillies about the charges, he told her that he had committed everything reported in the papers, except that he did not kill the lady. Logan had done that alone.

Hackworth asked if she would testify in court to what she had just told him, and Connie said she would. He also advised her to hang on to those two letters.

A few weeks following Logan's arrest, Rhonda's sister, Karen, visited him in jail. He expected a friendly, even sympathetic, talk, but instead she shouted at him. She reminded him that when she had asked where his money came from, he looked her in the eye and said his grandfather had died. Instead, he had murdered a woman for it! She was enraged that he would lie to her; then she abruptly ended the visit.

Logan was surprised at her reaction. Here he was accused of murder and she was offended because he had lied. It made no sense.

Once Gillies and Logan were indicted, Hotham prepared for their joint trial. Since the Gillies arrest, two of the wranglers had moved from Weldon, and Hotham had difficulty locating them. He found one working at a dude ranch near Wickenburg. On March 11, Hotham had them brought in for a series of interviews, and when he was finished, sat in while they were interviewed by Mesh.

Hotham lived in Arizona, but until now his dealings had always been with urbanites. This was his first experience with cowboys and he found it foreign territory. None of the four was especially willing to cooperate, none was particularly bright, and none was well educated. Two of the men were already experiencing difficulty remembering what they had heard originally, as opposed to what they heard from one another. One of the men embellished his story, and the last lied outright.

Hotham covered the same territory with each of them, matching what they were saying now with their earlier statements in the police reports. At least one was required to take the witness stand and relate what he had heard and seen in a convincing manner.

None of the four had the remotest concept of the judicial system, or what was taking place. They were the quintessential good ol' boys, and when Hotham's telephone rang or someone came into his office, whichever wrangler he was interviewing would sit in his chair, gawking and fidgeting, smelling of hay and horses.

There was also an undercurrent that Hotham detected. These wranglers were afraid of Logan and Gillies.

Hotham completed his interviews wondering if even one man was up to the task of testifying at the trial. Then it was Mesh's turn with the wranglers. He had spent enough time with Gillies to know that selling his winning personality to the jury was not an option. Mesh also matched the wranglers' present statements against what the police noted the night of the arrest. With some discrepancies, they told essentially the same story. The picture he formed of the wranglers was very different from that of Hotham.

These men had his client "holding court" up in the loft, and confessing to murder. Even worse, Gillies had told two of the wranglers independently before telling the group. None of the men vacillated on his story, and each of their versions was fundamentally the same as the others'. At least, two of the men at Weldon had gone to the police.

Mesh pictured Hotham placing each cowboy on the stand in turn to repeat the events of the murder as described to them by Gillies, while a horrified jury hung on every word. These men were the salt of the earth, with their cowboy morality and homespun sense of justice. How could a jury not believe them?

More than one wrangler told Mesh that as long as he believed Gillies was wanted for traffic tickets, or for stealing a car, they were prepared to help shield him from the police. But killing a lady? "That ain't right," one said, speaking for them all. Mesh found their accounts devastating. "I think," he said to himself, "I have an uphill battle this time."

The March 23, 1981, edition of Time magazine featured "The Curse of Crime in America" as its cover story. The article focused on several particularly horrible murders around the country. The first was entitled "Brutality in Phoenix," an account of the killing of Suzanne Rossetti.

Hotham interviewed Schneider alone, a few weeks after he talked to the wranglers. The tall cowboy with his narrow hips, bowed legs, boots, western shirt, and huge black cowboy hat, was stereotypical.

His moustache had blossomed, and Schneider had taken to twisting the ends with wax.

Unlike his former employees, Schneider was eager to talk and regaled Hotham with stories of his cleverness and bravery. Hotham would put the interview back on track, but soon Schneider would be off on another tangent.

The most frustrating aspect of the interview was that Schneider was a bright man, with an excellent recall of events, and he was potentially an outstanding witness. Hotham believed most of the other stories he was telling had been manufactured, or embellished, for Schneider's ego, but when he spoke of Logan, and especially about what Gillies had said to him, he related the same facts, the same way, each time. Clearly, he was deeply offended by their crime, and was interested in justice taking place.

So what was it to be? Inarticulate wranglers unable to recall clearly what had taken place, or Schneider, apparently eager for the limelight, a runaway witness who could blurt almost anything in court to look and feel important? Or a confusing mix of all of them?

Logan had languished in jail since Suzanne's body had been located, and was increasingly angry with himself for not leaving immediately after the murder. Lying on his bunk in the county jail, he had long hours to consider Gillies, and was coming to hate him. Clearly, his partner had turned him over to the police, otherwise Logan would already be in Australia.

Logan reasoned they would want him to testify against Gillies. As much as he hated Gillies, he despised snitches even more, and the last thing he wanted to take with him to prison was a reputation as a snitch.

Logan knew the moment he was arrested what had happened, and he understood then it was to be him or Gillies, which was why he had helped the police find the body. If anybody received a break, it was going to be Logan, and not Gillies.

On April 15, Hotham received an urgent telephone call from Schneider, who said he had been accosted by friends of Logan. Hotham informed Hackworth, who went to interview him. Schneider told Hackworth he had been at a truck stop on the Black Canyon Freeway at 2:00 A.M. the day before. Three men had approached him in a hostile manner, one aggressively brandishing a stick. The man said, "Logan is my brother. You're an asshole to do what you did." Not intimidated, Schneider walked up to the man and took away his weapon. Then he slapped him, and the men took off.

When Hackworth asked what kind of stick this had been, Schneider did not know. Was it a stick or a pipe? the detective asked. Schneider was not certain if it was either. He could not even provide the most elementary description of their vehicle.

Hackworth concluded there was nothing to this story, that Schneider was looking for more attention. Two months earlier, a local newspaper columnist had written a gratuitous piece concerning Schneider's participation in Gillies's capture. Hackworth believed the story of Schneider's confrontation at the truck stop was a flimsy attempt to see his name in print again.

In dealing with a defendant, Mesh would present the State's case and solicit a response. He would then tell his client how the State would counterattack. Often, his role was to lead the client into accepting a plea agreement that was in his best interest. These were not always pleasant encounters.

So Mesh was not surprised when, on May 2, 1981, he found himself in court with Hotham, responding to a request from Gillies that he be assigned new counsel. When Judge Scott asked if Gillies had anything to say about why he wanted another lawyer, Gillies replied, "No sir, just from the things I have discussed with my lawyer, I feel like my PD prosecutor here is conspiring against me."

Mesh informed the court of the frequency of his visits with Gillies, often two or three times a week, and of the need to discuss the possible resolution of the case. Perhaps Gillies thought collusion was occurring between him and Hotham. He pointed out that the State would be seeking the death penalty, and "I suspect Mr. Gillies might not like the type of information I am relating to him."

Mesh pointed out that the date of Gillies's request was one day after he had met with him to discuss the most recent developments in his case. "That leads me to believe that my client is dissatisfied with the things I am relating to him in my professional judgment."

Gillies's request was denied.

One of the many street lawyers, as they were known, who took court-appointed cases was initially assigned to Logan. After a few weeks, he withdrew, and James Kemper assumed the case. Kemper had worked as a deputy public defender from 1969 until 1973, and then went into a private practice. After receiving Logan's appointment, he visited his new client in the downtown county jail.

On its surface, the case against Logan was formidable. He had been arrested in possession of Suzanne's ATM card, been photographed using the card, been observed driving her car, had made a confession, and led the police to her body. His guilt was apparent, and from Kemper's first look at the evidence, it appeared his client was a likely candidate for the death penalty.

The only good news was that Logan had helped find the victim's body, which at least made him appear remorseful. As it was, the best Kemper could wish was to spare Logan execution. It was apparent Logan recognized the seriousness of his predicament.

When the evidence was as damning as this, Kemper searched for leverage, a weakness in the case. Sometimes leverage came from interviews with the witnesses, sometimes it never came at all. This time, it came when he read Hackworth's police report.

21

In May, Peter and Louise flew to Arizona to retrieve Suzanne's possessions, and to discover for themselves what had befallen her. No parent is ever prepared for the loss of a child, but when Peter and Louise had first learned that Suzanne was mountain climbing, and fully understood the risks she was taking, they had come to terms with her possible death. If Peter had received a telephone call informing him that his baby had been killed while climbing, he could have accepted that. The Rossettis could even have accepted her death in a car accident, or by illness. Those tragedies had happened to others they had known and only good fortune had spared them.

But to lose a daughter to murder? That was incomprehensible. Who could imagine such a nightmare happening to one of their children?

In the months since Suzanne's death, her parents each had had many sleepless nights. More than once, Peter had awakened in the dead of night to hear Louise quietly crying beside him. They rarely mentioned the tragedy, and worked to move on with what remained of their lives. They hoped this trip to Arizona would provide them with answers to their many questions.

The Time magazine cover story had generated a fresh wave of sympathy calls just at the time when the couple was learning to cope with their loss. Then a few weeks later, one of the national crime magazines that specialized in gruesome murders, featured the crime, complete with photographs of Suzanne's body. The piece had been filled with inaccuracies and innuendo about Suzanne's possible relationship with the two men.

In Phoenix, the Rossettis met with Hotham at his office. He was in the middle of an exhausting trial and could barely spare a few minutes to see them. He told them what he could, that both men were still in custody and scheduled for trial, that he believed he had a good case, and was hoping for the best. Peter and Louise were not impressed.

They met Hackworth next and found him even less forthcoming. At one point, when he moved his file, the mug shots of Gillies and Logan fell onto the floor.

"That's the man who drove Suzanne's car!" Louise said, staring at Logan's photograph.

They picked up Suzanne's personal belongings from Hackworth, then went to meet others who were involved in the case. At Weldon they met with Schneider, who was very apologetic over what had taken place and spoke at great length about what he had seen and heard. He told them that Logan had arrived at Weldon with a load of horses from Michigan. According to Schneider, Gillies and Logan had caused other kinds of trouble as well.

They had their good points though. One time, according to Schneider, Logan had talked to him about founding a western Boys' Town in Arizona to help rehabilitate wayward youths. The Rossettis thanked him for his time.

They drove to Tempe and spoke to Sarah Kokat. She told them what she knew, and said of Gillies and Logan, "They looked horrible."

Peter and Louise had no luck finding the U-Totem clerk. The company sent them to the wrong store repeatedly, and by the time they finished packing Suzanne's personal effects, they still had not spoken with him.

They returned to Saugus, satisfied they had made the effort, grateful to Schneider and Sarah Kokat for their time, and troubled by the conduct of the police and the prosecutor.

For one court hearing, Logan and Gillies were transported from the jail at different times, by different detention officers. Contrary to accepted practice, the men were placed in the same holding cell in the Superior Court building. No sooner had the officers left them alone than a ruckus erupted, although neither man was able to do much damage, with their hands handcuffed to their waists, and their ankles in shackles. The officers broke the men apart and moved one of them to another cell.

Following the devastating interviews with the wranglers and Schneider, Mesh decided his best route lay in testing Gillies for mental competency, known in Arizona as a Rule 11 motion. He was not certain any psychiatrist would find his client unfit for trial, but there was always that possibility, and even if Gillies were subsequently convicted, the information from the report would be helpful to Judge Scott. It had to be developed at some point, so why not now?

Such motions were not routinely granted, and it was up to Mesh to demonstrate adequate cause for it. He prepared a Rule 11 motion in which he suggested that his client may have been committed when he was a teenager, that the Arizona Department of Corrections had performed a previous evaluation on him as part of its intake process, that there was likely a long history of alcohol and drug use which may have caused a personality change, and, finally, that Gillies was a heavy drinker.

The motion was argued on May 28. Judge Scott told Mesh there were simply no facts to support such an order and denied the motion.

Mesh contacted Yolanda Gillies in San Francisco, telling her he required more information on her son if he was to defend him properly. He asked that she write as forthcoming a letter as possible, describing Gillies's upbringing.

James Kemper met with Hotham to discuss a plea agreement for Logan. At one point, Kemper suggested a reduced sentence if Logan would testify against Gillies. Hotham said he would consider that, but then Kemper reported back that testifying was not acceptable to Logan.

Hotham had told Mesh in February that if Gillies would help find the body and if Mesh could convince him that Gillies had not held the rock that killed Suzanne, he would be willing to discuss plea-bargaining the death sentence. At the time of the discussion, Logan did not have legal representation and could not be approached by Hotham. He had told Hackworth what he was willing to do, and that offer was available to either man.

During his questioning, Hackworth made no promises to Logan in exchange for his help, but Hotham felt at the least a moral obligation to honor his tacit offer, since it had been available to either man.

Kemper was not so certain; no offer for his client had been extended to him. At this meeting, he read Hackworth's police report and pointed out that Logan had agreed to talk to Hackworth and had answered his questions. Logan told the detective that Gillies might have had something to do with the death, but that he did not.

Then, Logan said he did not think he wanted to answer any more questions.

It was at that point, Kemper argued, that his client invoked his right to remain silent. And what did the officer do? He went out, poured coffee, came back in, and told his man that he did not think he was very compassionate for not considering the feelings of the dead woman's family. True, he had not asked any additional questions about the murder, but he had solicited Logan's assistance in locating the body, and his client had agreed.

That should never have happened. Logan had the right to remain silent, and having apparently expressed his desire, Hackworth should not have engaged him in conversation again. Kemper reached over and pointed to the place in the police report where Logan said he did not want to talk any longer. Nothing Logan had done, nor any evidence obtained thereafter, was admissible, in his opinion. Kemper wanted leverage, and there it was.

Hotham found much of Kemper's argument persuasive, and he did not want a reversal on appeal. His research indicated that in death penalty cases, many appellate courts would reverse, finding a Miranda violation. He considered that he had offered to give up the death penalty to the defendant who helped find Suzanne's body, and Logan had done so. Even if Hotham did not drop the death penalty, and Logan were convicted in trial, his assistance in finding the body would very likely spare him the gas chamber anyway.

The decision made, the men negotiated the other charges against Logan.

Before Yolanda's letter arrived, Mesh received a telephone call from Kemper. Because each of their clients was accusing the other of the actual killing, they had been preparing their cases without consultation. Kemper informed Mesh that Logan was entering a plea that did not call for him to testify against Gillies.

When Yolanda's two-and-a-half-page, single-spaced, typed letter arrived, it staggered Mesh. In all his years, he had never before read such a document. It began, "Jesse has displayed psychiatric disorders since the age of one." She then recounted in considerable detail his years of antisocial behavior, and her own inability to cope. There, outlined by the woman who had borne this man, was a life out of control.

The mother's plea for her son concluded, "It is of course my fault he did [not] receive psychiatric treatment as a child and though I know if he is guilty he should be put in an institution for the criminally insane for many years of extensive treatment. I do not believe he should die because he is very sick."

Mesh was able to obtain the Department of Corrections evaluation prepared on Gillies the previous fall. With that, and the mother's letter, he prepared a second Rule 11 motion. Judge Scott granted the motion and ordered evaluations.

Gillies refused to meet with the psychologist when he learned he was black. After Mesh assured the court that his client would cooperate, Gillies was provided a second opportunity to be evaluated. When neither the psychological nor psychiatric report concluded that Gillies met the legal requirement for mental incompetence, Hotham was satisfied. The reports' findings would be of use to the State when it came time to sentence Gillies.

Mesh had not expected to win this maneuver and now turned to his basic dilemma: finding some semblance of a defense.

Following his testimony before the grand jury, Hackworth's primary involvement in the case was ended. As murder investigations went, this one had not been especially difficult; it was the other aspects of the case that were disturbing.

Hackworth had been very impressed with Donna, particularly when she told him how she and her sister had decided they would conduct themselves if they were ever raped. It was clear to Hackworth that Suzanne had responded as she said she would to survive. Logan had suggested at one time that Suzanne had given the two men no trouble, had done everything they told her to do, yet they had killed her anyway.

Hackworth thought, here this woman had done everything she could to be kind to these assholes before her abduction, and had done what she was told afterward, and these shitheads had taken advantage of her and killed her when it wasn't even necessary. He had worked many homicides, but this had been the most cold-blooded of them. These men had driven for a long distance into the mountains to kill

Suzanne, knowing the whole way what they were going to do. They could have left her behind, or kicked her out of the car anytime. Hell, Logan was used to being on the run, what was this to him? But they had mistreated her until they killed her in a sloppy and godawful way. Each guy was trying to be more macho than the other, wanted to show how tough he could be.

Hackworth considered the two killers. Gillies struck him as a creep out to make a name for himself. Why else would he have talked about what he had done? "He wanted to be a star," Hackworth thought. "He wanted to be big time." And killing that woman had been his way of doing it.

There was something else about Gillies; he never once claimed Hackworth had the wrong man. Hackworth had given him his chance when he asked him to help find the body, and Gillies had said, "Fuck you, Hackworth!"

"Well," Hackworth thought, "piss on him."

And here was Logan, the con, smarter than Gillies by a long shot, egging Gillies on, all the while afraid of him. "Logan was a pussy," Hackworth thought, and basically an asshole. Once he was arrested, Logan understood the system, he had been around it many times, and had done what he believed would get him a better deal.

Logan may have helped them find the body, but he was never forthcoming about the whole story. He behaved as if he knew this was going to make him look good. It was disgusting.

Hackworth's final conclusion was the one he had formed early on, these men killed Suzanne because they wanted to. Neither of them felt the slightest remorse for what they had done, they weren't sorry in the least, except for getting caught, and they were sorry as hell over that.

When Hackworth heard that Logan was going to receive life in prison instead of the death penalty, he accepted it as the way of the system and was not surprised.

On August 3, a day as hot as the morning had been cold when Suzanne was murdered six months earlier, Logan stood before Judge Scott to enter a plea as agreed between Kemper and Hotham. The agreement was a typed form that Logan had initialed and signed.

Mesh attended to hear what Logan would say. It was possible, though unlikely, that he would take the whole blame himself and let Gillies go free.

Logan admitted that he had used the name of George Richardson and claimed to have had two years of college. Judge Scott read him the various charges to which he would be pleading. "Therefore," the judge said, "you understand that if your pleas of guilty are accepted, you will be sentenced to the Arizona State Prison on each and all of the five counts to which you are pleading guilty?"

"Yes, sir," Logan replied.

"Are you now on probation or parole for any other offense?"

"No, I am not. I am a fugitive from Michigan."

"You are not on probation, not on parole at this time?"

"No."

"What I said is correct?"

"Yes, it's correct." If Logan was on either probation or parole, the judge had another set of waivers he was required to read to him.

"In Count One you are charged with the crime of kidnapping, as a class-two felony. How do you plead to Count One?"

"Guilty."

"In Count Two you are charged with the crime of sexual assault, a class-two felony. How do you plead to Count Two?"

"Guilty."

"In Count Three you are charged with the crime of aggravated robbery, a class-three felony. How do you plead to Count Three?"

"Guilty."

"In Count Four you are charged with the crime of first-degree murder, a class-one felony. How do you plead to Count Four?"

"Guilty."

"In Count Five you are charged with the crime of first-degree computer fraud, a class-three felony. How do you plead to Count Five?"

"Guilty."

Judge Scott instructed Logan to examine the plea agreement, and confirm that his signature and initials were on it. He reminded him of the constitutional rights he was giving up, including the right to a trial by a jury of his peers, the right to remain silent, the right to be represented by counsel during a trial, the right to compel witnesses, and to testify in his defense if he so wished. He then secured Logan's waiver of these rights.

Judge Scott read into the record the terms of the plea agreement, then moved to establishing a factual basis for each count. In years past, once criminals were in prison, they often argued their innocence and disputed the plea entered by their lawyers. Now defendants were required to state in their own words what they had done, at least enough to establish a basis in fact for the charge. If Logan could not, or would not do so, the plea agreement would be withdrawn and Logan would go to trial.

Logan said that Gillies had tied Suzanne up and denied that he helped him. He said that he and Gillies had discussed taking her money before speaking to her. He said that Gillies had struck Suzanne in the head, opened the door, pushed her out, and then raped her and put her into the Pinto. He denied they had discussed raping her beforehand.

Hotham questioned Logan because Hackworth's report said that Logan acknowledged putting Suzanne into the rear of the car. Logan denied it before Judge Scott.

Moving on, Judge Scott said, "On January 28, 1981, did you have sexual intercourse with her?"

"Yeah, I did."

"Did you actually insert your penis in her vagina?"

"No, I didn't," Logan said.

"What did you do to engage in sexual intercourse?"

"Well, I just did it."

"What did you do?"

"I didn't do nothing. I got the disease called multiple sclerosis and I can't."

"Just a moment ago you told me you had sexual intercourse. What did you mean?"

"I tried."

As he listened to this exchange, Hotham was not surprised in the least. The worst crime for which one could go to prison was child molesting, the second worst was rape. Many times in the past, he had heard men freely admit to murdering someone, robbing them, assaulting them, only to pull back and refuse to admit raping them. There was something unmanly about the crime, and in prison it was viewed with disapproval.

Despite that, this was a worthwhile exchange. Neither he nor Judge Scott had any personal contact with Logan, and Kemper had always done the talking for his client. The attempt at an explanation was a tiny window into Logan's character. Both he and Judge Scott could see for themselves his pathetic machinations as he attempted to weasel around his conduct.

Judge Scott established that Gillies had had intercourse with
Suzanne based on what Logan had reported. Judge Scott returned to
Logan. "Are you telling me you didn't penetrate at all?"

"I can't," Logan said, "it is physically impossible."

"How is it you even tried, then?"

"I was trying. I was drunk as could be and I was trying." He told
Scott that Gillies raped Suzanne at the stables and later in the Superstition Mountains, where Logan had tried again. Logan claimed
that while Gillies was raping her, he went for a walk in the hills.

Judge Scott turned to Hotham and asked if these were the facts.

Hotham argued that clearly Logan was at least an accomplice.
Scott turned to Kemper and asked what he thought.

"No question about it," Kemper said.

Judge Scott decided to move on. "Count Four charges you with
the crime of first-degree murder, on or about January 29, 1981. Is that
the correct date?"

"Yes, sir," Logan replied.

"It says on that date you and Mr. Gillies caused the death of
Suzanne Maria Rossetti. Did you cause her death?"

"Yes." Judge Scott asked how. Logan said that Gillies crushed
her head with a rock while he had been sitting down on the ground
one foot away watching it. "I thought I was going to get struck by
the rock too. Then I helped bury her." He explained that he believed
they were going to leave her tied up in the mountains. After her fall
from the cliff, Suzanne was trying to rise and Logan kept saying, "Lay
down, lay down," and he pushed her down by the shoulder. That was
when Gillies bashed her head in with a rock.

Hotham suggested to the court that a factual basis had been laid
for felony murder, murder that occurs in the commission of a felony
and for which even the person whose hand did not cause the death
is guilty. Judge Scott accepted the pleas and referred Logan to the
Adult Probation Department for a presentencing report.

22

The trial of Jesse James Gillies began on August 21, 1981, at 11:30 A.M. Frances Chubinski, Suzanne's aunt, was in attendance. Her sister Louise had requested that she observe the trial, and inform the family of developments following each day's proceedings. Two weeks earlier, Frances had been injured while riding her bicycle. Ordinarily, she could not have taken the time from work to attend the trial, but she was still recuperating. When Judge Scott called the courtroom to order, Frances was seated with a friend on the front row with a notepad on her lap. In the months since the murder of her niece, she had often wondered how anyone could take advantage of little Suz, and now she was going to find out.

Hotham had been pleased with the jury selection that morning. He dismissed any juror who did not seem to support law and order, any seemingly without a stake in the system, or who appeared receptive to humanitarian arguments. He had also been satisfied when the selection was concluded early in the day. Juries selected after lunch were those that had been rejected in other proceedings, thinning the pool of good jurors. He believed that jurors formed a collective wisdom, and he wanted people who would participate in the process.

Fourteen jurors had been selected, six of them women. All were to hear the case. When the jury was impaneled to deliberate, two of the fourteen would be selected by lot and excused. In this way, should anyone became unavailable during the trial, there would be sufficient jurors to prevent a mistrial, and because no one knew who would be the alternates, everyone paid attention.

One of the jurors, Carl Everet,* was a manager at an electronics company. He had served on two previous juries, both in trials where the defendant had been accused of driving while intoxicated. He had no objection to being called, since he considered it his duty as a citizen. He had been startled when he realized this was to be a murder trial, and when Jesse James Gillies was announced as the defendant, the first two names immediately caught his attention.

Mesh also was pleased with the jury selection. It had been his experience that people generally do not want to serve on juries, but for reasons other than the inconvenience they usually claim. People are not accustomed to standing in judgment of others and seek to avoid it, especially in a crime for which execution is a potential outcome.

Before entering the courtroom, Mesh spoke with his client. He often explained to the other public defenders that proper courtroom demeanor was essential, particularly if you wanted the jury to suspect your client was mentally unsound. Mesh would tell his client to stare at his shoelaces and keep his eyes glued on them as long as he was in the courtroom. There was to be no calling out or glaring at witnesses.

It was vital that the lawyer never consult with his client in view of the jury. If you wanted the jury to believe your client was of unsound mind, you could not be observed taking his advice or explaining the law to him. It was not necessary to have an expert witness; the jury knew a crazy man when they saw one.

So it was that when Gillies entered the courtroom, he was staring straight down almost exactly at his shoelaces.

Hotham had dressed meticulously, as did Mesh. In his twenty-two previous felony trials, Hotham had developed a standard opening statement, which he now prepared to deliver. He was allowed one investigator to assist him, so beside him sat the white-haired Hackworth with his neutral expression.

Despite the *Time* magazine article, the trial was lightly attended. There was a newspaper reporter, Frances and her friend, and perhaps three other spectators, young lawyers from the Public Defender's office.

* Pseudonym

"Mr. Hotham," Judge Scott said, "you may at this time make your opening statement."

"Thank you, Your Honor." Hotham rose from his table and stood before the jury. "Mr. Mesh, ladies and gentlemen of the jury, my name is Jeff Hotham. I represent the People of the State of Arizona in this case.

"As the judge told you, this is the time set aside for opening statements from the lawyers. What we usually do is to tell you what we anticipate that the evidence will show. The evidence, quite simply, is what you will be hearing from the witnesses and seeing as exhibits.

"I like to think of evidence in a criminal trial as individual interlocking pieces of a jigsaw puzzle. The more pieces involved, the more difficult it is to visualize the end result. That simply is why we have opening statements. An opening statement is like a picture on the cover of a jigsaw puzzle box. It describes to you what the whole case will look like, so that later on in the trial, when you hear an individual piece of evidence, you will be able to understand how that one piece fits into the overall picture.

"Now, this case is really very simple, at the same time it is very tragic, very ugly. The defendant, Jesse James Gillies, is charged with the crimes of first-degree murder, sexual assault, kidnapping, aggravated robbery, and first-degree computer fraud. In our proof, the State will prove each and every material element of each and every crime."

Hotham briefly outlined the events of that night, then said, "This is essentially the evidence that the State expects that you will hear at the trial. After all the evidence has been presented to you, I will ask you to do your duty, and find the defendant guilty as charged.

"Thank you for your time and attention."

As Hotham returned to his seat, Judge Scott said, "Ladies and gentlemen, the defense counsel has the right to make an opening statement at this point, or reserve that statement until the conclusion of the State's case. Mr. Mesh, what would you prefer to do?"

"Your Honor," Mesh said, rising briefly from his table, "the defense would reserve its opening statement until the beginning of the defense's case."

"Thank you. Mr. Hotham, call your first witness."

"Thank you. The State would call Jo Ann Heckel."

Jo Ann had followed the case of Gillies and Logan in the sporadic news coverage. Hotham had interviewed her and put her at ease about testifying. Then, unexpectedly, Mesh had met her in the hallway just a few minutes before the trial. He told her who he was and said that any questions he would be asking would not be of an emotional nature and that she should not be concerned when he questioned her. She was surprised at this chivalrous courtesy and as a consequence was not nearly as nervous taking the stand as she might otherwise have been.

She knew that Logan had entered into an agreement to plead, in exchange for life imprisonment, and she had accepted that as the way of the system. At least, Logan had admitted in open court what he had done. Jo Ann was outraged that Gillies was still denying involvement.

When she took the witness chair, she stared directly at Gillies because she wanted to know what such a man looked like and, as she suspected, he had the appearance of a loser. Gillies refused to meet her eye, and instead was staring at the floor and off to the side. It seemed to her he was behaving as if he were not a part of the trial.

When Hotham asked his first question, Jo Ann turned in her seat to face the jury directly as he had suggested earlier. It was to them she was to direct her answers. One of the women was pretty and sat toward the center, so Jo Ann focused attention on her.

Jo Ann testified that she had been a friend of Suzanne and they had worked together. Hotham handed her a photograph of Suzanne in a pinafore sundress, with shoulder-length hair, parted in the middle, a friendly smile as she looked directly into the lens, and Jo Ann identified her. The night of the murder, they had attended a performance at Grady Gammage Auditorium at Arizona State University, then said good night in the parking lot at Monti's at about 10:30 P.M.

Hotham handed her a plastic bag containing a corduroy jacket, once blue, now turned a vile brown, and asked if she could identify it. Yes, it was the jacket Suzie had worn that last night. He handed her other items, and she identified each of them: nylons that were Suzanne's size and design, a ring with a blue star sapphire, a necklace, and a daypack Suzanne kept in her Pinto. And yes, Suzie made it a practice to wear underpants beneath her panty hose.

Judge Scott sustained Mesh's objection when Hotham tried to solicit testimony from Jo Ann concerning Suzanne's character. As she left the courtroom, Jo Ann made eye contact with Frances, but was unable to stop and speak to her.

Next was the clerk who had worked at the U-Totem that night. He testified that two men had been talking to this young woman and helped her into her car with a screwdriver borrowed from him. The woman bought a six-pack of beer for the men, then left with them. He recognized one as a frequent customer and identified a photograph of Gillies. Gillies and the other man had talked to him earlier about wanting to party and not having any money. As for the woman, she was "very attractive, very neat."

When it was Mesh's turn to question him, he asked the clerk if he had ever seen Gillies high. Certainly, he replied, high and under the influence of liquor a few times.

Following the lunch recess, Hotham called Dr. Jarvis. He testified he had been a medical examiner for twenty-one years.

"Directing your attention to February 6, 1981," Hotham asked, "did you have occasion to examine the body of Suzanne M. Rossetti?"

"Yes, sir."

"Would you describe to the jury your physical observations?"

In his smooth courtroom voice, Jarvis, who had testified in thousands of cases, delivered a recitation of what he had observed, outlining the injuries in detail. Jarvis explained that during the autopsy, he had instructed the identification technician to take photographs, that he took a liquid sample from Suzanne's vagina that tested positive for seminal fluid, and took swab samples from other areas of her body.

Hotham handed him a photograph from the autopsy. It showed Suzanne, still framed by the body bag, fully clothed, stretched on the autopsy table. Next, Jarvis was handed a photograph of the side of Suzanne's head, one that depicted a large gash, then another one of gashes to the back of her head, with twigs and desert burrs stuck in the hair. Still another showed her partially eaten right hand, the surviving skin heavily bruised, and one of the same hand, taken from a different angle. Next he was shown a photograph of her left hand, also heavily bruised, then one of her legs, severely bruised and nearly black from the collected blood. Dr. Jarvis identified each of them.

Mesh and Hotham had met with Judge Scott previously for the selection of these photographs. As graphic as they were, they were not nearly as hideous as many others. Hotham could not use photographs that would inflame the jury, and had experienced trouble in finding ones that could show the extent of the injuries and were not inflammatory. The effect of these photographs, following the lovely picture of Suzanne in the summer dress, was intended, at least in part, to demonstrate graphically the awful consequence of murder.

Hotham solemnly handed the photographs to the jury. As they

were passed hand to hand among the jurors, one of the women began crying softly and could not bring herself to look at the other pictures.

Frances watched the jurors closely and could see the effect the photographs were having. There were gasps as some jurors laid eyes on them. Others closed their eyes and passed them on.

Hotham resumed his questions. "You also testified that there was some indication of blood in the lungs and in the airway, trachea, and bronchi. Can any medical conclusions be drawn from those observations, based upon your experience?"

"Yes, sir."

"What is that?"

"That again, she was alive when at least some of injuries were inflicted, in that particularly with reference to the blood aspiration pattern in the lungs indicates that she breathed, actually was breathing while blood was gaining access to the mouth or upper airway or throat in some manner, and that she was alive and breathed and aspirated the blood into the lungs in a mechanical way. Blood in the trachea and bronchi would lead me to much the same conclusion, but with less assurance, it might possibly run down into her trachea after death, but it will not be aspirated out into the lungs in that pattern without actual breathing."

"Doctor, do you have an opinion as to the cause of the victim's death?"

"Yes, sir."

"What is that?"

"It's a compound cause of death and I listed it as follows: exsanguination, loss of blood, which is supported by the extensive soft tissue injuries of the head previously described, and the absence of any significant amount of blood in the circulatory system, so she bled out, you know, is the colloquial term. Aspiration of blood into the lungs also contributed in inhibiting the ability to breathe because blood displaces air spaces, and extensive head injuries. So, I listed cause of death as exsanguination, aspiration of blood, head injury."

"And the head injuries, from your testimony I take it there was a multiplicity of head injuries?"

"Yes, sir."

"Those head injuries indicated that there was more than one blow?"

"Yes, sir."

"How many different areas were there head injuries that you found?"

"It is difficult to say. I can say that there were at least five, probably many more." Jarvis explained the problems in making an exact determination.

"Thank you, Doctor," Hotham said. "I have nothing else."

"Cross-examination," Judge Scott said.

Mesh rose. "Thank you, Your Honor." This was one of those impossible situations for a defense attorney. If Mesh let the testimony go unchallenged, he would miss an opportunity to distance his client from the most horrifying aspects of the crime, or to create doubt so an alternate theory of death could be suggested later. If he asked questions, the brutality of the act was accented repeatedly while the jury glared at his client.

During his questioning of Jarvis, Mesh suggested that the injuries were consistent with an accidental fall.

On redirect, Hotham asked, "Doctor, on this accidental falling theory Mr. Mesh has presented to you, I would note that your report, as far as manner of death, your standard form has six boxes, one of which is accident, another of which is homicide. Do you recall which box it was that you checked after your examination?"

"Object, Your Honor," Mesh said. "That is immaterial as to the doctor's opinion as to whether it was an accident or homicide. That is the alternate issue for the jury to determine."

"Overruled."

Dr. Jarvis said, "I recall."

"What box," Hotham asked, "was it that you checked?"

"Homicide."

"Thank you; nothing further."

Sarah Kokat was called to the stand and testified to what she had told the police about the two men arriving and doing their laundry, one of them leaving two pairs of pants for alteration, giving him a receipt, and watching the men clean out the car. She saw towels in the trash they had tossed out, and a day or two later showed them to the police officers.

Asked to identify one of the two men, she pointed to Gillies, seated next to Mesh, staring at the floor.

Next, the Tempe police detective who had first examined the

Pinto at the Phoenix Zoo testified to the condition of the car and what he found inside it. Handed a number of items by Hotham, he identified each of them; racing tickets, receipts from purchases, the cleaners receipt with the name of Chess Gillies. These were placed into evidence.

During the afternoon recess, Hotham and Mesh met with Judge Scott in his chamber for an on-the-record motion. Mesh argued that both he and Hotham were material witnesses to this case, and therefore was moving that Hotham be disqualified and he be permitted to withdraw as Gillies's counsel.

Mesh stated that on February 4, he had received a telephone call from Hotham and been informed of this case. Hotham had said that if Gillies would assist in locating the body and if Mesh could convince him that his client had not held the rock that killed the young woman, he would be willing to deal away the death penalty. Mesh had talked to his client, and could not divulge that confidence, but he did call Hotham back and told him that he could not help him.

Clearly, this had been an effort on Hotham's part to determine if his client was the killer, because only the actual killer was in a position to accept such an offer. Hotham and he had, in a sense, become investigators in the case and should be called as witnesses.

Mesh had searched for a defense for months and was still looking. When a case appeared hopeless, it was his practice to try outlandish motions, in the theory that one of them might stick. So here he was doing just that.

"This is the most convoluted, illogical motion to withdraw I have ever heard," Hotham said. "I don't really understand any part of it." He argued that what had taken place was a standard plea offer, that Logan had benefited from it ultimately.

Judge Scott denied the motion.

Mesh returned to the courtroom to resume the trial. He had hoped the judge might grant the motion and let some other poor bastard defend Gillies.

23

Tempe detective Mike Palmer had been in an automobile accident and dislocated his shoulder. He was in excruciating pain and was taking heavy sedation. He wanted a clear head for the trial, so that morning, and all day as he waited to testify, he had not taken any medication. When he talked to Hotham earlier, he had apologized about the shoulder and his general condition, because he did not think he was going to make a very effective witness. Just as he entered the courtroom following the break, he removed his sling since he did not want the jury thinking it was a phony pitch for sympathy. The pain was exquisite as his arm hung limply at his side, and already he was sweating a dull sheen.

Palmer identified a number of the items he had taken from Suzanne's Pinto, including the panty hose with the heel of a woman's shoe pushed through it, Suzanne's jogging shorts, and a twelve-inch strip of towel; these were placed into evidence. He described his investigation that day and the general condition of the car. He testified to arresting Gillies that same evening and described the scene at Weldon. Asked about the panty hose and shoe, Palmer testified that he had formed the opinion that the shoe had been pushed down into the stocking to form a weapon.

Officer Fender testified briefly to his activities at Campus Cleaners, then the trial stood in recess for the weekend.

· · ·

Carl Everet had observed a change come over his fellow jurors when the photographs from the autopsy were passed among them. Everet could sense the sudden awareness that this trial was a unique experience. For him, the brutality of murder was never clearer.

Everet had paid close attention to Gillies throughout that day's testimony and wondered repeatedly why he was showing no emotion. Gillies sat there, not looking happy, not looking sad, looking instead, from time to time, very smug. Everet was genuinely puzzled at Gillies's reaction.

That night, Frances telephoned her sister in Saugus to provide the trial update the family had requested. She could not relate what the testimony had been; it was too horrible for the family to bear. Instead, she described the participants and gave a broad overview of what had occurred.

When the trial resumed, Hotham called the uniformed officer who guarded Logan the night of his arrest. He asked the officer to tell the jury about discovering Suzanne's ATM card in Logan's pocket. This was to set the stage for the introduction of the Ugly Teller photographs that pictured Gillies standing in the background.

Connie Parks then testified that she was once Gillies's girlfriend and pointed him out for the jury. She related that she had informed the homicide officers about seeing Gillies and Logan the day of the murder, and Gillies asking, "Wasn't the Superstitions fun?" She told how he was driving a Pinto he claimed he was leasing, and said he had $3,500. She testified to his telephone conversations to her from jail, and to his admission that he was guilty of everything except killing the lady.

Until now, Mesh had asked questions only intermittently during cross-examination of Hotham's witnesses. His motion to disqualify the two of them had been a long shot, so now he presented on cross-examination the only defense he could devise. He asked Connie if she believed that Gillies really had $3,500, and she allowed that he was just trying to impress her.

"You had known Jesse since April of that year; is that right?" he asked.

"Right."

"You knew him to be a person who, shall we say, liked to be a little boastful about his abilities?"

"Well, like what are you talking about here?" she asked.

"The things that he could do, type of person that he was. You knew he fabricated when he was with you on occasion, didn't you?"

Hotham stood up. "Your Honor, I am going to object. Mr. Mesh did not want the jury to know anything about what type of woman the victim was. I don't think it would be fair to inquire as to what type of man the defendant was. I believe that it's misleading, not appropriate, or relevant at this time."

"It goes to motivation in regard to the statement, Your Honor," Mesh responded.

"Objection overruled."

"Do you know what a braggart is?" Mesh asked.

"No, I don't."

"Do you know what a person who is boastful is?"

"Yes."

"Have you ever heard the expression, a B.S. artist?"

"Yes, I have."

"Would that expression, B.S. artist, be an appropriate label for Jesse Gillies?"

"I don't know if it would be appropriate."

"The short and long of it is you never saw the thirty-five hundred?"

"Correct."

"You knew that thirty-five hundred dollars, for a man who is a stable hand, from working, to have that much money on his person, to be given money owed to him for work he'd done in the past few months, is a little farfetched; is that right?"

"Yes."

"It's not your opinion that Jesse was trying to impress you at that time with his wealth, whether he had it or not; is that correct?"

"You are saying it's not my opinion?"

"Is it your opinion?"

"Well, at that time that's what I thought, yes."

"That he was trying to impress you; is that correct?"

"Yes."

"You also told us that about two weeks after his arrest he told you on the phone that he had done everything that he was accused of except the murder; is what he told you?"

She said he had. Connie also testified that Gillies had been depressed, and sounded frightened during the calls.

Next were technical witnesses to identify and place into evidence Gillies's latent fingerprints lifted by Palmer from the car, and to establish the similarity of the blood type determined from semen samples taken from the victim with Gillies's own blood type.

When the jury was absent from the courtroom, Mesh raised objection to Hotham introducing the photographs Hackworth had taken from the Valley National Bank videotape. In one of those peculiarities that plague nearly every serious felony trial, the tape itself had been destroyed later during rewinding, and all the State possessed was those dozen photographs Hackworth had taken as a precaution.

Mesh's argument against the photographs was novel. He feared that if the jury saw them, they might conclude that one of the two men depicted was his client.

Hotham argued that "they show a crime in action," and must be shown to the jury. Jurors could decide for themselves if the pictures were sufficiently clear to identify the man standing in the background.

Gillies had assumed an air of indifference and bravado as the trial progressed, behaving like a man who knew that something would intervene to prevent his conviction. No longer did he stare at the floor, but rather cast his eyes about the courtroom with disdain, and apparent unconcern to the proceeding.

With the jury back in the box, the head of Valley National Bank security testified to the ATM transactions on Suzanne's account until the following Saturday night, when it was believed the two men had parted ways.

With more than a little trepidation, Hotham called Jerry Schneider to the stand. In the months since he had first met Schneider, the two of them had spoken by telephone as often as twice a day, nearly always at Schneider's instigation. Hotham believed that Schneider saw himself as the star of this trial. Following the adverse publicity of Suzanne's murder, business at Weldon had fallen to the point where he was on the verge of closing.

It was customary for the prosecutor to pump witnesses up, to make them feel important to the process. Schneider had required none of that. The newspaper columnist's article had had a profound effect on his ego, and the alleged incident at the truck stop the previous April had caused Hotham more concern because it appeared to demonstrate another measure of Schneider's desire for attention. In this case, there was substantial corroboration to support what Schneider had to say, and Hotham did not doubt him. It was other areas that worried him more.

Hotham was not surprised when Schneider entered the courtroom, but only because he had observed his appearance briefly earlier. His star witness was decked out in all his western finery, with high-heeled, shiny-toed cowboy boots, hip-hugging western-cut pants, and a bright ivory western shirt with metal snaps that glistened from the overhead lights, and on top of his thinning hair was the largest black cowboy hat Hotham had ever seen. Schneider's moustache had grown to immense proportions, and he had waxed the ends and twirled them into a point. With a sweep of his hand, he removed the enormous hat to take the oath, then eased solemnly into his place at the stand.

It had been Hotham's experience that many witnesses held a fantasy that their individual testimony would make the difference in the trial. It did not matter if the testimony contributed only one link in the chain of damning evidence. Hotham had seen a change in demeanor in a witness at just this very moment, even in those he thought would be immune to such a reaction.

This could be useful because it tended to make witnesses very conscientious, but it could also backfire and cause ordinary people to stretch the truth, and twist the facts, in order to make their mark on justice. For a prosecutor asking the jury to believe his witnesses, it can be a frightening experience.

To Hotham it was all there in Schneider, out of control, ready, eager to spill out, and to make that difference.

Schneider established that he was the owner operator of Weldon Riding Stable and had employed Gillies. He described Gillies and Logan arriving with a Pinto that aroused his suspicion, and recounted the story the pair had first told him about their new jobs in Globe. He related how Gillies had damaged the car driving it cross-country, then repaired it, but came back when it broke again. One of the wranglers had helped retrieve his belongings from the car.

"Was that in the Phoenix Zoo—"

"Right."

"—parking lot?"

"Yes, sir."

Schneider testified that he had left on a horse-buying trip, then returned Monday night. "I came back into the driveway and pulled my trailer up by the barn. Everyone, usually when you drive up, the employees working, they come out and see what I need to unload and, if I do, I back up to the chute and they help me unload the truck." Instead, on this night, only one of the wranglers came up, and he said they were in trouble.

Before Schneider could relate what the man had told him, Mesh objected; the wrangler's comments were not admissible. Hotham volunteered to rephrase his question.

"Did you eventually see the defendant when you returned to your stable?"

"Yes, sir."

"And did you have a conversation with him?"

"Well, he asked me to go in my office. He said he had a lot to tell me about. He had a long story."

"What did you do then?"

"I was carrying some money, so I went in my office and put it up. Then we went to the bunkhouse and everybody cleared out and he proceeded to tell me what was the deal on the car."

"What did he tell you?" Hotham asked, taking the plunge with an open-ended question.

"He told me that he was in a lot of trouble, his conscience was bothering him, he was involved in a murder. And when he started telling me about it, I was kind of at a place where I didn't know exactly what kind of—it was like a fantasy—I didn't understand exactly what was being said as far as facts of someone talking about killing, or something like that. I was shocked to understand exactly what was being said.

"The fact that sticks in my mind is him telling me about Mike taking a rock and hitting Suzanne in the head. She wasn't dead and she said, 'Leave me alone, I am going to die anyway.' He said, 'That's right, you bitch, you are.' And from there he just more or less—"

Mesh objected. "Can we have some foundation in regard to who 'he' is?"

"Let's start from the beginning of that conversation," Hotham said. "Do you recall how he first told you that he was involved in a murder?"

"In what way? That he and Logan had been involved in this?"

"What do you recall?" Hotham asked patiently.

"He started explaining about the car, what reason the car was there."

"What did he tell you about that?"

"He told me that they had picked up a girl at Fifty-second Street and Van Buren at a U-Totem store—"

"When he was referring to 'they', did he say that it was himself and Mike Logan?"

"Yes, sir."

"What did he tell you then?"

"He said that the lady was locked out of her car and that they helped her get into the car and they had taken—as far as exact times and everything else, what happened there was the fact that they had taken her to the park where he said, 'I guess we kind of raped her,' and he said, 'The bitch wouldn't shut up, she just kept talking.' And he said. 'Then we went to her place,' and then started elaborating about the fact that Mike had the money."

"What money was he referring to?"

"The money that they had taken from her bank."

"Did he tell you that the money was taken from the bank or from her purse, or somewhere in specific?"

"Really, just the way I understood it, that it was, I thought I understood him from the Ugly Teller or something similar to that. It was a mechanical device where they could only get two hundred and fifty dollars out at a time."

"Did he tell you how much money they had taken?"

"He said that Mike had the majority of the money. Mike Logan had the money."

"Was any number given to you?"

"The way I understand it, it was over a thousand dollars. That was the reason he was after Mike. He wanted to get Logan."

"You testified he told you that the rape occurred in the park. Did he tell you where or what park?"

"He said it was in Papago Park. This part is not really clear to me, but I know when they took the police officer down, detective down, they found some panties in a gully down in one of the lower —bottom of the unlit part of the park, the part right next to Van Buren."

"Your recollection is that he told you that is where the rape occurred?"

"The first rape was there at the park."

"His statement was, though, 'I guess we kind of raped her'?"

"Yes. I will never forget that as long as I live." Schneider testified Gillies had told him they raped Suzanne again at her condominium, but Gillies was primarily angry because Logan had taken the money they had stolen.

"What did he tell you after the fact about taking the money out of the Ugly Teller, as you call it?"

"He said they were on their way to Globe and the Fish Creek Canyon area is where they pulled off, and he said that Suzanne Rossetti told him, or them, 'I guess you are going to kill me now.' And he had made the statement that—she had made the statement, excuse me, that 'I have got you clowns by the balls. You are not going to get away with this.' He said she wouldn't shut up, she just kept on. He said Mike kept getting madder and madder."

"Did he say whether, at the time of her statement. 'I guess you are going to kill me now,' if anything occurred at that particular time?"

"I believe that she was raped again."

"I object to the manner of the testimony," Mesh said. "He knows or he doesn't know. Not what he believes."

"Mr. Hotham," Judge Scott said, "make sure the witness understands you are asking for conversation, what was said by the defendant at this point."

"Did the defendant indicate anything to you, that any further sexual assaults occurred in the Fish Creek Canyon area?" Hotham asked.

"To be honest, there were so many rapes here and there, and I couldn't keep them straight, I will be honest with you. Just put yourself in my position. When you are being told a sickening story, you can't hardly—"

Mesh rose again. "Object to the narrative form of the witness's testimony. It is immaterial what the witness's feelings are in this matter."

"Sustained. Ask him another question."

Hotham asked Schneider if he remembered telling one of the detectives that Gillies had said they both raped Suzanne again at this time. He did remember this. Hotham asked if he recalled what Gillies said next.

"Well, the procedure of the killing, that it went down, as far as I was concerned, the way I understand it, sir, was—"

"Just what the defendant told you," Hotham said, attempting to hold Schneider on track.

"Right. The way I understand it was that they had taken her to a rock ledge, she was pushed over, she had a big gash in her head, she was still conscious when they walked down the side to get to her, that at that time there was a rock picked up and her head was, the way it was told to me, was bashed in and she lay there quivering."

"Did the defendant tell you that when they got down to the cliff area, whether or not the victim made any statements to them?"

"Yes, sir."

"What did he tell you?"

"She said, 'Leave me alone. I am dying. I am going to die anyway,' and Mike said, 'That's right, bitch, you are.' "

"What did the defendant relate to you happened next?"

"He said a rock was picked up, she was bashed in the head and he got sick."

Mesh objected to the lack of foundation for "he."

"Do you recall the defendant telling you who picked up the rock?" Hotham asked.

"Yes, sir, Mike Logan. He said Mike picked up the rock that bashed her head in."

"Do you recall in your interview with a detective telling him that the defendant told you that Mike then told Jesse to give him a rock and that he would kill the bitch, and that Jesse told you that he did give Mike a rock and that Mike then hit her in the head with it?"

"Yes, Jesse told me that he picked up a rock and give it to Mike and he used it, Mike used the rock to kill her with."

"Do you recall the size of the rock that he said he picked up and gave to Mike?"

"It was a heavy rock. He said it was a big rock."

"Did he tell you how many times she was hit in the head?"

"As far as I know, that's not really clear to me, as far as how many times she was hit."

"As he was telling you this, what was his manner, his mood, his frame of mind?"

"My main way of looking at it was the fact that he was nervous.

I think his conscience was bothering him, but he had kind of a little smirk to him that made the matter even more impressive in my mind, kind of a little giggle, it's done, there's not much I can do about it."

"Did he tell you what was done with the body?"

"He told me they covered, he and Mike, covered it up with rocks, then sat down and smoked some cigarettes right there on the grave."

Schneider testified that Gillies said the men then returned to Phoenix. During the next few days, he had seen them driving the light blue Pinto up and down Washington Street. After Gillies related this story to him in the bunkhouse, Schneider said he had called the police. He met them, and returned to Weldon and assisted in the arrest. He then identified Suzanne's bedroll in which Gillies had been sleeping at the time of his arrest.

Schneider told about finding Gillies's shirt the next day with Suzanne's department store credit card in the pocket, and turning the shirt and card over to the police. He identified the items and they were placed into evidence.

Hotham asked, "How long did Logan work for you?"

"Mike really was not employed there as such. I had obtained Mike through—he came over to oversee a load of horses from another stable on the south end of Phoenix and Mike was more or less just hanging around there and when Mike asked me if I needed help, could he have a job, I told him, well, he could stay around for a while if he didn't have any other place to go. He was fired over at South Mountain for drinking."

It was bad enough the newspapers were reporting that one killer had worked for him, let alone two. Schneider was attempting to show Logan was not actually an employee. Hotham had him identify a photograph of Logan, then concluded his direct examination.

Mesh stood to begin cross-examination. "How long had Mike Logan been hanging around the stables?"

"When I said hanging around, sir, I meant to say that he was working but was not on the payroll. In other words, he was working for his room and board. He'd been there probably three to five weeks."

"And during that time I take it you had the opportunity to observe him as a worker and in a social environment; is that correct?"

"Yes."

"You knew Logan to be a man of violence, didn't you?"

"Yes, sir. I had seen an act that he had done to a girl at the barn one night. Would you like me to go into detail? I will explain."

"Your Honor," Hotham said, "may we approach the bench?" Logan was not on trial here, but without the court's involvement, Mesh was very likely to lead Schneider down the path of Logan's conduct. Following a discussion at the bench, Hotham's objection was sustained.

Mesh resumed. "Had you ever heard Mike Logan use the term 'bitch' when referring to women?"

"Yes, sir. He used that term frequently. As a matter of fact, I corrected him one day about using the term in front of a customer."

"When Jesse told you that Mike had killed this young girl, was that in, shall we say, line with the type of individual you knew Mike Logan to be?"

"Yes, sir."

"Did Jesse tell you why he was telling you these things that night in the bunkhouse? Why the girl had been taken away and sexually assaulted?"

"He said his conscience bothered him, that he felt bad about it, he wanted some help."

"Did he indicate to you at any time that he wanted your help in leaving the Phoenix area?"

"Yes, sir. He asked me if I could help him get away."

"Did he ask you to loan him money so he could do that?"

"Well, he was always asking me to loan him money. I don't exactly remember."

"Now, did there come a time after that night when Jesse was arrested at your place and he had some form of communication with you again?"

"Such as? I don't understand."

"Did he ever write to you?"

"Yes, sir."

"When he wrote to you, did he indicate to you things he had told you about what had happened that night were somewhat of a fabrication on his part?"

"He said that he had lied about it."

"Did he explain in the letter why he had lied about being with Logan when Logan had killed that girl?"

"Well, he was trying to make himself feel big."

"Now, is there any question in your mind but that when Jesse related that story to you, it was shocking to you?"

"I don't understand what you mean, is it shocking to me?"

"You had no difficulty remembering the details of what Jesse told you when the detective came by, did you?"

"No, sir."

"It was kind of shocking, the recitation of what had happened to that woman; is that correct?"

"That is correct."

"It really, shall we say, got seared into your mind. They are things that you are not probably ever going to forget; is that correct?"

"That's true."

"Given the nature of things that were told to you, as a matter of fact, any human being would have difficulty trying to forget that they had heard those things; is that so?"

"That's true."

"Now, when Jesse told you these things, he indicated to you that he had in some way had sexual relations with the woman; is that correct?"

"He had said that he raped her."

"You have also become aware that men like to talk about their sexual prowess; is that correct?"

"Yes, that's correct."

"The information that Jesse told you about his being with the girl, raping her, did it ever cross your mind that he was just saying those type things to make himself a big man in your eyes?"

"That he was making himself a big shot in my mind? No, sir."

"But during the time that he worked for you, you knew him to be somewhat of a fabricator, is that correct, make up things?"

"I knew Jesse to be a hard worker and I didn't know what he did after I went home at night."

"You didn't know him to be what is sometimes referred to as a B.S. artist among the boys or with you?"

"He was more or less just a—like I said, hard-working guy that acted like he was going to take care of business, but sometimes when I would go home at night, there would be things going on I didn't know about, wild parties, hot-wiring trucks, running around here. You know, I really couldn't answer that honestly."

"Given what you have been telling us about the recitation of things that were done to the girl, it struck you as being totally out of character for Jesse; is that correct?"

"It struck me as just sickening. Out of character, maybe."

"If somebody told you Jesse had done those things, about this fellow who has worked for you and you knew to be a hard worker—"

"As far as believing something like that, unless you hear it from the horse's mouth, you take it as just what it's worth. I heard it from his mouth."

"That's correct, but I am saying if somebody else related it to you, you—"

"But no one else did relate it to me."

"What I am asking you is this: Were the things that he related to you, was that within the character of the individual you know, to in some way assist in the killing of a woman, to rape her, to brutalize her in the car?"

"The only—when I made up my mind firmly what I was going to do about this matter is when he told me, 'Well, I guess we kind of raped her. Then we beat her in the head with a rock. Then she was dead so we buried her, you know, covered her up with rocks.' "

"Okay, I realize he told you all those things—"

"You have to understand the way I felt about it, it was all this hitting me at once and the fact of just murder, was—"

"I think we better get back to my question, and if you'll be so kind, see if you can answer this with yes or no."

Hotham objected to the suggested form of the answer and was overruled.

"Specifically," Mesh said, "you had an opinion as to the type of person Jesse Gillies was prior to the time he told you about the incident with this woman; is that correct?"

"Yes, sir."

"And when he told you about the things that had taken place with the woman, did those things strike you as being part and parcel of the character of Jesse Gillies, the man who worked for you?"

"As far as anything else besides being a trail guide working in the barn, doing this and that, I don't know what out of character would be, sir."

"Let me ask you some specifics. Did you know Jesse Gillies to be a man of violence prior to the time he told you about the death of this woman?"

"I formed an opinion of Jesse when I saw him chase a little boy about this big," indicating with his hand, "over a little bitty kind of mouselike incident and he had the boy cowed down."

"Am I correct, then, you thought him to be a man of violence at that time?"

"I had an opinion of him at that time. I thought, what's a big guy doing beating on a little guy? You know what I am saying? It was over something just minor."

"Had he ever talked to you about his sexual prowess or conquests with women, the manner in which he received his sexual satisfaction?"

"As far as sexual satisfaction, I don't elaborate with my help as far as that would be, sir."

"Am I correct, then, the answer to the question is no, sir?"

"I am not really sure. That's the reason I am beating around the bush. I really can't answer that honestly."

"The answer is you can't answer the question?"

"That's right."

"Prior to the time that Mike Logan disappeared from hanging around, was that KJ night? Was he there that night?"

"Yes."

"Who would you say was driving the car most of the time that you saw Jesse and Mike with that car, the blue Pinto?"

"I saw Jesse driving only two times. I never noticed the car besides when it was parked at the facility. I was, like I said, when I saw Jesse and Logan going down the road on Washington, Jesse was driving, he looked at me and waved."

"Did you ever see Logan driving the car?"

"I don't remember."

"Did you see Logan in the car?"

"Yes, sir."

"During the time that Jesse was telling you about the things that had happened to Miss Rossetti, was anyone else present at that time or just you and he?"

"At intervals, there was someone walking in and out."

"But there was nobody there consistently listening to the whole story?"

"People were walking in and out, sir, and had already heard the story before I had."

"The jury is going to hear about that very shortly. I have nothing further."

Mesh returned to his place beside Gillies, and Hotham stood for redirect. "Mr. Mesh was asking you essentially, I take it, whether or not you believed the defendant when he told you he had raped and murdered a woman. Did you believe he had done that when he told you that, as you said, right from the horse's mouth?"

"Everything fit together, the car, and I know most all the ranchers in Arizona and there's no woman that runs a ranch near Globe, Fish Creek Canyon, they are all owned by Flying S. I know that area. I deal with these ranchers, so the story didn't fit from the beginning. That's the reason I called Crime Stop on the Saturday before I left, because I thought the car was stolen."

"But from what you knew of the defendant, from what you knew of everything else, Mr. Mesh and I are both interested in knowing whether you indeed believed him when he told you he had raped and murdered someone?"

"When I looked at Jesse's eyes and the smile on his face and the way he told me of what happened, I do believe that he was involved in the murder of that girl."

"Thank you; nothing further."

Schneider stepped down from the stand, placed his black cowboy hat on his head, and sauntered out of the courtroom. Hotham was relieved that his testimony had gone as well as it had, and the court recessed until the following day.

Hotham began with one of the wranglers, who testified that Gillies had told him a story about killing this woman. It was necessary to let the jury know that Gillies had told this story more than once.

"And what was his tone of voice when he told you this?" Hotham asked.

"Well, he was kind of laughing about it while he told me."

"Did he tell you any of the details of how he had killed the girl?"

"He told me that he met her at the store and that her car was broke down." He testified that Gillies said they had helped her, and she offered them a ride in gratitude. "On the way back to the stables, Jesse said that Mike, about halfway there, Mike grabbed her and they stopped the car, and I guess they got her out on the ground and raped her."

Mesh rose. "Object to that 'I guess,' Your Honor. It strikes me that the witness is speculating."

Hotham tried again. "Did he tell you what they did?"

Mesh was still standing. "Excuse me. I move that everything after 'I guess,' be struck from the record."

"It is ordered stricken from the record," Judge Scott said. The wrangler testified that Gillies said they had gone through her purse and he saw a credit card there.

"What did he tell you after that?"

"That they took her out to the mountains."

"Did he mention which mountains?"

"Superstition Mountains." Hotham asked what happened there. "He said that they got out of the car and that Mike told her to climb down the cliff and she said she didn't want to, then Jesse said he hit her, told her to do it, what Mike told her to do."

"Did he say where he hit her?"

"No."

"Did he say how he hit her?"

"No."

Hotham asked what took place next. "She started to climb down the cliff, then Mike kicked her and she fell down the cliff."

"What did Jesse tell you happened after that?"

"He told me that he went down to see if she was hurt or whatever and when he got down there, she said, 'Just leave me alone, I'm going to die anyway.' "

"Did he say whether or not she was bleeding when he went down?"

"Yes. He said she had a big cut on her head."

"And did the defendant reply to what she said?"

"He said, 'Yes, that's right, you are.' "

"And what did he tell you happened next?"

"He said that while talking to her Mike snuck up behind her, hit her in the head with a rock."

"Did he tell you why they killed her?"

"So that she wouldn't tell on them for raping her."

The wrangler testified that he took Gillies to Suzanne's car to retrieve his belongings. Then Hotham asked, "Do you know what brand cigarettes he smokes?"

"Marlboros."

"Do you know what kind of beer he drank?"

"Budweiser." Hotham asked him to identify the shirt the wranglers had found at Weldon with Suzanne's Broadway charge card in the pocket.

Mesh now resumed his defense. "You didn't really think he would go out and kill someone in the desert the way this woman was alleged to have been killed; is that correct?"

"Yes."

"And when he tells you the story the first time, you don't really believe him; is that correct?"

"Yes."

"Later on that evening, actually the following day, on the second, you were present with the other wranglers, and again Jesse related to you about what had happened, is that correct, by the barn, after the police had been there?"

"Yes."

"That's the second time that you heard from Jesse about what had happened?"

"Yes."

"After the group of people who worked there had been with Jesse, that's when Schneider came along; is that correct?"

"Yes, about an hour later."

"And part of the time that Jesse was talking with Schneider, you were there, too; is that correct?"

"Yes."

"So that you heard him talking about this woman out in the desert really three times?"

"Yes."

"In the course of up till the time he got arrested; is that correct?"

"Yes."

"Did the things that you heard change very much as he told the story from one time to the next?"

"No."

"Now, my understanding of it is that after you left Mr. Schneider, did you at that time head out to call the police?"

"No."

"Where did you go?"

"I stayed at the stables."

"Did you know anybody was going to call the police?"

"No."

"Would you say you knew Jesse the best of all the people that worked there?"

"Yeah."

"I take it that the reason that you didn't go to call the police after having heard Jesse say this thing is because you still didn't believe him; is that right?"

"No, Schneider told everybody to wait there and that he would go call his lawyer, not to do anything."

"That was in regard to calling his lawyer for Jesse; is that right?"

"Yes."

"But if somebody confessed to you they had committed a murder, you believed them, you'd call the police, wouldn't you?"

"Yeah."

"You didn't do that in this case, did you?"

"I was told not to."

"Not to call the police?"

"Not to do anything, just wait."

"So, you were just following instructions?"

"Yes, sir."

"It wasn't because you didn't believe Jesse because you knew him to be a B.S. artist?"

"No."

"No further questions."

Hotham rose and asked, "You have told the defense attorney that the first time when you heard the defendant tell you the story, you did not believe it. As you heard each successive rendition of what had happened, did you then come to believe what he was telling you?"

"Yes, I did."

"What was your feeling about that?"

"I felt that something should be done about it but I knew, or kind of knew, what Schneider was thinking, so I just went along with what he told me, to just wait."

"You knew Mr. Schneider would probably be calling the police?"

Mesh objected. What the wrangler thought Schneider had probably been doing was not evidence. Judge Scott sustained the objection.

"Nothing further," Hotham said. He called a second wrangler to take the stand. He repeated the story Gillies had told the men in the barn, especially about Gillies spotting the lady's exposed hand and taking time to cover it also. After the wrangler heard this story, he had walked up the street to the U-Totem and called the police.

When it was Mesh's turn to cross-examine the witness; he attempted another tack. "You previously described Mike Logan as kind of being a crazy man?"

"Yeah."

"What about Jesse, was he a crazy man?"

"When he was around Mike."

Next, Hotham called a series of officers to introduce various items taken from the Pinto and at the bunkhouse, then he turned to the man beside him and called Detective Jack Hackworth.

24

Hackworth testified that he had first interviewed Gillies early in the morning following his arrest. When Gillies declined to answer any more questions, Hackworth left the interview room, obtained envelopes, and a Polaroid camera, then returned to take pubic-hair samples and photographs. Gillies had inquired about the penalty for murder in Arizona, and when told had said, "All that just for killing that bitch?"

That afternoon following Gillies's arrest, Hackworth viewed the other videotapes from Valley National Bank and taken photographs from the screen. These were placed into evidence. Later that day, Logan was arrested and interviewed by Hackworth, after which they had driven to Fish Creek Hill to search for the body with no luck. Officers returned after daylight to resume the search, assisted by helicopters. The next day they returned with a dog and Logan was brought out again.

"How was the body found?" Hotham asked.

"Two deputies had located what appeared to be a grave down in the canyon. The deputies proceeded down in the canyon till they got close enough they could see a portion of a foot protruding out from underneath the rocks. They called out of the canyon and summoned myself and a couple of other people and we proceeded back down into the area of the grave."

"What did you do?"

"We took the ID technician with us, who took photographs on the way down, photographs of the grave, and myself and Detective Klettlinger. It took two of us to remove one of the rocks, the biggest rock on top of the body. We proceeded to collect certain evidence, such as a cigarette butt that was butted out on top of the grave, hair samples that were scattered around, and some blood samples I tried to pick up. We then proceeded to uncover the body completely."

"Where in relation to the body was this large rock that it took two of you to move?"

"It would have been directly on top, about the chest area, I guess."

"Where in relation to the body and the rock was the crushed cigarette butt you found?"

"Right in the center of the main rock, the big rock on top."

"Then what did you do?"

"Proceeded to then uncover the body completely, photograph it, examine it."

"What did you observe?"

"We observed it was a, what appeared to be a young white female. She was clothed in a blue jacket, heavy jacket type thing; blue and white, predominantly blue and white tennis shoes; stockings, blue, navy blue pair of pants; blue vest; no panties; the bra was torn open at the middle; the face, right cheek was crushed in; the eye was void; the lips, nose, eyelids, major portion of the face was completely gone due to insects or small rodents for the damage that was done to the face; there was blood on the hands; there was certain jewelry on one finger, it was a ring, and there was a necklace. Eventually, the body was bagged and carried out."

"And were photographs taken of the area?"

"Yes, sir, they were."

"The area where the body is found is in what area?"

"It would be right near milepost two twenty-two on probably halfway down the roadway on Fish Creek Hill."

"Is that located in Maricopa County?"

"It is, and off the roadway, down in the canyon, it was I'd say maybe one hundred twenty-five yards on an incline ranging from forty-five to sixty-five degrees from the roadway down the canyon side. It was strewn with small rocks, medium-size rocks, and huge rocks, rocks as huge as the area that the judge is occupying now. It took us probably a half hour to forty-five minutes to get her out of there."

"With the angle of the slope of the hill and the distance from the road (where) the body was found, is it possible at that time the body had been thrown to that location?"

"Virtually impossible."

Hotham handed Hackworth the photographs taken at the scene, which he identified. They were placed into evidence.

"What does Exhibit Forty-L depict?"

"A pile of rocks with a blood spot on it."

"What does Exhibit Forty-N depict?"

"This is the gravesite itself, blood on rocks. You can see a portion of the victim's head, there's some hair protruding from a rock, one rock about the middle of the chest area with a butted cigarette on top of it."

Hackworth testified that the cigarettes at the scene were determined to be Marlboros. He identified other items for admission: a latent print, a towel.

"And did you then attend the autopsy at the Medical Examiner's office?"

"I did."

Hotham had him identify those photographs taken from the autopsy that had already been screened by the court. After reviewing these, Hotham asked Hackworth to relate his conversation with Connie Parks when she told him what Gillies and Logan had said at her house about having a good time in the Superstitions.

Now it was Mesh's turn for cross-examination. To the extent possible, he wished to establish that this had been Logan's killing. Hackworth testified that he had questioned Logan for up to an hour and that a uniformed officer had provided him with the ATM card he discovered in Logan's pocket. No, Gillies had never given him any directions to the location of the body when he spoke with him; those had all come from Logan.

"The information that you related to your brother officers concerning the manner in which Miss Rossetti's body could be found was that it was basically under a pile of rocks; is that correct?"

"I was told she was buried under rocks, yes, sir."

"And you were told that by Mike Logan, weren't you?"

"That's correct, yes, sir."

"In fact, that's where she was buried; is that correct?"

"The body was under a pile of rocks, yes, sir."

"Given the manner in which the body was found by your brother officers, would it be a fair statement to say that only someone who actually knew where the body was located could have given you the type of instructions that you got from Mike Logan?"

"I believe it was a stroke of luck we found the body."

"You mean Mike Logan didn't bring you within a quarter of a mile or half mile of where the body was actually buried?"

"We searched the area from the top of the hill all the way to Roosevelt Dam." But yes, it was Logan who took them to the site.

"As far as the general area, he was pretty close?"

"He was on Fish Creek Hill, yes, sir, and probably within a half mile."

"You also had information that some things had been taken from Miss Rossetti's home in Scottsdale; is that correct?"

"Yes, sir, I did."

"Now, did your department, or any of the other departments that you cooperate with, do any type of fingerprinting to identify anyone who might have been in that apartment?"

"Yes, they did."

"What were the results of that?"

"I went back into the apartment with two ID technicians to dust for latent prints, was advised by Miss Rossetti's sister that there had been about fifty to sixty people in the apartment the previous evening before I got there. What prints we obtained, we couldn't identify as being either suspect."

"Am I correct there is no physical way for you to say that my client was in Miss Rossetti's home?"

"No physical way, no."

Mesh moved on in the questioning process. "You have been a police officer twenty-three years. How long have you been in the homicide unit?"

"Approximately three years now."

"I take it during that time you have had lots of experience in talking with people who were accused of homicide; is that correct?"

"Some, yes."

"My client, when you arrested him, talked with him, was he nervous?"

"Oh, yes."

"That's really not unusual under those circumstances, is it, Officer?"

"It's not unusual for anybody to be nervous when arrested."

"When he inquired of you, 'What do they do to you in Arizona?,' you had already told him he was a suspect in a murder case; isn't that right?"

"Yes, I told him he'd been arrested for murder."

"He really was fishing out information from you, even though you were conducting the interview, wasn't he? 'What do they do to you in Arizona when they kill you? How do they do it?' That's what he was asking you?"

"That's what he asked, yes."

"You told him that it was death by the gas chamber; is that correct?"

"Yes, sir."

"Are you aware that there are lots of people that have, shall we say, objections to the death penalty under any circumstances?"

"I am sure there are."

"By the same token, given your experience as a police officer you have met men who are not genteel and refer to women as 'bitches,' haven't you?"

"Yes."

"That's the language you say my client used, he referred to Miss Rossetti as 'that bitch'; is that correct?"

"Those were his words, yes, sir."

"Not 'a bitch,' 'that bitch'? "

" 'That bitch,' yes."

"You made note of that at the time, I am sure, did you not?"

"Yes, I did."

"A mental note or written note?"

"I made a mental note then and put it in writing, yes."

"Now, Officer, you put the exact statement—I am trying to find it—give me—do you remember exactly the way it was said, exactly? I am trying to find it here."

"Which statement?"

"Give me the quote as to what it was that he said to you that you put in your notes. I believe you testified to it on direct."

"I believe it was 'All that for killing that bitch.' "

"Okay. Would it have been as impressive to you if he said, 'Just for killing that woman'?"

"I imagine it would, yes."

"Would 'All that for just killing a woman'?"

"Yes, it would have been very impressive also."

"That statement really is in response to your admonition that people who commit murder, murder in the first degree, generally end up by death in the gas chamber, correct?"

"I made a similar statement to that, yes."

"His response to your statement is 'All that for killing somebody,' but he used embellishing terms, didn't he?"

"It didn't quite come out the way you put it out that time, Counsel."

"The reason that you put it in, Officer, is that it sounded bad about my client; isn't that true?"

"No, sir, I put it in there because that's what he said."

"The reason that you put that in there, as opposed to other things that you two talked about, was that you thought it showed that he was making references to the particular lady whose death you were investigating; is that correct?"

"That had something to do with it, yes."

"Even though you are the one who told him, 'The reason you are here is because I am investigating the death of some lady.' Did he ever acknowledge to you that he had anything to do with Miss Rossetti's death?"

"No, he didn't admit it."

"But it's the innuendo of that statement that you want the jury to have; is that correct?"

"It's the statement he made, Counsel."

"And if it wasn't for the innuendo you attached to it, Officer, you wouldn't have put it in your report, would you?"

"I would have put it in there, anyway."

Mesh turned to the black-and-white photographs taken from the Valley National Bank videotape of ATM transactions. Hackworth acknowledged they were not as clear as the tape itself, but they were the best he had. Mesh had Hackworth testify they had established that Curly, Logan's short-lived friend from the KJ party, had been with Logan on occasion when he had extracted money from the machine.

Hackworth's testimony concluded the State's case. Hotham rested, after which the court recessed for the day.

Carl Everet had faithfully watched the progress of the trial. He was also very impressed with his fellow jurors. Two of them were retired, one was a mechanic, there were some professionals, and several housewives. Ages varied from the early twenties to the late sixties, and all of them were paying close attention. No one was speaking openly of it, but Everet knew that they, like him, were aware that a man's life was at stake.

The defendant's demeanor was not making it easy for him in the courtroom. Gillies was exhibiting no emotion whatsoever and, considering the seriousness of the charges, that struck Everet as odd. After staring at the floor for a time, Gillies had taken to looking around the courtroom with obvious disinterest, even a certain nonchalance.

The two witnesses who had seized Everet's attention were Dr. Jarvis, with his professional, even routine recitation of facts, and the detective, Jack Hackworth. Everet had been riveted when Hackworth was on the stand, and for the first time the juror had been able to follow how the case had unraveled. It had been like reading a murder mystery.

Judge Scott struck Everet as remarkably evenhanded in dealing with the opposing attorneys and having seen to the routine comforts of the jury. Hotham had impressed him with his organization and emphasis on facts. This was especially impressive because Hotham was such a young man.

Everet found himself comparing the two attorneys and was not as moved by Mesh, though he admired his aggressiveness. His interest was piqued, however, and he had worked to hold an open mind as he prepared to listen to the defense.

The next day, Hotham and Mesh, along with Gillies, met in Judge Scott's chambers. Mesh informed the court that he would rest without calling any witnesses. He asked Gillies if that was correct, and if he believed it was in his best interest not to testify in his own defense. Gillies said yes. One of the unstated tactical reasons for this decision was that if Gillies testified, the jurors would learn of his prior felony convictions. Also, Mesh had an ethical obligation to avoid perjured testimony. The lawyers then turned to the instructions the court was to deliver to the jury.

On August 27, 1981, a large contingent from the Public Defender's office was present to witness the closing arguments, and one or two new prosecutors had dropped by as well.

Judge Scott began. "Yesterday the State rested. Mr. Mesh, you may proceed."

Throughout the trial, Mesh had treated Gillies with respect and dignity. Whenever his client indicated that he wished to speak, Mesh had politely leaned to him and listened. He had delivered his customary million-dollar defense. He rose from the table.

"Your Honor, at this time, the defense will rest."

Judge Scott addressed the jury. "Ladies and gentlemen, both sides having rested, you have heard all the evidence you are going to hear in this trial. Now is the time for the attorneys to present to you their closing arguments. I will remind you, as I have before and will probably again, that what the attorneys say in their closing arguments is not evidence. It is offered to help you understand the law and the evidence. Mr. Hotham, you may proceed."

Hyperbole and animation were not the tools this prosecutor used in these situations, or for that matter in his life. Hotham believed he had presented a step-by-step case that demonstrated beyond the legal doubt that Gillies was a vicious murderer. He approached his closing presentation with concern anyway. This was a capital case and some jurors, in spite of their stated beliefs, possessed an unconscious reluctance to convict if they believed their vote would cause a man to be put to death. At least part of Hotham's job was to help any juror with such reservations see where his duty lay.

Hotham rose and stood before the jury with his notes placed on the table just behind him. He would address the jury first, followed by Mesh, but Hotham would then have the final words. He had prepared a chart that contained the elements of the crimes he had endeavored to prove, and these first remarks would focus on the legal aspects of the State's case.

"Thank you, Your Honor. Ladies and gentlemen of the jury, thank you for your kind attention and patience throughout this trial. As the judge just told you, this is the time for closing arguments and what we attorneys are about to say is not evidence. It is simply to guide, to help you understand the evidence that you heard, evidence that you saw. The final determination of what that evidence means is up to you."

Hotham reviewed the already agreed-upon instructions that Judge Scott would deliver in a short while. "Those are the instructions that you will be getting, and in order to have me explain the case as it proceeded according to the elements, I have broken it down into simple terms so I can explain it easier." He indicated the chart beside him.

"There are two types of first-degree murder. If you find either type of first-degree murder, you must find the defendant guilty.

"Type one has three basic elements: Defendant causes death, intends or knows that his actions will cause death, and premeditation. All right? What did the State present to you that proves first-degree murder of this type?

"Number one, the defendant causing death. You heard Dr. Jarvis of the Medical Examiner's office, he told you that the cause of death, in his medical expert opinion, was multiple fractures to the victim's head, loss of blood, and the fact she choked on her own blood. Besides medical evidence, we have the defendant's own admissions that he and Mike Logan killed a woman and buried her in the Superstition Mountains.

"Intends or knows it would cause death. What do we have to prove that? We have the defendant's statements and we have other items of physical evidence that verify that. The medical evidence of intent is the fact that the Medical Examiner told you there was more than one blow, there were several discrete, as he called them, separate blows. He said at least five, perhaps as many as ten. This is the medical evidence that you heard. Defendant's own admission, that he told the wrangler that he hit the victim, that she fell down, cutting herself, gashing her head. He went down to look at her, and that when Mike Logan came down, Mike told him to give him a rock so he could kill the victim. He also admitted, essentially, the same thing to two other wranglers. Certainly when you hit someone in the head with a rock, you know that that person is going to die or you intend for that person to die.

"The third element is premeditation. Simply, that means time to reflect. What do we have to prove time for reflection? Defendant's statements again. He admitted to several of his friends that they killed her because they didn't want her to report the rape, which shows he was thinking about why he killed her. The other fact that is important is the fact that they drove all the way out to the Superstition Mountains. Obviously he was thinking, planning. Why would they go all the way out there unless they intended to kill her and dump her body there and to hide it so no one would ever find it? That's premeditation. That's first-degree murder, type one.

"There's another type of first-degree murder, simply called type two for our purposes today. Again, it causes death. What do we have to prove that? Again, it's the same as in the first type of murder, we had the doctor's medical opinion and the defendant's admissions that he killed the victim, buried her under a pile of rocks.

"The new element, different element between first and second type, is that in this type death occurs in the commission of a sexual assault, a kidnapping or robbery. What do we have to prove that? Sexual assault. We know that seminal fluid was found in the victim's vagina. We know that a pair of panties were found in the location where the defendant said that he had raped someone, and that pair of panties had seminal fluid stains. We also know from the defendant's own admissions that he raped her in various locations.

"Kidnapping; what do we have to prove that? We have common sense. That's the main reason why each of you was picked as a juror, to cut through nonsense. Mr. Mesh will be telling you in a few minutes to get down to the basic realities of this case. Weighing the testimony and using your common sense, there's only one logical conclusion: Defendant is guilty.

"The State has proven beyond a reasonable doubt that the defendant robbed the victim, kidnapped, sexually assaulted, raped, and murdered Suzanne Maria Rossetti. It is your duty to evaluate the evidence and the State would request that you return a verdict of guilty on all counts. Thank you."

"Mr. Mesh, do you want to proceed," Judge Scott asked as Hotham returned to his place beside Hackworth. Mesh stood before the jurors.

"Your Honor, Mr. Hotham, ladies and gentlemen of the jury. Right about now you are probably wondering what is it that this fellow is going to say to you? I represent Jesse Gillies, the man who has been accused of this crime. I am his appointed representative. What I am about to tell you has already been broadcasted to you as being non-sense. I hope when I conclude with this, you will find that my remarks are perhaps worthy of some other type of classification besides nonsense.

"I think it would be fair to say that for all of us, this has been quite a week. Most of you have never been called upon before to assist as, I suspect, jurors in a murder, first-degree case. That's a big thing, your official capacity as jurors. Most people don't get that type of opportunity but perhaps once in a lifetime. Really, you have been called upon to sit as judges in judgment on Jesse Gillies. To determine, in effect, whether or not the things that the State says about him are sufficient in your individual minds and collective judgment, to meet some legal standards that the judge is going to give you, concerning whether or not he has committed those things.

"My experience as a practicing attorney for a few years has been that most jurors that are plucked away from their businesses, homes, have to leave children behind, view their service here as, especially a case of this magnitude, as a very, very heavy responsibility. I have been trying to throw an eye over from time to time as we had the opportunity to do that, and I noticed many of you taking notes. I don't think there was anybody who wasn't really paying attention just about a hundred percent of the time I was looking. I thank you for that, because it's your recollection what the testimony was that's going to be really the basis upon which you then fashion your verdict."

He described to them how the American system of justice works and their place in it. Mesh was not unaware of the jury's probable reaction to his client by this time. They had watched him for a week, had heard his statements from a number of sources, seen the snapshot of the lovely Suzanne Rossetti, and viewed her brutalized, murdered corpse. What kind of man, they would be asking themselves, can defend such a person?

His purpose was to demonstrate to them that he was not just some sleazy lawyer, that he was appointed to his role, and was as much their servant as the judge or prosecutor.

"Evidence comes in two ways in the courtroom. Number one is the physical stuff over here. You are going to get to bring all of this into the jury room, the big box full of things the State has seized either from Jesse's bunkhouse, pictures involving Miss Rossetti's car, things like that.

"There's a second kind of evidence, that's testimonial evidence, things that people said here in this courtroom. It comes to you, in regard to testimonial evidence, in two ways."

This was direct examination presented by the State; "that is half the story." Then there is cross-examination, the other half. He turned to the potential outcome of this proceeding.

"One of the instructions that the judge will give you is that you are not to consider penalty. He gives you that as a kind of stock instruction because jurors are not supposed to consider penalty in regard to any case." This, he reminded them, was a capital case.

"The magnitude of the matter that we are going to talk about in a few moments concerning whether or not Jesse Gillies is responsible for this girl's death and the other things involved here, is the type of thing you want to be reflective about. In that regard, to be frank with you, I think you kind of turn to me and you say, in effect, you are the appointed representative of the defendant, you are asked, I am asked—as a matter of fact, I am commanded by the system to go into that place where they keep him in jail, talk with him, learn his side of the case, and through the cross-examination of the witnesses against him, try to present to you all of the evidence that might in some way be valuable to you in fashioning your verdict.

"You asked me to talk to him, to get up, as I am doing right now, point out to you things that might interfere with the State satisfying their burden that the defendant is guilty beyond a reasonable doubt. You want me to do that, I think, because of, number one, the magnitude of the matter. How horrible it would be if someone like me didn't bring to your attention something that might allow you to make a mistake and, so, in that regard, really, I am not only Jesse Gillies's appointed representative, in a way, I am kind of your servant, and I have a responsibility cast upon me to present to you evidence that makes you uncomfortable. Because when you sit down in that deliberation room, you start to think about what it is that he actually said, what are the judge's instructions, what does the evidence mean, hopefully some things I am about to say to you might be ringing in your ears, because later on, after you have had the opportunity to vote, you are never allowed to go back and change it. You have to come to a decision in that deliberation room that says, 'If I am satisfied beyond a reasonable doubt, it's forever, but if I am not,' then the judge will command you to vote not guilty.

"That doesn't mean he didn't do it. That means that the system of justice under which you and I live and of which Mr. Hotham is a servant as well, says that unless the State has established pursuant to certain rules and regulations and the standards have been met concerning the quality, the nature of the evidence, you may not say guilty, because the stakes are just too high."

Now Mesh turned to the evidence. In several instances, he suggested there was more flash and less substance than there initially appeared. "One of the things I think we've established is that a pair of panties were found in the park area. No one knows if they would even fit Suzanne but, hey, in a case like this, bring them in and show them to the jury, because maybe that's impressive." There is even seminal fluid on those panties, he conceded, but it is only circumstantial and proves nothing.

The same for a can of Budweiser beer found in the area. His client "drinks Bud, therefore it's probably his," the State would have them think. "That's just not so. There is no evidence tying it in to him." The same for the cigarette butt. "An individual Marlboro cigarette left on a rock out in the desert. The defendant smokes Marlboro. So do millions of other people, but they don't want you to know about that.

"But the real key to this case is not physical evidence but, rather, what Jesse Gillies was reputed to have said to other people." This was the crux of his defense. By this time, Mesh was prepared to give up most of the State's case. He was willing to admit his client had raped the poor woman, robbed her, and kidnapped her. His goal was to avoid conviction for murder, or persuade the jury to convict him of felony murder and set the stage for a life sentence rather than the death penalty. If the jury could be convinced that Gillies had done many bad things but was only technically guilty of murder because he was with Logan, that was a major victory.

"Now, I believe that when the time comes most of you are going to sit around and say did Jesse sexually assault this girl? If you believe that Jesse sexually assaulted her, if he forced himself upon Suzanne, you are going to find him guilty of sexual assault, that's one of the offenses. If you do find him guilty of sexual assault, it's going to be because you believed the people who came in here and said that Jesse told them that he had done those things. It also means that they basically and you believed Jesse was telling the truth when he told those people those things."

He led them through each of the lesser charges in the same fashion: If you find him guilty, it is because you believe what the others have testified he told them, because you believe Jesse told the truth about those crimes.

"We get down then, I guess, to the final issue, the big one, the reason we are here. The State is not satisfied to charge Jesse with these things he has admitted to doing, to each one of the people that he brought in to you. Let's say Jerry Schneider and the other wranglers were present, these people, at the time Jesse said those things, there's no doubt about it, that all of these people came in here and said yes, he said that, he took the girl by force sexually, took her property, and he was out there using the card.

"But, you see, at the same time he wants you to believe he is telling the truth to these people, and when he turns around and he says, 'But I didn't have anything to do with her death,' he wants you to call him a liar, you can't believe him when he says that. The State is willing to accept eyewitness accounts through the mouths of other people as to what happened in the mountains in regard to everything, where it was, that she was taken by force sexually, how they stole her money from her, where they went with the credit cards, but not in regard to the eyewitness account of her death.

"Mr. Hotham will say to you that Jesse is Logan's accomplice in the death of Suzanne and, therefore, he's equally culpable. That's kind of a broad sweeping statement. He's got charts up here to show you.

"There is absolutely no testimony in this courtroom that the administration of the lethal blows to Suzanne were inflicted by anyone other than Logan, that stands unrefuted in this courtroom. It's a shame that she's dead, but we know that it was Logan who did it."

He asked them to use common sense when considering who is an accomplice. Gillies never urged Logan to hurt the woman, nor did he order Logan to do anything. Gillies made no plan and finally, Gillies provided no opportunity for Logan to commit any of the offenses. "Take a good look at the pictures," Mesh told them, indicating the photographs taken by the bank video camera. "Logan is the one getting into the driver's side of the car."

Directing the jury's attention toward the other man, Mesh said, "Logan is the one who brings the cops up to where the girl's body is located, where it was left.

"Jesse has told us that Logan is the one who threw the body over the ledge and Logan is the one who had administered the fatal blows to her.

"Now, in what regard was it that Jesse provided a means or opportunity? What Mr. Hotham will tell you is we have the testimony that he gave him a rock and that's the means or the opportunity. Now, take a look at the area, it's an area strewn with rocks. Even assuming that that was true, Jesse had given Logan the rock, what have they forgotten? Where is the premeditation, or anything else along those lines, that Jesse in fact knew what Logan was going to do?

"Mr. Hotham draws the assumption that if they drove into the Superstitions, they had been planning it all the way. Or was it, if you will, a crazy act, the impulsive, craziness of Logan that 'We better get rid of her before she might tell on us'? "

Explaining that this will be his only chance to speak to them, Mesh apologized for taking so much time, then summarized the case as he had argued it.

"What evidence," he asked rhetorically, "have they presented to you that there was any conspiracy, plan, that Jesse went along with him? None. That mouth of his, that has brought him into the court-room, but the State has failed to reveal any evidence of that nature. But God only knows, evidence was presented to you that most of you I think will feel comfortable with in fashioning a verdict of guilty in regard to some of the other conduct that clearly he's admitted to.

"If you take a look at the felony murder situation, which the State wants you to believe is the basis upon which Jesse Gillies is guilty of murder in the first degree, you will have with you I believe the indictment in this matter, which is nothing more than the charging document which says here is what the man is charged with. I would ask you to read it because what it says is:

" 'Acting either alone or with one or more other persons committed or attempted to commit an offense, to wit: kidnapping, sexual assault, or aggravated robbery, and in the course of and in furtherance of such offense or immediate flight from such offense, caused the death of Suzanne Maria Rossetti.'

"I think you have listened attentively to the evidence. I think the State has presented evidence to you that sexual assault, robbery, and kidnapping all took place in Papago Park. The death of this girl, as tragic as it may seem, is not to be attributed to the hand of my client. We know, through his mouth, who the actual killer is. That actual killer led the police to her body.

"For that reason, ladies and gentlemen, I ask you to find my client not guilty of murder in the first degree. Thank you."

Hotham, as was his practice, had saved the fire for his rebuttal, but he began slowly. He spoke in a measured pace, his voice quiet and unassuming.

"You will be instructed by the judge that the State must prove the defendant guilty beyond a reasonable doubt. Mr. Mesh commented upon that, described for you in his own fashion, but there is nothing magical about reasonable doubt, it means exactly what it says. Reasonable doubt means doubt based upon a good reason, a logical doubt, not just a possibility, not just a guess. The State is not required to prove guilt to an absolute certainty. After all, nothing in life is absolutely certain. The State gladly accepts the burden of reasonable doubt, it's not nonsense. The State has proven the defendant guilty beyond a reasonable doubt.

"Now, the defense attorney said a few things that I would like to respond to.

"Mr. Mesh spent a great deal of time telling you about the American system of justice and all the rights that the defendant has. Well, Suzanne Rossetti had some rights too: She had the right to live, she had the right to be safe from violent crimes. Society has rights also. Society has the right to expect that when people commit violent crimes, that they be convicted and punished.

"Mr. Mesh would, I am sure, agree with me this case is a perfect example of the American system of justice. The defendant had his day in court. The State proved him guilty beyond a reasonable doubt. The system works with you in your own position as an important part of the system.

"Mr. Mesh also mentioned, basically, arguing to you that it was Mike Logan who killed the victim and not the defendant. But you know under the laws of Arizona, as explained to you and as you will read the instructions, that it doesn't matter who actually hit the victim in the head with a rock. Both men are equally culpable, as each are accomplices to the other in the murder. All of the evidence shows that there were two men involved throughout the whole unfortunate series of events.

"The clerk at U-Totem saw the defendant, identified him and another man with the victim leaving in the car. Photos, video photos taken from various banks, show two men, the defendant and Logan, and the victim's car.

"Detective Hackworth told you some of the rocks on top of the victim's body out in the mountains were so heavy that it took two men to remove those rocks from the body.

"All other evidence points to the defendant. His cigarette on the rock on top of her body, as in the car, all the physical evidence that she had been taken from the vehicle, all her property. He didn't try to explain that because he couldn't. All of that evidence shows that there were two men involved and the defendant was one of the two men.

"Now, Mr. Mesh argued to you that the defendant was only bragging, he was B.S. 'ing to his friends, essentially that he was lying about his participation. But you saw those men, they told you that they believed the defendant. They thought he was telling them the truth when he told them the grisly details of the rapes and murder. They knew him very well, they knew him better than anyone else. They were friends and they would have no motive to lie.

"The defense attorney also argued it was Logan who took the police to the body, that therefore he is the actual killer. The fact that Logan took the police to the body doesn't mean anything other than the fact Logan was also in the mountains.

"You will be instructed that you don't need to worry about Logan. You will be instructed that it is no defense to the crimes charged against the defendant in this case that another person not now on trial might have participated or cooperated in the crimes. You are not to guess the reason for the absence from the courtroom of such other person, as the only matter, only matter before you for your decision is the guilt or innocence of this man.

"The defense attorney also tried to explain away the insensitivity of the defendant when he said, 'All that for killing that bitch?' That statement alone shows the defendant's guilty knowledge. He knew that he was in big trouble for the murder of Suzanne Rossetti. Detective Hackworth made a point to put that exact quote in his report. That's not an innuendo, that's the exact quote and that shows that he was feeling guilty. That was an inquiry as to what was going to happen to him.

"Defense counsel also conceded that perhaps the defendant is guilty of everything except the murder. I think that it's pretty apparent that he's guilty of the other four counts, as he's guilty of the murder. As he told Connie Parks, he was guilty of everything, but he was very clever when he talked to Connie, he said, 'I am not guilty of the murder.' Well, you have to recall, he called her after he was arrested, and he knew, probably, that the State would find her and bring her back in as a witness, and he was trying to plant something there that he would be able to use at a later time."

In the months since that early morning telephone call when Hotham had been shocked at the depravity of this crime, he had struggled to contain the anger he felt. In these crucial final moments, he no longer suppressed it. Now was the time for the well of emotion he genuinely felt to come to the surface for the jury to see.

"The defense attorney also argues that there is no proof that the defendant actually sexually assaulted, raped the victim. But the defendant admitted, through witnesses who are believable, say they believed him, that he raped her at least three different times, three different locations, and he admitted this to five, six, perhaps even as many as seven different people. The witnesses told you that they believed that he did that, and the physical evidence corroborates everything that he said.

"When he told the wrangler he raped her by the maintenance gate at Papago Park, he goes out there and finds her underwear at the maintenance gate in Papago Park exactly where he said, and that underwear had semen stains. The Medical Examiner's office told you that there were seminal stains, fluids in her vagina. Everything that he said is corroborated by physical evidence to show that he was telling the truth.

"The defense attorney will also argue to you that the videotape photographs do not show the defendant. You be the judge of that yourself, but remember that Detective Hackworth identified from those photographs the defendant and Logan. Detective Hackworth also told you that he had the defendant's jacket in property that is shown in one of the photographs.

"Mr. Mesh also argues that the defendant was not an accomplice of Logan in the murder. Read the instructions about the accomplice and I am sure you will see it does apply to the defendant. What does he call hitting the victim in the head? The wrangler told you that the defendant said, 'Yes, I hit her in the head while we were out in the mountains.' Isn't that what an accomplice does?

"What does he call the defendant giving the rock, the actual murder weapon, to Logan? Remember, Logan says, 'Give me a rock, I am going to kill that bitch.' The defendant picks up a rock, gives it to Logan. If that's not an accomplice, then nothing is."

It was important that the jury know Hotham felt as strongly about this murder as Mesh had shown he felt about his client, that he was moved personally, that it was not just another case. He wanted them to know that he experienced moral outrage at what Gillies had done to Suzanne.

"There were over one hundred twenty-five people killed in our community last year. All of those deaths were tragic, yet none was more senseless than this killing.

"Violent crime, as you are well aware, is on the increase in the

United States. Last year one person was killed every twenty minutes, one every twenty minutes. Seventy-two lives taken every day.

"But we are not talking about abstract figures here, we are talking about Suzie Rossetti. One minute a beautiful, living, breathing human being, the next moment just an ugly, beaten, battered body lying on the ground in a pool of her own blood, under a pile of rocks."

Hotham paused for a moment to slow the momentum of his presentation.

"Take a minute, think about death. Death is very ugly and is very final. Who determined that it was time for Suzie to die?" Hotham turned and pointed directly at Gillies. "That man right there. Who determined that this"—he held the photograph of Suzanne in her pinafore—"would become this?" He held up the picture of Suzanne on the autopsy table.

Hotham pointed again at Gillies. "That man right there. And why? Because he was afraid that she was going to turn him in for raping her."

There were tears in his eyes, and each member of the jury was fixed on him. "Defense counsel conceded that this was a tragic event and ashamed it happened. The defendant quite callously referred to it as a lot of fun in the Superstitions.

"What it really was, was a brutal act of violence with the victim's head being smashed five or ten times by a rock, being buried alive, left to die, choking on her own blood, and bleeding to death. That's first-degree murder.

"The State has proven the defendant guilty beyond a reasonable doubt and it is your sworn duty to find him guilty. Thank you."

Silence followed Hotham's final remarks to the jury. It was as if he had taken the legalisms of these past several days and told everyone in the courtroom why this trial was taking place:

This man, Gillies, murdered this woman, Suzanne, and you will now stand in judgment.

Judge Scott read his prepared instructions to the jury, then the two alternates were selected at random, thanked, and dismissed. At 3:10 in the afternoon, the jurors filed from the courtroom and entered the jury room for deliberations.

Frances Chubinski left the courtroom satisfied with the prosecution. She had been moved by the closing argument. She thought

Hotham had been marvelous, building his case relentlessly until she could see no other possible verdict but guilty.

Mesh had remained calm and done his job. He was too good a lawyer for the case. Probably it had been best for Gillies not to take the stand; what could the man say in his defense?

She had seen Logan at an earlier proceeding, and he had looked to her exactly like an instigator, a con. Having watched Gillies all these days, she could understand how the two of them together were dangerous and capable of something like this. Poor Suz never had a chance.

25

The first duty imposed on the jury was the selection of a foreman. The twelve took their seats around a rectangular table, and each waited for someone else to speak. Finally, one person asked, "Has anyone ever been on a jury before?" No one had except Everet, who said he had served on two previously. He was elected foreman by acclamation.

Everet had been touched by the closing arguments, and though he had not found Mesh to be persuasive, he was impressed with the passion the public defender had brought to his cause. Hotham had been sobering, and Everet could see his influence on the others as well.

One individual who had been part of the events of the previous January had not been present at the trial. Everet had formed a mental image of the missing victim, Suzanne. She came across as a petite and attractive young woman, very bright, trusting, and cheerful. He was struck with her youth and how her promising life had been cut short.

They had been provided with verdict forms for each of the five counts. As foreman, it was Everet's duty not only to conduct the deliberations, but to complete the forms and deliver them to the court. He reminded each juror that this was not just a murder case, that there were four other crimes charged as well, and that they must discuss and decide each one of them also. He said, "Now everyone has to make their decision, then we will vote."

They took the first count, kidnapping, and discussed it briefly.

No one expressed any doubt. Everet asked if everyone was ready to vote, and no one dissented. They voted verbally and unanimously for conviction. Everet completed the form, then turned to Count 2 and repeated the process. For each of the first four counts, there was little anyone wanted to say, and each ended in a unanimous vote for conviction. Finally, he turned to the last count, murder, and began the discussion.

When the closing arguments were complete, the few prosecutors present came up to congratulate Hotham on his presentation. Mesh was standing nearby accepting the compliments of the large group of young public defenders. To Hotham's surprise, several came over to offer congratulations on his performance, and that was a special point of pride for Hotham. He knew about the Mesh entourage and looked at his adversary with a gleam in his eye as he spoke to them.

This was also a moment for Hotham to admire his adversary, because despite what he had viewed as a hopeless situation, Mesh had been charismatic and aggressive. The men crossed the floor and shook hands, congratulating each other on a good job and a clean fight.

Sometimes there were rare cases that could be savored, and this was one of them for Hotham. The young lawyers, both prosecutors and defenders, loitered to talk, to absorb that special feeling that comes from the completion of a capital prosecution. A newspaper reporter asked for a statement, and finally Hotham returned to his office. When he arrived there and was asked how it went, he said he thought it had gone well and he was optimistic about the outcome.

The adrenaline was running so strong in him he felt incapable of working. It was Hotham's custom to meet with his supervisor and do an immediate postmortem on the prosecution. This discussion continued for a time as he analyzed every aspect of the case, pointed to his successes, then pondered his shortcomings to decide how to handle it better next time.

In the jury room, the discussion was no longer perfunctory. This had been an emotionally draining experience for the jurors, who all knew a man's life was at issue. Three of the jurors were not certain that what they had heard was really murder in the first degree. There had been no evidence that Gillies had actually killed anyone. The case pointed to Logan.

There was considerable discussion as to the nature of premeditation. Even if Gillies had participated, he might have acted without thinking; there had been no time for him to reflect on his actions. The most senior juror proposed a verdict for manslaughter.

Someone else thought Gillies was guilty of first-degree murder, but could not decide if he was actually the killer or guilty by association. Did they have to decide that?

It was suggested that they ask the judge for clarification. At 4:20 P.M. Everet wrote two questions on a slip of paper and handed them to the bailiff for Judge Scott.

In chambers, Judge Scott summoned Hotham and Mesh, then read the first question from the jury. "We need clarification on amount of time for reflection. What is considered legal amount of time?"

Judge Scott read his response to the attorneys and neither had objection to it. "Any period of time, however long or short, that is sufficient to permit reflection, as long as that period of time is longer than the time required merely to form the intent or knowledge that conduct would cause death."

Then he read the second question. "Do we have to state which type of first-degree murder?"

Judge Scott's reply: "No, simply use one of the two forms of verdict relating to first-degree murder."

"Does either counsel have any objection to that response?" he asked. They did not.

For those few in the jury room who were uncertain, others were impassioned in their belief that the State had established its case. More than one pointed at the brutality of the murder, the long drive to a remote location. One juror reminded the others about the crushed cigarettes on top of the grave. The man who had suggested manslaughter jumped on that detail and suddenly agreed; he had forgotten about the cigarettes.

When Everet received the answers to their questions, he read them to everyone. Someone suggested that they take a look at the physical evidence, and slowly Suzanne's personal items were passed around the table, followed by the photographs. Not all could bring themselves to look at them, having been so disturbed at seeing the pictures the first time.

Everet watched the mood of the room alter at that point. Three jurors were moved to tears at the sight of the savagery of the attack on Suzanne.

When they returned to discussion of the murder count, the jury's collective mind had solidified. This killing had been so cold-blooded, so inhuman, no one argued a lack of premeditation any longer, no one talked about manslaughter. Everet took a verbal vote, and the verdict was unanimous. He asked each of the jurors if they were comfortable with their decision. He wanted them all to be of a single accord. When they assured him they were, Everet completed the last form and informed the bailiff the jury was ready with its verdict.

At 5:00 that afternoon, the court reconvened to hear the verdict, almost exactly seven months following Suzanne's murder.

"The record will show the presence of our jury, roll call waived, presence of both counsel and the defendant," Judge Scott said. "Who is the foreman?"

Everet rose. "I am, sir."

"Mr. Foreman, have you reached a verdict in this matter?"

"We have."

"Please hand your verdict to the bailiff." Everet handed the forms to the court bailiff, who turned them over to Judge Scott. He checked them to be certain they were completed properly, then handed them to his clerk. "The clerk at this time will read and record the verdicts."

The clerk rose in her place. " 'We, the jury, duly impaneled and sworn in the above entitled action, upon our oaths, do find the defendant, Jesse James Gillies, guilty of kidnapping. Carl Everet, foreman.'

"Is this your verdict, so say you one and all?"

The jurors said yes. The clerk read the verdict for sexual assault, guilty, then for aggravated robbery, guilty.

" 'We, the jury, duly impaneled and sworn in the above entitled action,' " she read, " 'upon our oaths, do find the defendant, Jesse James Gillies, guilty of first-degree murder. Carl Everet, foreman.'

"Is this your verdict, so say you one and all?"

"Yes," the jurors responded in unison.

Everet knew Gillies to be a murderer now. During the trial, he had watched the defendant from time to time and wondered if he hadn't just been the victim of bad luck. Now Everet knew better. He wondered how Gillies could sit there, especially as the verdicts were read, and show no emotion.

Everet looked at Mesh with fresh respect. The juror had been genuinely puzzled when Mesh presented no defense. He had anticipated Gillies taking the stand and telling them his side of what had happened. His respect for Mesh suddenly rose as all became clear to him. There had been no defense, because there was no defense. It had been a hopeless cause from the beginning, yet Mesh had fought aggressively and successfully raised questions in Everet's mind at various points during the trial. Mesh had been in a tough spot, and Everet sympathized with him.

From time to time, Everet had watched Frances Chubinski sitting behind the rail taking notes. He did not know her, nor did they ever meet, but he sensed that she was a member of the victim's family. He knew how very hard this had been on her and wished there was something he could do.

The final verdict convicting Gillies of first-degree computer fraud was read. Neither lawyer asked to have the jury polled. Judge Scott said, "Ladies and gentlemen, thank you very much for your services. This case has now come to a conclusion." He referred Gillies to the Adult Probation Department for a presentencing report.

Judge Scott met briefly with the jurors in private once court was in recess, and thanked them for their time and service to the State. He told them they were free to discuss the case now if they wished. Specifically, members of the press were present and would approach them. They could comment or not, it was their choice.

As for the verdict, Judge Scott said they should feel comfortable with their decision. In his many years in the law, he had never seen a more certain case for conviction. His comments allayed the lingering concerns of several jurors. He advised them to call him later if they wished, and he would tell them what sentence he had decided to impose. With that, they were free to leave.

When Carl Everet arrived home, he was emotionally exhausted. He told his wife the trial was over and that they had reached a verdict. She had known he was sitting on a murder case and had followed the only such trial closely in the newspaper, clipping the small reports of the proceedings to give her husband when the trial was finished. She told him she knew about it because she had seen it on the television news. She handed him the clippings, and Everet sat down to read them.

For the first time, he learned Logan had confessed, and he was even more reassured about the verdict. His wife told him he had done the right thing, and he nodded his head slowly as he reread the clippings.

In the months since the murder of his friend, Pug had avoided closely following the legal proceedings because of the pain it caused. Slowly, however, he had come to learn of the terror that Suzanne had experienced at the hands of Logan and Gillies those last desperate hours of her life. Pug was a gentle man of charitable disposition, but he believed that he could kill those two in a heartbeat if asked. If given the opportunity, he would volunteer for the chance.

Four days later, Logan was brought before Judge Scott for the formal acceptance of his plea agreement and to be sentenced. He was one of several that afternoon, and sat shackled in the jury box waiting his turn.

Under the terms of the plea agreement, the State could not present aggravating circumstances, nor could the defendant present any in mitigation. Judge Scott had received a report from the Probation Department that contained a description of the crime, Logan's social history, and his prior criminal record.

Logan looked unrested as he stood before the bench, with James Kemper beside him, at 4:00 P.M. Judge Scott indicated that he had computed that Logan was entitled to receive 209 days' credit for time already served in the county jail.

"Is there anything you wish to say in your own behalf before I impose sentence for these offenses?" he asked.

"No. There are so many things I would like to say, I don't know, just—I don't know."

Judge Scott sentenced Logan to the terms outlined in the plea agreement, then decreed they would be served consecutive to the life sentence for murder, life plus a total of sixty-seven years.

"The law requires that I put on the record my reasons for consecutive sentences. They are fairly easy in this case: One, the plea agreement calls for it; two, you were an escapee from the state of Michigan at the time you committed these offenses; three, it is necessary, in my judgment, to impose consecutive sentences in order to protect society from you for the period of time I deem necessary." He then informed Logan of his right to appeal this sentence.

It had taken only fifteen minutes. As Kemper escorted his client to his place, he reminded him that he had been spared the death penalty under the terms of this agreement, and he should not do something so foolish as to appeal his sentence.

On September 28, 1981, Gillies was present before Judge Scott for an aggravation-mitigation hearing and sentencing. Hotham had the right under the law to present reasons why Gillies should be sentenced to die. Gillies had the right to present evidence as to why he should not.

Jack Hackworth had never attended the sentencing of one of the murderers he had previously investigated, but decided to make an exception in Gillies's case. So while he had no part in this hearing, he was present as an observer.

Hotham called Billy, the man Gillies had robbed and threatened with death, to testify as to that offense. Billy had a serious speech impediment, and appeared very vulnerable with a slow intellect.

"Do you know a person by the name of Jesse James Gillies?" Hotham asked.

"Yes, sir."

"Did you know Jesse James Gillies on June 19, 1980?"

"Yes, sir."

"Was that at the Wigwam Riding Stable in Litchfield Park?"

"Yes, sir."

"Did you go to the stable that date to ride your horse?"

"Yes, sir."

"What happened when you got to the stable? Did you meet Mr. Gillies?"

"Yes, I did."

"And when you met him, did he tell you something?"

"Yes. He took my money."

"He took your money?"

"Yes, and then he choked me."

"How many hands did he use to choke you?"

"One hand."

"Where did he put his hand?"

"Here." Billy held his hand around his throat.

"Around your neck?"

"Yes. I tried to take it off but I can't do it."

"Then what happened?"

"Then he hit me here." Billy pointed to his face.

"Hit you in the face?"

"Yes."

"What did he hit you with?"

"With his fist."

"Do you remember which hand it was?"

"Right hand." Billy then testified Gillies stole his radio as well.

"What did he do after he choked you, hit you, and took your money and your radio?"

"Then I come with him to come to eat."

"He took you with him somewhere?"

"Yes."

"Did he threaten to do anything to you or your parents?"

"Yes."

"What did he say?"

"Kill me."

"He threatened to kill you?"

"Yes."

"And what did he threaten to do to your parents?"

"Kill them, too."

"Kill them, too?"

"Yes." Billy testified Gillies wanted $1,000 by the next day not to kill all of them.

Next, Hotham called another Weldon wrangler, who said he knew Gillies from working at the stable and had considered Gillies to be his friend. He related how Gillies had twice told him how he and Logan had killed this woman. After reciting what he heard, Mesh had his final opportunity to point the accusing finger at Logan.

"Did he say who pushed her off the cliff?" Mesh asked.

"He said Mike pushed her."

"Did he also tell you who hit her in the head with the rocks?"

"He said Mike hit her in the head with the rocks, yes, sir."

"You had worked with Michael Logan at the Weldon Stables for a while, hadn't you?"

"Yes, sir."

"Did you know him to be a man of violence, Mike Logan?"

"Sometimes he was, yes, sir."

"Did you ever see him beat up on a woman there?"

"He slapped a woman around, yes, sir."

"Had you ever seen Jesse employ any violence toward women during the time you worked with him at Weldon's?"

"No, sir, not towards no women."

"Your evaluation of Mr. Logan, as far as the type of character that he was, did you think him to be a man of violence?"

"Yes, sir."

"Did you know him to do drugs?"

"Yes."

"Did you think he was stable in the head mentally?"

"No, sir."

"What about Jesse? Is Jesse stable in the head mentally, as far as you know?"

"Yes, sir, he is, as far as I know."

"As between Jesse and Mike Logan, which individual do you think was more truthful?"

"Jesse would be more truthful."

"When Jesse told you these things the first time, you really didn't believe him, did you?"

"At the time, it seemed like he was telling a story or joke."

"Kind of pulling your leg?"

"More or less, but then I believed him."

"When you heard it a second time, you started to believe him, though, didn't you?"

"Yes, sir, me and one of the other wranglers."

"You believed him when he said that he had raped that woman out in Papago Park, that was the reason you went to the police, among others; is that right?"

"Yes, sir, one of the reasons."

"You believed him when he said he went to her apartment for the purpose of either taking things from there, or whatever?"

"At first I didn't believe him until he showed me this bag containing some of her stuff."

"At that point you believed him?"

"Yes, sir."

"He told you that he had used the credit card or that he and Logan had used the credit card; is that right?"

"He said they were trying to use it but could not get it without written permission on paper."

"Did he indicate to you they were able to get any money out of the Ugly Tellers?"

"Yes, sir."

"They did?"

"Yes, sir."

"You believed him when he told you those things?"

"Yes, sir."

"You believed everything that he told you about what had happened to this woman, didn't you?"

"Yes, sir."

"You believed him when he told you that Mike Logan was the man who actually pushed her off the cliff and smashed her head in with the rocks."

"Yes, sir."

"Nothing further." Mesh had lost the verdict, but no client of his had ever received the death sentence. He had argued unsuccessfully with the probation officer who prepared the presentencing report on Gillies, that it was unjust for Gillies to be sentenced to death because he had exercised his constitutional right to a trial while Logan had elected to plead and receive life.

Hotham handed the court a more explicit photograph of the dead Suzanne Rossetti to demonstrate the depravity of the crime Gillies had committed.

"The facts here show that the defendant was a coequal in all circumstances, all of the crimes, starting from the kidnapping, sexual assault, all the way through to the final end in the murder.

"And I think it's nondisputed as to the testimony from the witnesses as to what actually happened, that the defendant says, even if we assume that he was telling the truth to the witnesses who testified, that the evidence shows that after she had been pushed off the cliff, that he went down to the victim who was lying there crying and begging for help, and he actually told her something to the effect, 'Yes, bitch, you are going to die.' Then when Logan came down and asked him for a rock, the defendant gave him a rock and then Logan smashed her in the head. Even if we assume that's what happened, and the defendant Logan told this court that's not what happened, but even if we assume that's what happened, the act of giving the codefendant Logan a rock to smash her in the head and the prior statement to her, 'Yes,' in effect, 'you are going to die because you are a witness to the rape. We don't want you around anymore,' those are facts stronger than in other cases, yet the death penalty was imposed in those cases also.

"The State has proven beyond a reasonable doubt four separate aggravating circumstances and the defense has not been able to prove any mitigating factors substantial enough to call for leniency. That's why the death penalty is appropriate and indeed it's mandated by statute. As Mr. Mesh told you, the word says 'shall' if the court makes that determination. Therefore, the State requests the court give defendant the death penalty. Thank you."

Judge Scott ordered a brief recess to prepare for the actual sentencing and retired to his chamber. He had listened to the testimony during the trial and reviewed all of the evidence. He had prepared a presentencing work sheet, listed all of the factors he should consider, and could find absolutely no cause for leniency.

This had been his first murder trial and he had never previously faced a decision such as this. He had spent long hours pondering the right course. He wanted to be absolutely certain in his own mind; he wanted no room later for doubts. He had found the death of Suzanne to be sickening and the crime to be senseless. It never should have happened.

He had seen the photographs. He knew Gillies's long history of antisocial behavior. He had read Yolanda Gillies's letter about her son with special interest. It was not enough to consider only the innocent victim, he must also take into account the character of the convicted.

Judge Scott could not account for a man like Gillies. It was, he thought, a shame that the system of justice he served could not prevent crimes such as this, only address them after the fact.

In his chamber he thought back to what it had been like for Suzanne that terrible night. She must have been terrified during those long hours these two men had held her against her will and abused her. She had been bound, helpless, raped repeatedly, thrown from a cliff, stoned until she was unconscious, then buried alive.

Lying under those rocks, she had slowly choked to death in her own blood. The horror of it. Judge Scott gathered his papers, and considered for a moment what it must have been like, what it would be like, to be buried alive. Then he entered the courtroom for the sentencing.

• • •

"Mr. Mesh," Judge Scott said, "would you have your client please come forward?" Gillies, dressed in jail garb, stood with Mesh before the bench. "Is your true name Jesse James Gillies?"

"Yes, sir, it is."

"Mr. Gillies, in a previous proceeding in this matter, specifically a trial by jury, a determination was made that you are guilty of the crimes of first-degree murder, sexual assault, kidnapping, aggravated robbery, and first-degree computer fraud.

"I have considered the evidence that I received at trial; I have considered the presentence report that has been written in this matter; I have considered the evidence that I have received at the hearing that we have just concluded; I have considered arguments that have been made by both counsels; I have considered letters, all of the attachments to the presentence report, and also a letter that was written to me directly by your mother; I have considered the fact you have been in custody on these charges two hundred thirty-seven days prior to this morning. Is there anything, sir, you would like to say in your own behalf before I impose sentence for these offenses?"

"Just for the record," Gillies said, "I want to point out that I should have had my choice of a lawyer to defend me. I didn't feel, you know, I can confide completely with this lawyer here, that he could defend me completely within his capabilities.

"I'd say also I am not guilty. I have never sat on the stand or anything, just want to put on the record now that I am not guilty."

"All right, sir. Is there anything else you would like to say in your own behalf?"

"No, thank you."

"Mr. Mesh, is there anything you would like to say on behalf of your client?"

"There are several things I would like to address some comments to. If I might just have my client sit down while I do this, because I think I will be probably ten or fifteen minutes, Your Honor." Gillies sat at the table. "I, too, reviewed the presentence report and just for the purposes of the record, I would like to point out some inaccuracies that I believe have crept into Mr. Gillies's presentence report."

For the next several minutes Mesh outlined those concerns. He pointed out the injustice of one man, Logan, taking a plea and receiving a life sentence, while his client, Gillies, who asked for the trial guaranteed by the Constitution, was facing execution.

"If it's wrong for a judge to exercise the uncontrolled arbitrary exercise of power, then it has to be equally so for the State.

"I am told that the jury is instructed not to consider what happened to the other defendant in this matter, that's no concern of theirs. I really don't have a lot of trouble with that, but I find, as I stand here now, the thought that the State has picked between these two gentlemen, and I use the term loosely, because no right person can read the presentence report in regard to both of them and come away and say they are very nice people.

"But yet the State, for whatever reason, turned around and said, as well as the chief investigating officer, the prosecutor, investigating officer at the Probation Department, every one of them has said he is probably equally culpable with the other defendant, but he was smart enough, had a lawyer who was good enough to whisper in his ear, 'Take the deal, plead guilty, turn the key on yourself for the rest of your life. Maybe somewhere down the line something good will happen to you and maybe you will get out.' Whatever went into that decision, it was done, it is a fact, it's reality.

"But as to this man, he either didn't have the power to stand up before this court and say, 'I am guilty, I did it,' or didn't have the intestinal fortitude to turn the key and remain the rest of his life in prison.

"That State in its total power in this situation turns around and says, 'Boy, for not cooperating, because of the absence of remorse, for that we are going to send you to death.' I think you can draw a distinction, if you will, because Mr. Logan did provide the State with the body. He did that out of urging by Detective Hackworth. It was the appropriate thing for the detective to do and I will even submit to you the appropriate thing for Mr. Logan to do. I don't know what mental process went into Logan's part concerning whether or not he should cooperate with the State, but I will tell you this: This man sat in the jail and the only contact he had with the outside world has been through me.

"As I told you in my motion, I feel the State tried to make me their agent to go in and find out is he the actual killer. He can have life provided that he can give us the body, is not the actual killer. If he doesn't give us the body, that means one of two things: Either he is the actual killer and does know where it is, or we know where it is. We know he knows where it is. That leaves us with the assumption he was the actual killer. We are not going to accept things that we have out of his mouth from the people who tell us that they believe he's telling the truth when he relates the story in regard to what happened to that.

"Our Supreme Court has said you can't limit the number of mitigating factors. I submit to you that the State's treatment of an equally guilty individual under these circumstances should be sufficient for this court to say mitigation is that this community will never know who the actual killer is. This defendant was involved and should fare no better, certainly, than his codefendant, but as to putting him to death because of the exercise of his constitutional rights, that would be inappropriate.

"Your Honor, I ask you to sentence my client in the same fashion that you did Mr. Logan, because a fair reading of the presentence report, a fair reading of all the information in this report, leads me to the conclusion these are two men who are so totally similar in background, involvement in this case, that the only difference between them is the facial impression that they leave when you look at them. I would have nothing further."

"Mr. Mesh," Judge Scott asked, "is there any legal cause why sentence should not now be pronounced?"

"No legal cause, Your Honor."

"Mr. Hotham, do you wish to make a statement on behalf of the State?"

"I wasn't going to, Your Honor, but Mr. Mesh made a very eloquent argument to the court. But what I would like to have the court direct its attention to is the fact that we are sentencing the defendant Jesse James Gillies, not Logan.

"Mr. Mesh's implication that the State is requesting death for the defendant because he exercised his constitutional rights is a slur upon my handling of the case, which I will not idly sit by and take. That's not true, and Mr. Mesh knows that. The State is requesting death in this case because death is appropriate, death is mandated. This man deserves death. He took another person's life under the aggravating circumstances which our community has determined to be so grave that the death sentence is required; that is why the State is requesting death. I think that it is appropriate and the death penalty should be imposed."

"Anything further?" Judge Scott asked, looking at Mesh.

"Nothing further, Your Honor."

Gillies was brought before the bench. "Mr. Gillies, I am going first to address the offenses charged against you in Counts One, Two, Three, and Five. In relation to those offenses, I have considered all the circumstances that have been presented to me. I have determined that there are aggravating circumstances, and that those aggravating circumstances are sufficiently substantial to call for a greater term of imprisonment on each count than the presumptive sentence the statutes provide."

Judge Scott imposed the maximum term for each of the four offenses and ordered they be served one after the other rather than at the same time, a total of seventy-two years.

As for the murder itself, he listed those aggravating factors he had determined. "The evidence that I have had presented to me establishes clearly that this victim was bound and terrorized for approximately eight hours prior to her death. The evidence establishes that she was raped by you as well as your accomplice on at least two different occasions, once at Papago Park area and the second time back at her condominium. The evidence establishes that you and the codefendant either threw or pushed the victim down a forty-foot embankment, causing serious injuries to her at that time. The evidence has established that when you went down to the victim, she was injured, she was bleeding, she begged for mercy. The evidence establishes clearly that you showed a gross indifference to her situation. The victim was struck several times in the head by a rock. While she was still alive you and your accomplice buried her under a pile of rocks. It was only thereafter she died.

"As our courts have defined the terms in this aggravating circumstances, I find this offense to have been committed in a cruel manner. It is apparent to any person that the victim in this case suffered terrible pain and mental anguish prior to death.

"The crime was committed in a particularly heinous, depraved manner. The murder was senseless. This was one lady against two men. She was absolutely under your control, there was absolutely no reason to murder that woman. She had done nothing to you. You didn't even know her prior to that evening. It was a completely senseless murder.

"The manner of inflicting death, by striking her in the head, by piling rocks on top of her prior to her death, shows to me a shocking and evil and depraved state of mind. I find that aggravating circumstances do exist in this case." He discussed other, more technical aggravating factors.

"I do not find your participation was relatively minor," he said. "I do agree with Mr. Mesh, however, that it is a mitigating circumstance in your case that Mr. Michael Logan, your accomplice, received a life sentence as his sentence, I consider that as a mitigating circumstance. However, I think there are several things that need to be stated on the record concerning that mitigating circumstance.

"The first thing is that Mr. Logan has confessed to his participation in the offenses and has shown remorse for what occurred.

"Clearly, you are certainly under no circumstances being punished for exercising your rights to remain silent or your right to a trial by jury; neither one of those is considered against you at all in this case in any manner whatsoever. They are clearly things that can be considered in determining whether to enter into a plea agreement and whether or not that plea agreement should be accepted in relation to Mr. Logan. Logan also did show the police the location of the victim's body, that's something considered in relation to his sentence.

"In the mitigation-aggravation hearing concerning Logan, the State presented no information, evidence concerning aggravating factors, as the law requires the State to do before the court can impose a death sentence. However, the fact that none were shown at that hearing does not mean that the aggravating circumstances did not exist. The reasons for the plea agreement between the State and defendant Logan were particularly peculiar to the case against Mr. Logan. The reasons for the plea agreement with Logan were totally unrelated to the existence or nonexistence of aggravating circumstances or mitigating circumstances as they relate to you or, for that matter, to Logan. They are totally immaterial to the determination of what your sentence should be in this case. However, the fact Logan received a life sentence is a mitigating circumstance that I have weighed in my decision as to the sentence to be imposed in this case.

"Mr. Gillies, I have considered and considered and considered the circumstances in this case. I have found both mitigating and aggravating circumstances and, therefore, I have had to weigh the two against each other to determine if the mitigating circumstances are sufficiently substantial to call for leniency.

"I find, sir, that they are not.

"It is therefore ordered that as your sentence for the crime of first-degree murder, that you be sentenced to death, and death is to be inflicted in the manner as prescribed by statute.

"The judgment that I have entered on all of these counts, sir, will be the authority for the director of the Department of Corrections to incarcerate you for this period of time as provided by law, by my sentencing.

"It will also be the authority for the Department of Corrections to inflict death upon you as provided by our laws."

Judge Scott advised Gillies of his appeal rights, thanked counsel, then adjourned, and left the bench. Gillies turned in his place, glared at Hackworth, made a face, then flipped his middle finger at him and shouted, "Fuck you!"

Hackworth smiled back benignly and said, "I'll see you at your last walk."

Gillies was led away to his cell for transportation to death row at the Arizona State Prison in Florence.

Hotham had witnessed Gillies's actions and was not surprised. It was entirely in character. The problem with a trial like this was that it tended to focus the guilt on the man who had not taken a plea offer. Logan was, Hotham felt, an equally pathetic, rotten, worthless human being, as despicable and as guilty as Gillies. Witnessing Gillies's display made that easy to forget.

Hotham put away his papers with a sense of satisfaction at the outcome, but as he walked to his office, he experienced a feeling of utter sadness for Suzanne. Justice had not brought her back.

Hackworth walked out of the Superior Court building onto the street. In that moment, in the courtroom upstairs, he had had every intention of attending Gillies's execution, but he realized, as he stepped into the lingering desert heat, that he would never go, it was just not in his nature.

However, there was something about Gillies that pissed him off and made him think things like that.

Well, Gillies had wanted to be tough, to make a name for himself, and now he had done that. He would sit down there in a little cell with the other tough boys. Senseless, this had all been so senseless.

There was a moment when Gillies had let down his guard and revealed himself to one of the wranglers. The cowboy had asked why

Gillies had killed the lady. Gillies had wanted Suzanne to grovel, to be debased and humiliated in front of him. Instead, she had maintained her composure, even attempted to reason with him as he was preparing to kill her.

"She would not give in," he said, she would not break.

EPILOGUE

"I miss her."
—Debbie Crisafulli

On a cool winter day in central Phoenix nearly ten years after the murder of Suzanne Rossetti, Superior Court Judge Jeff Hotham removed her autopsy photographs from a file and grimaced as he looked at them. The smell of the autopsy came back to him vividly. Jeff Hotham was appointed to the bench in 1987, a position in which he has served with distinction. The month he reexamined the autopsy photographs, Hotham was facing his first sentencing of a murderer. He conceded it was much more difficult to face the prospect of imposing a death penalty as the judge than to ask for it as the prosecutor.

In the years since the murder of Suzanne Rossetti, life has gone on for all those who remained. Steve Scott stepped down from the bench in 1985, and now practices law. Dick Mesh resigned as a public defender; he is now a county prosecutor and chief of the Organized Crime and Racketeering Bureau. Jack Hackworth retired from the Phoenix Police Department in 1984 and is a self-described "gentleman farmer" near the town of his birth in Kansas. Pug finally remarried in late 1990. Gary Reid resigned from the FBI and runs a business with his wife.

Both Peter Jr. and Donna have been in counseling at various times since the death of their sister. Peter Jr. proceeded with his plans and married Geri that spring. Peter and Louise have avoided counseling, believing they must work this tragedy through by themselves. They have sought ways to keep the memory of Suzanne alive, fearing perhaps that they would be engulfed if they ever fully grieved. They still live in the house in which they raised their children. The Rossettis filed suit against the state of Arizona for having improperly released Gillies from prison. With the court settlement and from contributions received at the time of the funeral, they established the Suzanne Maria Rossetti Memorial Foundation, Saugus, Massachusetts, which provides college scholarships to needy graduates from Saugus High School.

The Arizona Mountaineering Club named a 9.7 trail on Pinnacle Peak the Rossetti Rose in honor of Suzanne. Eric Gregan prepared a bronze plaque in her memory and climbed South Mountain in Phoenix, where he placed the plaque at the site they had last camped together. Each year the Berkshire Dance Theater in North Adams, Massachusetts, presents the Suzanne Maria Rossetti Dance Award to the most deserving student to help advance his or her career. In Dallas, Pennsylvania, a local artist named Sue Hand read the account of Suzanne's murder in *Time* magazine and contacted the Rossetti family. Every year since then, she has held the Suzanne Maria Rossetti Memorial Juried Art Exhibition for students in grades 7 through 12.

Jo Ann Heckel also proceeded with her scheduled wedding and was married two months following Suzanne's death. Suzanne was to have been one of Jo Ann's four bridesmaids, and the dresses had already been ordered when she was murdered. Jo Ann could not bring herself to substitute another friend in Suzanne's place and so had only three bridesmaids. She left the dress order as it was, but when she went to pick the dresses up, the clerk explained that the company had sent only three. The dress for Suzanne had never been delivered.

The victims of the murder of Suzanne Rossetti have continued to accumulate. Two who were close to Suzanne and are portrayed in this book, and one who is not, suffered a complete emotional collapse as a result of her murder. All three were hospitalized for significant periods and have been in continuous treatment for the decade following her death.

Joanie Saltzberg took self-defense training, worked at a rape crisis center and, most recently, at a hospice, all as a result of Suzanne's murder.

Carolyn Peters and another friend who had been very close to Suzanne each named a child for her. The second friend fell to her knees in prayer to thank God when she learned she would have a daughter she could name after her.

Because Suzanne had lived away from Saugus for over three years, her friends had grown accustomed to not seeing or speaking to her every day. Seven years after her murder, a close friend phoned Carolyn Peters, sobbing hysterically. She had suddenly realized that Suzanne was not simply living in Arizona far away but really and truly dead.

Debbie Crisafulli still sees Donna Rossetti. She tells of visiting Donna after Suzanne's death. She was impressed with how much of Suzanne was in the home, how alike the two sisters had been. When she saw a picture of the Rossetti girls smiling at the camera, Debbie left the room and broke down in sobs.

As the years of Debbie's marriage have passed and she has watched her children grow, she realizes more and more just how much Suzanne lost. To take a life is to take a lifetime. "We thought we were so grown up," she once said. She realizes now that when Suzanne was murdered, all her friends were still in their twenties and the joys of a long life were ahead of them. Each year, and the pleasures it brings, increase her sense of loss over the death of her friend.

Donna avoided close relationships with people, never wanting anyone to be so close to her that she could be hurt in the same way again and she was plagued for many years by nightmares. In one of them, Gillies and Logan had abducted her. One day, long after her sister's death, Donna saw Suzanne in a dream. "Stop feeling bad," she told her sister. "Everything's fine." Donna rushed to find her parents so they could see her, too, but Suzanne said she had only come to visit with her sister. Today, Donna is more serious and less lighthearted than she used to be, but she has found happiness, darkened as it is by the loss of the person to whom she was closest.

Louise has also had dreams. In one, Suzanne was in her hiking clothes with a backpack and was leading Louise's four nephews, all of whom had died of leukemia, up a cloud bank. Louise called out to her daughter and Suzanne smiled back. "I'm fine," she said, then turned to her four companions. "Come on boys," and she led them over the cloud and out of sight.

Logan remains behind walls in maximum security at the Arizona State Prison in Florence. He claims that Gillies is the only person on Earth he truly hates, and he has passed the word that he will happily "drop the pill" for Gillies when his time comes to be executed by gas.

The prison staff have repeatedly recommended that Logan be reclassified to a reduced custody status and transferred to a less secure location. Arizona has historically permitted inmates serving life sentences for murder to be housed in minimum security facilities. Senior corrections officials have until now overruled those recommendations.

Logan does not expect ever to be released from prison. Given his past behavior and references he has made, it is apparent that he is hoping for a transfer from behind the walls so he can escape. He will not permit anyone to stand in his way.

Logan only received two write-ups for rules violations, and both of those were many years ago. The first was for arguing when he received the wrong size of pants. The second was for fondling the breast of a female visitor.

Gillies claims to have become a reborn Christian on death row. He persuaded a girlfriend who had a baby by him to see him for a time, but that has come to an end. During one stretch, he went seven years without a visit.

He is a less-than-model inmate. During his first nine years on death row, he received thirty-one disciplinary actions. He has threatened guards more than once and has attempted to suborn them to obtain help for an escape. He has threatened to kill another inmate, extorted goods from a second, and threatened still a third's family. He was caught providing an inmate in isolation with a prison-made knife, a shank.

Random searches of his cell have produced a map, hacksaw blades on two occasions, and a pair of wire cutters, sharp enough to get him through the fence surrounding his cell block. He was once disciplined for reading a contraband magazine, *American Handgunner*, and on another occasion a *Mother Earth* magazine was discovered in his cell. He had been reading an article on the building of a homemade crossbow.

Twice he has scoured concrete from around his air vent, and once there were signs he had attempted to remove it. On that occasion, he was found in possession of a blowgun and eight darts tipped with needles. Another time, his cell door was opened electronically in error. Gillies bolted from his cell and had to be physically restrained.

The Arizona State Supreme Court has twice issued a Warrant of Execution, authorizing his death. The first was in 1983; the most recent was in 1985. Both times, federal courts intervened to grant him another stay, procured by an endless stream of state-financed defense attorneys.

On May 30, 1988, a passing guard noticed Gillies lying face down in his bunk, his arm extending to the floor and resting in a pool of blood. Gillies had slit open the arteries of his forearm. Nearly dead, he was rushed to a nearby hospital where his life was saved. He was then returned to await execution in Arizona's gas chamber.

Found in his cell was a carefully written suicide note that said, "It is a good day for dying," a line from a movie to which he had taken a liking. He lamented the conditions under which he was imprisoned, calling them "unbearable," and wrote, "I'm tired . . . not that anybody does or will give a shit." His note concluded by saying, "Everybody dies."

In 1989, Gillies became obsessed with the thought that someone had murdered his sister. He demanded that officials contact his mother, who assured them that her daughter was fine.

Since that first attempt, other instruments that Gillies could have used to kill himself have been discovered in his cell, including a razor blade and a knotted rope. There have been no other attempts. He is today a chronically depressed, very frightened, and quite desperate man.

The only regret Gillies has ever expressed was during the pre-sentencing phase of his sentencing. He said he was sorry that he had once looked at a photograph of the murdered Suzanne because it gave him nightmares for several days.

In Saugus, the year following Suzanne's death, Freddie Quinlan purchased a home overlooking the Riverside Cemetery. From his deck, he can see her gravesite a short distance away, and several days each week he will cast his gaze there for a time. Every May 3, Suzanne's birthday, he walks the short distance down the hill to her grave and stands there for a time before laying fresh flowers on it. On Memorial Day, he takes his five children with him and again places flowers on her grave, and tells them of Suz.

ABOUT THE BOOK

LATE IN THE SUMMER OF 1981, I was working as an adult probation officer preparing presentencing reports for the Superior Court in Phoenix, Arizona. Altogether I worked for fifteen years as a probation officer. As a presentencing investigator, it was my job to present to the sentencing judge a defendant's prior criminal record, his social history, psychological makeup, record of substance dependency, and to provide a summary of the offense and its impact on the victim. The conclusion of the report was a discussion of issues that appeared most relevant, and an evaluation of all the facts that should be considered in imposing a sentence. The final portion of the report was the recommendation. Judges followed my recommendation in ninety-nine percent of all cases, and it was not without justification that I acted in the belief that in most cases, my report decided the outcome.

At this point, I had eleven years' experience and, as one of the veteran officers, was assigned the case of Michael David Logan, and later of the codefendant, Jesse James Gillies. Until then, I had never heard of the murder of Suzanne Rossetti.

These were the first reports I had ever been assigned for a homicide. In the case of Gillies, it was the only matter in which I affirmed the imposition of a death sentence.

At that time in my life I opposed capital punishment. It seemed to me that any civilized society must reject such a measure if it is to call itself just and humane. I had known a number of killers in my career, and in most cases found them no worse than the wide range of misfits, addicts, predators, and sociopaths with which I dealt each day.

I faced no dilemma with Logan, since he had entered into a plea agreement that prohibited a death sentence. Only if I had believed that the proposed sentence represented a serious miscarriage of justice would I have recommended the plea agreement not be followed. I had done that in a handful of cases, most recently with a lifelong pedophile who I believed was receiving an excessively lenient jail sentence. The judge had followed my recommendation, refused to accept the plea agreement, and set the case for trial. The molester was acquitted by a jury following fifteen minutes of deliberation.

In Logan's case, I was not willing to second-guess the prosecuting attorney and accepted the necessity of the bargain. My primary contribution was to recommend a succession of consecutive sentences, called "stacking," as to each of his offenses, i.e., kidnapping, sexual assault, computer fraud, aggravated robbery, and homicide. This ensured that, barring clemency by a governor or laxness on the part of prison officials, Logan would end his life in prison.

It was not long into my interview with Gillies that my personal conflict became apparent. Since I opposed capital punishment on moral grounds, I could not play any part in the legal process that led to a man's execution. Over the years, I had frequently been required to enforce laws that I personally opposed. I recall with particular distaste jailing marijuana smokers in 1969 and 1970. While Gillies's case was different, I could not accept the wisdom of a society that sanctioned the death penalty when I personally believed such an act was immoral.

I spent a long weekend revisiting my thoughts on capital punishment. My conclusion was that civilized societies still send their sons and daughters to war to kill and be killed. Could not such a society decree death as a fitting punishment for murder? I concluded that retribution is an acceptable act of society, given our state of affairs. I wrote the Gillies report and presented the issues as I saw them. Mine was the last essential legal step required to impose the death sentence on Gillies.

When one deals with criminals for as many years as I have, one develops a necessary distance from the most despicable of them, even in the face of almost daily contact with intimate details of their life. Criminals had amused and angered me, made me proud and caused me shame. A child molester I had supervised for three years once looked me up. He told me that of all the people with whom he came in contact after his arrest, I was the only one who had treated him with dignity and respect, and he wanted to thank me. I did not tell him that he repulsed me, nor that my frequent interviews with him had been among the most excruciating of my career.

I thought I could handle anything. Following my interview with Logan, I was nauseated. After my interview with Gillies, I threw up. In all my years, they were the only men who made me physically ill.

I have no regrets and no reservations about my role in either case. It was only with a great deal of prodding by my wife, Jo Ann, that I was willing to return to this case and write this book. For that encouragement, for her support and all her tireless hours of research, I publicly thank her. To paraphrase Robert Caro, others have research teams, I have Jo Ann.

To understand murder and its consequences, you must know the victim and how much the victim and those who knew her have lost. Suzanne Rossetti has not been glorified here; she was the wonderful person portrayed.

Nor have I made the two murderers into monsters. They were, and are, as depicted here, and I leave it to others more qualified than I to explain them.

This was a small murder; most murders are. The bodies of more than a dozen people are discovered in shallow graves in the desert surrounding Phoenix each year. The killing of Suzanne Rossetti received minimal media coverage in both Phoenix and Boston. The trial of Gillies and the sentencings of both men received scant mention. Yet for the people who knew Suzanne, this was a life-altering event. Even for those involved in the legal process, it was haunting. Again and again, I interviewed seasoned professionals who had dealings in countless homicides who told me this case was the one they remembered. The foreman of the jury told me he awoke from sleep for weeks after the trial because images of Suzanne tormented him. It was in part my desire to illustrate the extended victimization that results from a murder that was not a media event that led to this book.

I have considered the place of both Logan and Gillies in society and have concluded that they have met the end they would have faced whenever, and wherever, they had been born. Logan is a career criminal and alcoholic who would inevitably have spent his life in prison, if not all at once, then on the installment plan, as we used to say in probation circles. Gillies is a misfit, a mutant if you will, though not as rare as one would wish. Any society would have been provided with reason to execute him, because it is his nature to prey on others and his removal from society is the only protection from him possible.

None of the police departments involved in the Suzanne Rossetti missing-person report have altered their procedures. A daughter reported late for an appointment would not result in any action different from that received by Peter and Louise. An Arizona legislative committee did conduct hearings into the circumstances of the release of Gillies, motivated primarily by the lawsuit that Suzanne's parents filed, and some changes in the state's work-release program were made. The system for releasing inmates is essentially unaltered, however, and is motivated primarily by prison population pressure on the Department of Corrections and does not take the safety of the community into adequate consideration.

There is, finally, this to consider. Gillies and Logan did not simply kill Suzanne that early morning in 1981, they took her life. Because of their deed, she never married or bore children, never lived into her middle years, or grew old. She will never climb another mountain, or smell a flower. Her life was extinguished.

It was also taken from her family and those who loved her. Peter and Louise will never have grandchildren by her, Donna will never laugh with her over the telephone or walk with her on the beach, nor will they ever say again that they love one another. Pug will never have the opportunity to share his life with her; nor will any of her many other friends.

How different these lives are from the ones they would have led had Suzanne's life not been taken from them.

Prison has not been easy for either of her murderers. But what has Suzanne had compared to that? Gillies and Logan know the satisfaction of a full stomach, the embrace of sleep, the nether region of semiwakefulness, solitary orgasms in their cells or sex shared with male inmates. They occasionally feel the sun on their faces; touch, smell, and hear life. They have had some measure of living, while Suzanne has had nothing.

I thank Michael David Logan and Jesse James Gillies for their cooperation. My only assurance to each of them was to write the truth to the best of my ability, and that I have done.

My special thanks to Jeff Hotham, Steve Scott, Dick Mesh, Jack

Hackworth, Brayton "Pug" Willis, Debbie Crisafulli, Carolyn Peters, Freddie Quinlan, and Gary Reid for giving so unselfishly of their time and for trusting me with their stories.

My profound appreciation to my gifted editor, Lisa Drew, senior editor and vice president of William Morrow and Company, for her keen ear and gentle touch with the manuscript, and to her skilled assistant, Bob Shuman, who held my hand by long distance countless times and contributed so effectively to the final manuscript.

There are hardly any words to adequately thank my friend and agent, Michael Hamilburg, for his confidence in me and his constant good cheer. Surely no writer was ever better served. And my thanks to his assistant, Joanie Socola, for giving of herself far beyond the requirements of her job.

My deepest appreciation to the family of Suzanne Rossetti who revisited the ugliest experience of their lives for a stranger, and treated me as a longtime friend. Thanks to Peter and Louise, to Peter Jr. and Geri, to Donna, and those I cannot name. I only hope the result has been worth the emotional price.

DATE DUE